HOW
it works
&HOW
to fix it

Contents

Staff

Lawrence Teeman, editor-in-chief; Judith Papier, managing editor; Charles Block, Jerold Kellman, Rick Kemmer, editors; Mort Schultz, contributing editor; Bill Gabbert, consulting editor; Sara Bangser, Marilee Wood, assistant editors; Linda Bishop, Leslee Fivelson, Barbara Jacobson, Marian Mirsky, Joyce Oellrich, Helen Parker, editorial assistants; Gregory Thornton, graphic arts; Grant Hoekstra, cover design; Frank Peiler, art director; Foster Silins, artist; Steven Feinberg, public information director; Ira Briskman, circulation director.
Louis Weber, president; Estelle Weber, assistant to president; Jack Lowell, business manager; Jack Lynn, production director.
Photos: Courtesy Appliance Service News
Automobile drawings courtesy National Automotive Parts Assoc.

Introduction

ADVANCES IN TECHNOLOGY make life easier and more comfortable — and far more complex. Where once a homemaker bound straw together for a broom and discarded it when it became worn to a stub, today's homemaker depends upon the vagaries of electrical supply and vacuum cleaner or electric broom components. Where once a family went down the road to a quilting bee or square dance or community play-reading for entertainment, today's family relies on the intricacies of an automobile or the equally mysterious workings of radio, television, and stereo. Where once a fireplace or wood-stoked oven met the cooking and baking requirements of a family, today's kitchens are furnished with an electric or gas range and one or more appliances from a list that includes toasters, rotisseries, blenders, mixers, roaster ovens, electric can openers, waffle irons, and electric coffee pots. And for cleaning up afterward, a dishwasher and a garbage disposer or trash compactor are standard items in many kitchens.

No more do we scrub clothes at a river bank — or even on a washboard at the sink: at the push of a button a clothes washer does the job, and a dryer replaces the clothes line. Bicycles are more common than scooters; refrigerators and freezers occupy the space where the old ice box stood; electric blankets serve where feather comforters once lay; electric and gas mowers have supplanted the scythe and hand mowers; and carpentry has become a brand new skill with power tools of all kinds.

And we have conquered the weather with home and auto air conditioning.

In other words, almost all aspects of modern life depend to some degree on electric energy, gears, wheels, switches, knobs, buttons, cords, and wires. All of which are far more complicated than the basic objects they replace.

It would be easy for a homemaker to become entirely dependent upon the army of technicians and service personnel trained to repair the hundreds of products we use throughout the year. But that would be an expensive proposition, and a frustrating one, with making telephone calls, waiting for the technician to arrive, trying to understand what the fee represents, and attempting to figure out how to prevent future problems, future frustrations, and future bills.

There is no need for such dependence. Most electrical and mechanical products are designed on basic principles which, once learned, can be applied to many problems once thought far too complicated for home repair. These principles are repeated again and again. A thermostat switch, for example, is basically the same whether found in an electric blanket, a toaster, a steam iron, or a room heater. Once you understand the working of a switch, and the way it is wired in the appliance, it becomes a simple matter to check it (is there a loose connection? is a wire broken? have the points become bent so they do not move properly?) and repair or replace it on most appliances.

That is the purpose of this issue of CONSUMER GUIDE Magazine. It is unlikely that any magazine or book will make you an instant expert in every electrical and mechanical field, but the information and diagrams in the following chapters should help you in several important ways.

You will learn the basic "How it Works" for the most familiar appliances, tools, and other products in your home and garage. This information is not written for the professional; it is for the average homemaker with a smattering of knowledge of electricity and gear operation, but with no background on how various components are fitted together and work together to produce a desired end — such as an iron

Introduction

hot enough to press clothes or a spray arm spinning soapy water to wash dishes clean. The description, together with the diagram (or diagrams), will give you that background and allow you to go to the next step.

With the knowledge of "How it Works" at your fingertips, you also have information on maintaining your equipment. CONSUMER GUIDE Magazine provides detailed instructions on what to do, and what not to do, to preserve the smooth functioning of each product and to prevent unnecessary repair bills. Maintenance is more than half the secret of long, trouble-free service, no matter what products you own.

Once you know "How it Works," you can define many problems. Some will be beyond you, either because they are based on principles and techniques too complex for anyone but those especially trained to handle them, others because they are located in areas too dangerous for you to explore (such as the picture tube of a television set). Many problems, however, are easily defined and easily solved once you understand your appliance.

When you have defined the problem, and checked to make sure it is one you can handle, this issue of CONSUMER GUIDE Magazine points to the solution: reconnection of wires, replacement of a switch, installing a new power cord, and so on. Where you should call an electrical or a professional service person, the text tells you to do so; there is no pretense here that everything can be done at home. But in this respect, too, the information in these chapters will be of help — even though you cannot make a specific repair yourself, you will be able to talk to the technician about the problem and understand what you should (and should not) be billed for.

With this issue of CONSUMER GUIDE Magazine, you will no longer be completely dependent upon technicians and service personnel. You will save significant amounts of money — service calls are among the highest-priced items in most homeowners' budgets. You will eliminate the frustration of waiting for someone to come and fix an item that you feel instinctively should be easy enough for a novice to handle with just a little more knowledge than you have.

The knowledge now is yours. Use it carefully and wisely; call for professional help when you know a problem is too serious for you to handle alone; and you and your equipment will both have longer, happier lives.

Types of Motors

OF THE MANY different kinds of electric motors that exist, these five types are commonly used in electrical appliances.

- the shaded pole motor
- the universal motor
- the split phase motor
- the miniature DC motor
- the synchronous clock motor

Figure 1 illustrates these motors and lists the appropriate appliances for each.

The part of a motor that rotates is called the rotor. The stationary part is called the stator, and contains field coils consisting of many turns of wire. End bells on each end of the motor hold the bearings on which the rotor shaft turns. Permanently lubricated bearings are used in virtually all present-day electrical appliance motors.

The Shaded Pole Motor

THE QUIET-RUNNING, economical shaded pole motor is found in appliances where the power requirements are not great. In the room heater, for instance, all the shaded pole motor does is spin the small fan blade that blows warm air out. In the can opener, a train of gears reduces the cutting speed to a small fraction of the shaded pole motor speed and thereby produces just enough power to cut out the top of the can.

Household power is delivered to a single field coil at the base of the shaded pole motor. Up near the rotor, two other coils, each of a single complete loop, are imbedded in the motor. These are the "shading" coils. The placement of the shading coils determines the direction that the rotor turns. Unlike some others, the shaded pole motor cannot be reversed by switching. In fact, the only way to reverse the shaded pole motor is to take it apart and turn the rotor end-to-end, then reassemble it. Now the rotor sticks out the other end of the motor, and even though it still rotates in the same direction as before, the object it drives will be rotated in the opposite direction.

It is difficult to damage a shaded pole motor except by deliberate abuse. Even when the rotor cannot turn — for example, when the appliance is jammed — current through the field coil will not do any harm. Overloading may stop the motor from turning, but will cause no electrical damage to the motor windings.

The Universal Motor

IF IT HAS brushes, turns at a high speed, and whines while running — you know it is a universal motor.

At one time, in some locations, one part of a community would have 110-volts AC, while another part would have 110-volts DC. The motor that worked on either AC or DC was called "universal," and that style of motor still carries the name.

The rotor in a universal motor is called an armature. It contains several windings, all connected to a cylinder made of copper segments — the commutator. In a universal motor with two brushes, the brushes are located on opposite sides of the commutator. The brushes have only one purpose — to carry current into and out of the armature coils.

Also, in the universal motor, there are field windings in the stator. Generally the motor is hooked up so that current enters one field coil, goes through the armature by way of the brushes, then flows out through the other field coil. Reversing the wires connected to the brushes reverses the direction of motor rotation.

When running free, the universal motor goes at a very high speed — several thousand revolutions per minute. However, at this high speed it has its least power. Putting a load on the motor slows it down, but it turns with more power. The electric drill is a good example: with a tiny bit, it turns full speed; with the largest bit it can hold, drilling through tough metal, the drill slows considerably, but bites in harder, and keeps going.

In appliances where speed control is a must, such as a mixer or blender, the universal motor is used. It is almost impossible to vary the speed of any other appliance motor continuously, but with the universal motor it is easy. Coils are switched in and out; resistors are switched in and out; rheostats are used to vary speed by varying resistances; and a governor-type speed controller is quite popular.

More recently, speed control by solid state devices has cropped up in electrical appliances. Solid state speed control offers full power in both the high and low speed ranges. One of its most successful applications has been in sewing machines.

The Split Phase Motor

THIS IS the big motor used on washing machines and dryers, food waste disposers, and dishwashers. In its stator there are two windings, each with four coils. One is the starting winding, the other is the running winding. As its name implies, the starting winding is needed and used only to get the motor going, then it is switched out of the circuit automatically. The motor continues to run on the running winding only.

Although it does not look like it, the rotor contains a "winding." It is imbedded in the steel cylinder that is the rotor. No brushes or wires carry current to this winding, but current flows in it nevertheless, "induced" by the magnetic fields while the motor is running.

This "workhorse" of appliance motors is ordinarily used in 1/6, 1/4, 1/3 and 1/2-horsepower sizes. It has a fairly constant speed — generally 1725 revolutions per minute — and is moderately quiet in operation. Reversing the wires to the starting winding reverses the direction of rotation. This reversing can be done by a switch that allows either direction of rotation to be selected.

The motor in hermetically-sealed refrigeration compressors is a split phase type. Where extra high starting power (torque)

Types of Motors

is needed, a capacitor is connected in the starting winding.

The Miniature DC Motor

LIKE THE UNIVERSAL motor, the little battery-operated motor has a wound armature and brushes. The field contains no coils; its magnetism is obtained from strong cylindrically-shaped permanent magnets. Current from the batteries goes directly into the armature to produce rotation.

While not exceptionally strong, these little motors have amazing power for their small size: witness the cordless electric knife cutting through a ham.

The miniature DC motor can be reversed, simply by reversing the wires to the brushes.

The Clock Motor

BECAUSE it "locks in" with the 60-cycle frequency of the power line, the motor used in electric clocks is called a synchronous motor. Its constant speed causes electric clocks to stay on time for months or even years.

They are not very powerful — after all, it does not take much to turn the hands on a clock, or flip the cards on a digital clock. By the same token, they use very little current. To operate an electric clock puts only a few pennies on the electric bill.

The built-in reduction gears and accurate timing make these motors ideal for use in operating the kind of timers found on washing machines and dishwashers. Usually the timer switch set is built so that a standard clock motor can be readily attached.

These motors are exquisitely built, but not made to be repaired. Being made in quantities, they are relatively inexpensive. When the clock motor stops running, "repair" consists of replacing it.

Where the Motors are Found

ON THE following pages are illustrations of each of the five types of motors described in this chapter, with a listing of the general application of the motor.

TYPE

SHADED-POLE MOTOR
- quiet operation
- for low-power appliances

Heating appliances with a blower, such as
- room heaters
- hair dryers

Electric fans

Can openers

Movie projectors, slide projectors, tape recorders, record players

UNIVERSAL MOTOR
- very high speed
- lots of power for its size
- noisy, due to brush whine
- good for speed control

Electric tools: drill, saw, sander, hedge trimmer

Vacuum cleaners

Mixers and blenders

Floor polishers

Range hood exhaust fans

Bathroom exhaust fans

Types of Motors

TYPE	USED IN
SPLIT PHASE MOTOR • heavy duty motor • quiet operation • used in major appliances	Washing machine Dishwasher Food waste disposer Clothes dryers Furnace blowers Ceiling exhaust fan Hermetically sealed compressors

TYPE	USED IN

MINIATURE DC MOTOR

- tor cordless appliances
- operates on battery current
- powerful for small size

Cordless appliances, including:
Shaver
Grass trimmer
Knife
Toothbrush
Portable record players and tape recorders

CLOCK MOTOR

- speed synchronized with power line 60 cycle frequency
- negligible power

Timers (range, washing machine, dryer, dishwasher)
Electric clocks — digital and pointer

Continuity Tester

ALTHOUGH THE appliance technician has available a variety of quality test instruments, he often bases his initial diagnosis on the indications of a very simple instrument called a continuity tester or test lamp. It is a quick and easy device to use, and you can pick up an inexpensive one at most electrical supply stores as well as many electronics shops.

Once you deenergize the appliance, you can test any component or circuit with a battery-powered light or test meter. Never rush to remove the service panels; frequently, you can diagnose the repair problem with the continuity tester while all of the panels are still in place. You can also use a continuity tester to determine if a ground fault exists in the appliance. Such an appliance should be disconnected and taken out of service at once. The same is true for components; test components for ground faults and replace any hazardous parts before using the appliance.

Touching the test prod tips together completes the circuit and causes a light in the tester to glow. Thus, the continuity tester makes it possible to check the condition of a switch, motor, cord, plug, etc., without having the appliance connected to a live electrical circuit. To test electrical components for continuity, just follow these simple instructions.

To Test a Switch

TO TEST A switch, touch the test leads to the prongs on the plug of an electrical appliance. Trip the appliance switch off and on. If the ap-

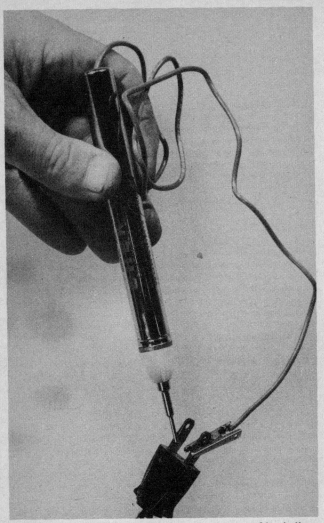

The Workman BZ5A continuity tester consists of lead clip for one side of the circuit and a probe for the other.

pliance switch is in good condition, the test buzzer or lamp should go on when you close the switch and off when you open the circuit. Thus, the continuity tester allows you to verify the condition of a switch without dismantling the appliance.

To Test a Thermostat

TO TEST A thermostat, however, you must take the appliance apart. With the appliance disassembled, touch the test leads to the wires that go to the contacts on the thermostat switch. If the switch is making good contact, the tester will indicate continuity. Now, manipulate the thermostat knob or lever that changes the temperature setting until you see the switch contacts open; the tester should then stop lighting or buzzing.

To Test a Heating Element

WHEN TESTING a heating element, touch the test leads to the end leads of the element. If the element is burned-out — that is, open-circuited so that there is no continuity through it — the tester will not light or buzz. If the element is in good condition, then the continuity tester will tell you so. If the heating element has a high resistance (a hot pad for instance), the tester light may glow only dimly. That tells you there is not much current getting through that high resistance; in other words, the element is still in good shape.

To Test the Brushes

TO TEST THE brushes in a universal motor, remove the appliance cover, disconnect the motor lead wires from the remainder of the circuit, and tag the wires so that you will be able to put them back in the right place. When you touch the test leads to the motor wires, the continuity tester should light or buzz. Now, slowly revolve the motor shaft by hand. If the brushes are bad, the tester light will flicker noticeably and even go off during some part of the shaft's rotation. Good brushes making good contact should produce a steady light or sound from the continuity tester.

To Test for Grounds

WHEN TESTING an appliance for grounding, touch one test lead to the frame of the appliance and the other test lead to the appliance cord (run the lead end through the little holes in the plug so as to touch both at the same time). If the continuity tester lights or buzzes, then you know that the appliance frame has a faulty ground and should be replaced.

You can test the safety ground (green wire in a three-wire cord) the same way. Touch one tester lead to the appliance frame, and the other to the pin on the three-wire plug. The tester should go on, thereby indicating that the safety ground wire is continuous from plug pin to appliance frame.

To Test a Solenoid Coil

TO TEST EITHER a solenoid coil or a field coil, disassemble the appliance far enough to allow you access to the solenoid wires. Disconnect the solenoid from the remainder of the circuit, and tag the wires. Touch the test leads to the solenoid coil lead wires. If you fail to get a response from your continuity tester, the coil is open-circuited; perhaps the coil contains a broken wire. If the coil is good, the tester will indicate continuity.

To Test an Appliance Cord

ON APPLIANCES where the cord is flexed constantly (like a vacuum cleaner), the cord can develop a break in one of the wires. When that happens, the appliance turns on and off erratically. To test the cord, remove it from the appliance and twist the wires together at the end of the cord. Touch a test lead to each of the plug prongs, and the tester should go on. Then, wiggle the cord at various points along its length. If at some spot the tester flickers off and on when you bend the cord in a certain way, there is a break in the wire. Discard the defective cord and replace it with a new one. Be sure to use heat-resistant cords on heating appliances.

Thermostatic Controls

THE PRIMARY PURPOSE of many electrical appliances is to produce heat. Examples are the electric iron, space heater, range, toaster and waffle iron. In all cases where heat is produced, electricity is changed to heat by running the current through a nickel-chromium alloy resistance wire — the Nichrome heating element. The amount of heat produced is stated as the wattage of the element — the higher the wattage, the more the heat. For instance, a 1000-watt element pours out twice as much heat as a 500-watt element.

If the wattage of the heating element is known, its resistance in ohms can be calculated. And, of course, it follows that if the resistance is known, the wattage can be calculated. The electric iron will do as an example. Suppose the nameplate says that when used on 120-volts the iron produces heat at the rate of 1000 watts. To calculate the resistance, divide the wattage into the voltage squared:

$$\frac{\text{VOLTAGE SQUARED}}{\text{WATTAGE}} = \frac{120 \times 120}{1000} = 14.4 \text{ ohms of resistance}$$

To figure the other way, if the resistance is known to be 12 ohms, when plugged into 120-volts the iron wattage is calculated as:

$$\frac{\text{VOLTAGE SQUARED}}{\text{RESISTANCE}} = \frac{120 \times 120}{12} = 1200 \text{ watts}$$

These two examples make another point. If, on 120 volts, a 14.4 ohm element produces 1000 watts and a 12 ohm element produces 1200 watts, then it is clear that lowering the resistance increases the wattage, and consequently, the heat produced. Higher resistance for lower wattage elements is obtained by a long slender Nichrome element suitably coiled to fit in the available space in the appliance. The shorter element made of thicker wire has the low resistance and the heat-handling capacity needed for high wattage.

For convenience of use, it is desirable to be able to select and to change the heat produced by an appliance. Still using the electric iron as an example, you, as the user, want an iron that heats up quickly (high wattage) and then can be adjusted to various ironing temperatures. To change the wattage by adjusting the resistance is possible, but very inconvenient. Another way is used; it is called cycling.

If the current to the element is repeatedly turned on and turned off, the heat ultimately given off will depend on the length of *on* time compared to the length of *off* time. An iron that is on for a second and off for a minute will scarcely get warm. Changing the cycle so that the iron is on for a minute and off for a second means it will get hot almost to its total wattage rating. These are extremes, used just for purpose of explanation; somewhere in between is the useful cycling on and off times. The cycling principle is used in many ways. In heating your home, for example, adjusting the way the furnace cycles on and off determines how warm the house will get.

Thermostat Heat Sensing

THE MOST POPULAR way of obtaining heat cycling is by use of the heat-sensitive switch called the thermostat. Although it comes in many shapes and forms, all thermostats contain switch contacts and a heat sensing device. Let's talk about the typical thermostat heat sensing device.

A familiar principle is used in the heat sensor. It is: when metals get hot they expand; when they cool, metals contract or shrink. Nothing new about that. But not all metals expand and contract to the same extent. Aluminum, for example, expands farther than steel for the same temperature increase. Now suppose that identical-size strips of two unlike metals are actually fused together, face to face, in one solid piece (called a bimetallic strip), what happens to the strip when it is heated or cooled? On heating, the one material will try to expand more than the other. But since the two metals are

Thermostatic Control

inseparably bound together, the strip curves; the metal on the outside of the curve has succeeded in expanding more than the metal on the inside. And, on cooling, the bimetallic strip uncurves. If chilled, the bimetallic piece will again curve, but in the other direction.

Now, let us fasten one end of the bimetallic strip to some part of the appliance — say, for example, near the heating element in an electric iron — and leave the other end free to move. Iron heat will cause the strip to curve and the free end will move. Let us further design the free end, in moving, to open and close electrical contacts carrying current to the iron. The iron heats; the strip bends; the contacts open. The iron cools, the strip unbends; the contacts close. This is thermostatic cycling.

An external knob changes the distance between the bimetal end and the switch contacts . . . thereby adjusting the length of *on* and *off* parts of the cycle . . . thereby changing the heat setting of the appliance.

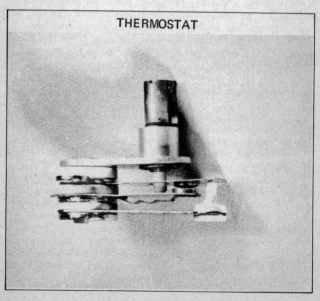

THERMOSTAT

Thermostatic Control

Bimetallic element thermostats are used in many appliances. A partial list includes:

room heaters
air conditioners
cooking utensils
refrigerators
toasters
electric blankets
coffee makers
electric ranges
clothes dryers
dry and steam irons

It is a rare occurrence for the bimetallic part of a thermostat to go bad. If a thermostat becomes defective, almost invariably the trouble is in the switch part. Contacts either "weld" together due to arcing from overload current, and then the thermostat will not "open;" or the contacts become pitted and fail to make a satisfactory electrical contact, in which case the thermostat will not "close."

In very sensitive thermostats, like the kind used to control furnace heat, the bimetal is a long, slender strip curled into a coil. A very slight temperature change — just a few degrees — separates the turn-on and turn-off points. By comparison, in an electric iron the rugged but less sensitive thermostat may stay "on" until the temperature of the appliance drops 10 to 20 degrees before cycling to "off."

One thing more about the thermostat. It does not control the heat produced by the heating element while the element is on. But by cycling, the thermostat controls the average heat over a period of time that is apparent at the working end of the appliance.

Grounding

ALMOST EVERYONE knows that the household electrical system that powers our electrical appliances is grounded. But what does grounding mean and how does it affect us as users of appliances?

In the wall behind the receptacle, two wires feed power to the prongs of the appliance cord — one covered with white insulation, the other with black. The white is the grounded, the black is the "hot" wire. Somewhere in the building, the white wire is connected to a metal conductor that is imbedded in the earth, thus the name "grounded." One popular way is to jumper (attach) the white-wire circuit to a water pipe — never a gas pipe — that comes in from underground. The same black and white color scheme is carried into some appliance cords.

The word "grounded" is also used in a different sense. In some appliances, a conductor goes from the ground end of the circuit to the metal frame of the appliance. The frame is grounded.

"Grounded" is used in still another way. When — due to some defect, fault or damage — a part of the circuitry inside an appliance is no longer protected by insulation, and a bare conductor touches the appliance frame or shell, an unintentional, or "fault" ground occurs. It is the fault ground that can be hazardous to you when you are using the appliance.

"Fault Ground"

THE TYPE OF ground that concerns us here is the type described above, caused by an insulation defect in an appliance. When you touch the appliance frame, a "fault

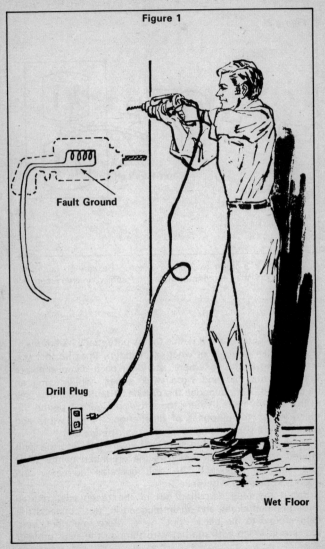

Figure 1

Figure 2

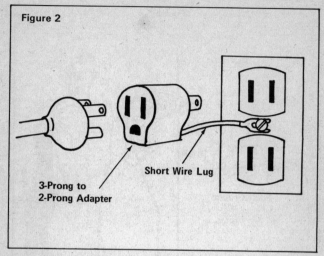

Short Wire Lug

3-Prong to
2-Prong Adapter

If you use a 3-prong to 2-prong adapter, be sure to fasten the adapter short wire lug firmly under the screw on the receptacle cover plate.

ground'' occurs — and it is this that is potentially hazardous.

Here is an example of what can happen. Imagine that you are working in the basement, standing on a damp concrete floor, wearing old and worn work shoes, while using an electric drill. And, suppose the drill has a fault ground — say at the end of the coil where the arrow in Figure 1 points. (In the drawing, for purposes of illustration, all the wires and windings are shown lumped together as a single coil.)

If the cord is plugged in so that the wire going to the fault ground end of the drill wiring is the grounded (white wire) end, nothing happens. The drill operates normally, and nobody knows the difference.

But if the plug is pulled out of the receptacle, rotated through a half circle, and again plugged in, this connects the fault ground to the black ''hot'' wire. More important, you, too, are in touch with the hot wire through the fault ground.

Current can and does go through you, through your electrically-leaky shoes, and through the wet floor right into the earth. The resulting shock causes your muscles to tighten, making you grip the drill all the tighter. It can be fatal.

Of course, the fault ground does not have to be at one or the other end of the internal circuit. A fault anywhere in the internal circuit can cause a fatal shock.

You will notice that recent advertising for appliances, especially electrical tools, uses the term "double insulated." The good insulating property of plastic housings and shells is being taken advantage of to help prevent shocks due to fault grounds.

Many of the appliances that are operated where the user might be in contact with the earth, such as power tools, lawn mowers, and hedge trimmers, have a 3-wire cord, and the plug on the end of the cord has two prongs and a pin. The third wire, usually covered with a green-colored insulation, goes from the pin on the plug to a screw in the frame of the appliance.

In the 3-wire receptacle, the hole for the plug pin connects to a wire that is deliberately grounded. Thus the green wire, acting as a "safety" ground, electrically connects the frame of the appliance to the earth. Now, if a fault ground should occur, the safety ground wire "shorts out" the fault ground, causing a fuse to blow, or a circuit breaker to trip, before the fault can give you a shock.

For safety's sake, do not ever do anything to circumvent the grounding provisions in an appliance. And, if you use the adapter that allows the 3-prong plug to be used in a 2-prong receptacle, be sure to fasten the adapter short wire lug under the screw on the receptacle cover plate as illustrated in Figure 2.

Repair

TO REPAIR a fault ground, the appliance must be disassembled, electrically tested, and the windings must be either replaced or rewound — obviously a task for the experienced technician. If the appliance is relatively inexpensive, buying a new one might be wiser than having the defective one repaired.

Air Conditioners

HOME AND AUTO air conditioners operate on the same principle as the electric refrigerator. The main difference is the way the principle is applied: the refrigerator cools a food-storage compartment, the air conditioner cools a living space.

The underlying principle of electrical refrigeration is the fact that evaporation is a cooling process. You can notice the cooling effect when stepping out of a swimming pool into a breeze.

Evaporation is the process of changing a fluid into a vapor. The "law" which applies is that when a fluid changes to a vapor it absorbs heat; conversely, when changing back into a fluid, the vapor gives off heat. The fluid is called a refrigerant; in refrigeration jargon, the refrigerant absorbs heat in evaporating; in condensing, the refrigerant expels heat.

In the air conditioner, the refrigerant fluid is totally contained inside the unit, and is repeatedly evaporated and condensed in parts of the system naturally called the evaporator and the condenser. Most air conditioners contain a refrigerant fluid called Freon, either Freon number 12 or Freon number 22. Both are specially compounded fluids that evaporate and condense at temperatures and pressures ideally suited for air conditioner use. (Actually Freon is the registered trade name of refrigerant made by a well-known chemical firm, but technicians use the name for the refrigerant fluid regardless of who makes it.)

In evaporating and condensing, the refrigerant goes through what is called a vapor cycle. Here is how the vapor cycle is accomplished.

An electric motor operates a compressor. The compressor pulls in refrigerant (as vapor) from the evaporator, pumping it into the condenser and applying pressure. Being under pressure, the refrigerant in the condenser tends to change into a liquid, but first must lose heat. A fan blows air through the condenser "radiator" coils, taking away heat and allowing the refrigerant to condense into a liquid under pressure.

From the pressurized space inside the condenser coils, the liquid refrigerant seeps through a small opening into the evaporator, which is also a serpentine coil with cooling fins. The "small opening" is provided either by a part called an expansion valve, or by a long, slender, copper tube called a capillary tube.

Because the compressor has been pulling refrigerant out, the evaporator becomes a low-pressure space. Liquid refrigerant seeping into the evaporator can and does expand and evaporate—actually it boils. But in evaporating, the refrigerant absorbs heat—remember, evaporation is a cooling process. A fan blows air through the evaporator coils; the air is cooled. This is the "conditioned" air that keeps your house or car comfortable in the hot summer weather.

Another thing happens. As warm air is cooled by being blown through the evaporator coil, some of its moisture is wrung out. The humidity of the air is lowered. In other words, simultaneously the conditioned air is cooled and dried, both operations adding to your summertime comfort.

The moisture pulled out of the air condenses on the cool evaporator coil, drips off and is carried away by a drain tube. (Perhaps you have felt it drop on your head while walking under a window unit.)

When the air in the room has cooled down to the temperature you have set on the thermostat knob, the switch in the thermostat turns off the compressor motor and the two blower motors, and the refrigerant stops circulating through the system.

There must be a separation, or wall, between the hot condenser coil and the cool evaporator coil to keep the evaporator from being heated by the condenser heat. With central air conditioning, the evaporator is inside the building, the condenser outside. With a window unit, a barrier separates the evaporator (room side) from the condenser (outside). In your car, the evaporator is underneath the instrument panel and the condenser is under the hood.

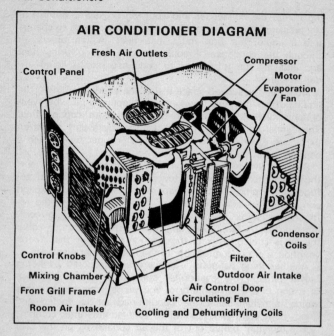

AIR CONDITIONER DIAGRAM

Fresh Air Outlets

Compressor

Control Panel

Motor

Evaporation Fan

Condensor Coils

Control Knobs

Filter

Mixing Chamber

Outdoor Air Intake

Front Grill Frame

Air Control Door

Room Air Intake

Air Circulating Fan

Cooling and Dehumidifying Coils

In your home air conditioner, the compressor and its drive motor both are sealed in what looks like a big black can—the so-called hermetically sealed unit. You cannot get inside it for any repairs. In your car, the compressor is driven by a belt from the auto engine.

Your home air conditioner contains as many as three motors; the split phase or capacitor motor in the hermetically-sealed unit, a motor for the condenser fan, and a motor for the evaporator fan. These are often shaded pole motors. Central air units with the evaporator in the furnace plenum use the furnace blower as the evaporator fan.

In your car with factory-installed air conditioning, the engine drives the compressor; the radiator fan cools the condenser coil, and the fan that blows heat in the winter blows cool air from the evaporator in the summer.

Troubleshooting Auto Air Conditioners

A PROFESSIONAL serviceman with special tools and expert knowledge will be needed to locate and repair problems in auto air conditioners. However, many times what seems to be an air conditioner problem is really caused by something else in the car's system. Being aware of these other causes could save you unnecessary bills.

Automobile air conditioner problems are almost always either a failure to turn on or poor cooling. Causes of a failure to operate (other than failure of parts of the system) include a blown fuse, bad switch, loose electrical connection, or a broken wire.

Lack of cool air may be caused by an improper setting on the air conditioner controls, an obstruction in the duct, a loose wire, a malfunction of the blower fan, or a loose drive belt.

Most if not all of these problem areas can be corrected by the owner or an auto mechanic at a local service station. However, if these possibilities have been investigated and the problem remains, the following should be done by a serviceman:

To correct an insufficient cool air condition, check the system for refrigerant leaks. Repair leaks and recharge the system with refrigerant. Or, check the receiver-dryer. If this unit is clogged, discharge the system, install a new receiver-dryer, vacuum it thoroughly, and recharge the system with refrigerant.

To correct all other problems, make a thorough check of all parts, particularly the expansion valve and compressor.

Maintaining Home Air Conditioners

CLEANLINESS is the rule. You must pay a small price for your bonus of filtered air. You no longer breathe dirt because the air conditioner has trapped it before it can get into your home; however, it can do real damage to the unit if you ignore it. The dirt particles clog the air conditioner coils, making the unit work harder and far less efficiently. Dirt also increases the chance of major problems, as well as running up the cost of running the unit.

The small cost you must pay is keeping the filter clean. In a room air conditioner, this must be done frequently. A dirty filter prevents the warm air from flowing over

Air Conditioners

the evaporator coils where the liquid refrigerant is circulating. If the first step in the cooling process cannot take place, none of the other steps will follow.

There are two kinds of filters. One is a permanent (that is, reusable) filter made of a tough, spongy material that traps dirt and dust particles. It can be washed in soap and water, rinsed, squeezed dry, and reinstalled. The other kind is made of fiberglass that also traps dust and dirt, but cannot be cleaned. When this kind becomes clogged, it should be thrown out and replaced with a new one.

The inside of room air conditioners should be cleaned out once a year. With one model, this presents little problem. This is the model that enables you to slide "the works" out as you would pull open a drawer. Everything is within reach. Other models are rougher to handle, because the only way to reach all the components is to remove the unit from the window or wall and open it up.

Once you have found the way to reach the components, use the brush attachment of your vacuum cleaner to clean the condenser and evaporator coils (see the diagram of the air conditioner). If your vacuum cleaner has a blower, you can blow the dust and dirt from hard-to-reach places, though this has obvious disadvantages; vacuuming up is much neater.

For other parts, including the compressor, fan motor, fan blades, and the tubing running throughout the unit, use a quick-evaporating cleaning solvent, available in hardware stores (tell the salesperson what you want it for). You may find it under the generic name *trichloroethylene*.

If your air conditioner had to be removed from the window or wall opening for cleaning, take special care with the way you reinstall it. Tilt it toward the outside at an angle of 1/8 to 1/4 inch. This angle will permit condensation to drain off.

During your once-a-year cleaning of the inside of your unit, check the outside case for signs of rust. If you find any, scrape them off with a small knife and touch up the area with a good quality metal primer and paint. If ignored, the rust spots will become larger and ultimately eat through the unit.

How to Repair Room Air Conditioners

THERE IS NOT much the average homeowner can do to

repair a malfunctioning room air conditioner. In most cases, special tools and training in refrigeration repair are necessary. CONSUMER GUIDE Magazine lists the following troubleshooting charts for owners who have some experience with air conditioners, and for those who want to know what a professional serviceman is talking about, recommending, and charging for.

PROBLEMS, CAUSES, REPAIRS

Problem: Unit will not run

Possible Causes	Repairs
1. Blown fuse or tripped circuit breaker	1. Replace fuse with one of correct rating, or reset circuit breaker. If fuse blows or circuit breaker trips again, do not operate unit. An electric failure exists that may start a fire. Call an electrician.
2. Broken or loose power cord	2. First spread the prongs of the power cord plug, reinsert into wall outlet, and try the unit. If this fails, check the service cord over its entire length for breaks and for a loose connection at the control switch end. Repair with electrician's tape.
3. Defective thermostat	3. Check thermostat for continuity. Replace broken wires; refasten if a wire has worked loose.
4. Defective starter capacitor	4. Remove starter capacitor and replace with new one.

Air Conditioners

Problem: Unit does not cool

Possible Causes	Repairs
1. Thermostat not properly set	1. Set thermostat to a lower temperature to provide more cooling.
2. Dirty filter	2. Replace or clean filter
3. Condenser coil dirty	3. Blow or vacuum dirt from condenser with brush attachment of vacuum cleaner.
4. Compressor not running	4. Check for a defective thermostat, bad run capacitor, an open overload switch, and broken or loose wiring. Finally, perform a compressor test.
5. Refrigerant leak	5. Check unit's tubes and components for leaks. Repair and recharge.
6. Unit too small for load imposed	6. If unit is undersized, it will not adequately cool a room. Substitute a proper size unit.

Problem: Air conditioner operates, but fan does not

Possible Causes	Repairs
1. Defective fan switch	1. Check switch for continuity (broken or loose wires).
2. Defective fan capacitor	2. Replace capacitor.
3. Defective fan motor winding	3. Check each winding of the motor for continuity.

Problem: Unit switches on and off in short cycles

Possible Causes	Repairs
1. Lack of good contact between evaporator inlet and thermostatic expansion valve bulb.	1. Make sure evaporator is not blocked by dirt or anything else. The thermostatic expansion valve bulb must be touching the evaporator inlet pipe.
2. Dirty condenser coil	2. Blow or vacuum dirt from condenser with a vacuum cleaner.
3. Defective condenser or fan motor	3. Check operation. If motor stalls when it becomes hot, be sure bearings are not binding. If the bearings are in order, the problem is with the motor; it must be replaced.
4. Defective overload switch	4. Lack of continuity across overload switch terminals indicates the need for a new switch.
5. Unit restarted too soon after being stopped	5. An air conditioner turned on too soon after it was stopped may cause a blown fuse or short cycling. Allow at least five minutes of idle time before restarting a unit that was just halted.

Dishwashers

DISHWASHERS are essentially simple appliances. They take in hot water, through a valve, for a specific period of time. Then one or more spray arms are spun by a motor so that they spray water over dirty dishes. The water dissolves detergent that has been held in a special dispenser; after the dishes are washed for a specific period of time, the water is pumped from the dishwasher, carrying with it all the food that has been left on the dishes and silverware.

This sequence usually occurs twice during a wash cycle, followed by a hot rinse cycle. The final step is a drying phase, accomplished by means of a heating element.

To the more technically minded, this brief description may seem an oversimplification. A more detailed description of a typical dishwasher washing cycle includes these steps:

1. Some dishwashers begin the cycle by pumping out water that may have entered the unit as dishes were being loaded. This phase is very brief.

2. The machine is filled with hot water by means of a solenoid-controlled water valve (see Figure 1). Solenoid control means that, in effect, the operation of the water valve is controlled by electric current. When current is allowed to go to the valve, the valve opens and hot water enters the dishwasher. When current is turned off, the valve closes and the flow of hot water ceases.

The component that controls the solenoid (and controls all phases of dishwasher operation) is an electrically-operated automatic timer driven by a motor similar to the one in an electric clock. As each interval passes, the timer switches control the dishwasher motor, solenoid valve, detergent dispenser, pump, and heating element. In this way, various operations occur in sequence. (see Figure 2)

3. When hot water enters the dishwasher, it mixes with the detergent that you have poured into its dispenser. The dispenser has either an electrically-operated or mechanically-operated cover that opens at the proper time, permitting the detergent to be washed out of the dispenser and mixed with hot water.

4. At the end of the "fill" phase, water and detergent are sprayed over the dirty dishes. The spray arm (or arms — there may be more than one) is similar to a lawn sprinkler. Water and detergent are forced through the spinning spray arm by a pump operated by a split-phase motor and are ejected out with driving force to cascade over dirty dishes. The driving force of the water removes food particles while the heat of the water sanitizes the dishes and silverware. This washing action continues for a specific length of time.

5. Dirty water is pumped out of the dishwasher. Most units have a pump that does this; in those that do not, water drains out by gravity. The pump is either a small separate unit, or it is part of the main motor. If the latter, a set of contacts on the timer causes the motor to reverse itself, which activates impellers that pump water out.

At the start of the pumping phase the automatic timer sends an electric "message" to another solenoid that causes the drain valve to open. These actions must be simultaneous so that the water can drain out as it is pumped.

6. The unit is filled with water again, followed by spraying of dishes with the clean water. This is generally referred to as the rinse phase. The only difference between the wash phase and the rinse phase is that washing is done with detergent, rinsing without.

7. The final phase is drying. This phase consumes one-third to one-half of the total cycle time. Drying is done by an electrically operated heating element that evaporates moisture from the dishes.

Most dishwashers are capable of performing more than one cycle, which you select by pushing a button or by rotating the timer dial. These other cycles are nothing more than one or more phases of the total wash cycle, arranged to suit purposes other than total wash.

Dishwashers

For example, a rinse and hold cycle uses no detergent. It allows you to rinse dishes only, without drying them. This cycle is useful when a dishwasher is partly filled with greasy dishes or with dishes that have food particles which could create offensive odors if allowed to stand or which could dry and harden to the point where the unit's spray could not wash them off.

When Purchasing a Dishwasher

WHEN SELECTING a dishwasher, there are four basic types from which you may choose: top-opening portable, front-opening portable, built-in, and under-sink built-in.

A portable dishwasher requires no installation and is ready to go to work as soon as you snap its hoses to the kitchen faucet and plug its electric cord into a wall socket. You can roll the dishwasher on its casters for loading and unloading at the table and you can push the unit out of the way when it is not in use. A portable is probably the most practical dishwasher for families living in rented houses, apartments, and second homes.

Features to consider when looking at portable models are the following:

● A power cord of convenient length with a three-prong grounding plug for safety.

● A power cord storage housing in the form of either an automatic reel that winds the cord into the dishwasher cabinet or a manual storage facility.

● A handle that permits easy movement of the appliance.

● Casters that allow the dishwasher to be rolled easily.

● Proper height if you want to store the dishwasher beneath a counter.

● A provision for raising water temperature if the water supply is below 140° F.

Top-Loading Portables

THE TOP-LOADING portable model takes up the least amount of space when it is being loaded and unloaded since you need no extra space in front to lower the door. However, other factors are involved. Using a top-loader requires bending to reach down inside the appliance. The top rack thus assumes a new importance.

Some top racks lift up and out of the way as the dishwasher cover is raised, allowing access to the bottom. Another type of rack folds up out of the way. This gives access to the bottom, but the rack must be loaded last and unloaded first.

Generally, the loading capacity of top-loading portable models is less than front-opening models.

Front-Opening Portables

FRONT-OPENING portable models are basically the same as built-in models, except for the addition of a top and casters. Also they must be plugged in to a wall outlet and their hoses snapped to faucets in the kitchen sink.

Most front-opening portables are designed for conversion to a built-in when a family moves to a more spacious home or when a kitchen is remodeled. A decision to purchase a front-opening portable, therefore, should be based at least partly on whether you ever plan to convert it to a built-in.

One feature to look for when selecting a front-loader is stability. The dishwasher must remain stable without rocking or tipping when full racks are pulled out for unloading. Also check the construction of the door hinges; they must bear the weight of the door for many years without giving way. A word of caution: never lean or kneel on the door; it is not meant to support you.

Built-In Dishwashers

BUILT-IN dishwashers offer the most convenience. Once one is installed, you can operate the unit without having to connect it to water and electrical sources, or disconnect it when you are not using it.

Built-in models are also the quietest. Surrounding cabinets help to muffle the sound of water action. In addition, a built-in gives a kitchen a unified appearance. You can usually order a front panel for the unit in the same wood as your cabinets.

Because a built-in dishwasher is permanently connected, its convenience features are used more frequently than a portable's. Rather than rolling the portable unit to the sink and hooking it up, most owners do their own rinsing, heating of plates, and so on, but a built-in will do this for them.

Dishwashers

Features to look for in selecting a built-in dishwasher include:

- Racks that pull out all the way, so back sections are easily reached.
- An automatic cycle that rinses partial loads and resets the timer for a regular wash cycle.
- A special scrubbing cycle for pots and pans.
- A special gentle cycle for fragile china and crystal.

Under-the-Sink Units

UNDER-THE-SINK dishwashers are designed for small kitchens with minimum cabinet space. Usually, the dishwasher, sink top, bowl, faucets and cabinet come as a one-piece unit. The dishwasher's upper rack is reduced in size to allow for installation. Therefore, capacity of the unit is smaller than other models.

Dishwasher Tips

THE FOLLOWING list suggests ways for you to use your dishwasher to attain more efficient and better performance, to prolong the appliance's life, and to help you avoid unnecessary service calls and repair bills:

- Successful dishwasher operation depends upon this minimum requirement: a water supply that flows at a rate of at least 2 to 2.5 gallons per minute at a pressure of at least 15 pounds per square inch and at a temperature of at least 140° F.
- See to it that your dishwasher works at full capacity whenever possible. A partial load of dishes uses as much hot water and electricity, and puts the same strain on a dishwasher, as a half load. You save money and preserve the unit by running it only when it is full.
- Use your dishwasher; it actually conserves hot water and saves energy. Studies reported by the General Public Utilities Corporation show that the average dishwasher uses between 11 and 16 gallons of hot water to wash a full load, while washing a comparable number of dishes by hand requires from 27 to 52 gallons of hot water.
- The temperature of the water that reaches a dishwasher should be 140° to 150° F. for best results. However, the

water temperature that reaches the dishwasher is not always the temperature at which you set your water heater thermostat. Water temperature is affected by the distance water must travel from the heater to the hot water outlet. The farther it travels, the greater will be the drop in temperature.

Check the temperature of the hot water by turning on a hot water faucet in the sink closest to the dishwasher and testing with a thermometer. Readjust the water heater thermostat as necessary. Incidentally, you can conserve energy needed to heat water by wrapping hot-water lines with insulating material found in hardware stores. Insulation holds in the heat.

● Scrape large food particles from dishes and empty glasses before placing them in a dishwasher. There is no need to pre-rinse dishes unless you will hold them all day before running the dishwasher. Otherwise, dishwasher action is sufficient to clean and sanitize dishes. If you feel more comfortable with pre-rinsing, then do so, but use cold water in order to conserve hot water.

● Some dishwashers are equipped with filter screens; others are not. Check the owner's manual which came with the unit when it was new to determine in which category yours falls. If yours has a filter screen, make sure that you clean it periodically to prevent food particles from being redeposited on dishes and to maintain the efficiency of the dishwasher.

● Use only detergents specifically made for dishwashers. Products made for hand washing of dishes, for use in a laundry, or for general household cleaning, can impede dishwasher action or cause the unit to overflow, which will lead to damage.

● Use only that amount of detergent the dishwasher actually needs. Read your owner's manual to find the proper amount. Excessive (or not enough) detergent will result in unsatisfactory washing.

● Each dishwasher detergent differs somewhat in chemical formula, and therefore each may serve a particular water condition better than others. If you are not getting good results with your present detergent, give other brands a fair trial. You may find one better suited for your water conditions.

● Never put dishwasher detergent into the dispenser until you are ready to wash dishes. Moisture that may be in the

Dishwashers

dispenser will cause detergent to cake and harden as it stands. Hardened detergent will fail to dissolve.

● Frequently, using a rinse agent or additive in a dishwasher will help overcome the water spotting of dishes brought about by excessively hard water. Many dishwashers are equipped with separate dispensers that automatically eject a few drops of additive during the final rinse cycle. If your dishwasher does not have a dispenser, rinse additive in solid form that you can hang from the silverware basket is sold in food stores. If water is extremely hard, not even rinse additive will help. You should consider installation of a water softener.

● When adding or removing dishes from a dishwasher while it is in the middle of a cycle, unlatch the door or lid and wait for water action to cease. Then, open the door or lid slightly and allow hot, moist air to escape.

How to Repair a Dishwasher

MOST TIMES, dishwasher problems are caused by carelessness in washing rather than mechanical failure. Such things as improper stacking of dishes and using a weakened detergent result in poorly washed dishes. These problems, and causes and remedies, are outlined in the troubleshooting charts below.

However, mechanical failures and repairs are also listed to make you aware of what might be wrong and actions that should be taken. Scan the chart before calling a serviceman. Some problems can be remedied by any homeowner. Homeowners with technical ability can solve more problems, but even if the action to take is not within your area of ability, at least you will have an idea of what a professional repairman should do.

Caution: The combination of water and electricity makes a dishwasher a lethal appliance if extreme care is not taken. If you are working on a portable unit, *be sure the power cord is disconnected* from the wall outlet before doing work in an area where there is danger of contact with wiring. If the appliance is built-in, locate the fuse or circuit breaker that serves the unit, and *remove the fuse or trip the circuit breaker* before tackling repairs involved with electricity.

Dishwashers

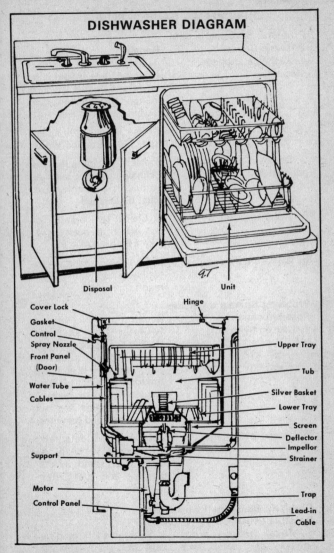

DISHWASHER DIAGRAM

Disposal

Unit

Cover Lock
Gasket
Control
Spray Nozzle
Front Panel (Door)
Water Tube
Cables
Support
Motor
Control Panel

Hinge

Upper Tray
Tub
Silver Basket
Lower Tray
Screen
Deflector
Impellor
Strainer
Trap
Lead-in Cable

PROBLEMS, CAUSES, REPAIR

Problem: Spotting or film.

Possible Cause	Repair
1. Dishes improperly stacked	1. Stack so there is space around dishes. Avoid clutter. Soiled sides of cups in top rack should face toward center of rack.
2. Insufficient detergent	2. Use full quantity specified in instruction book.
3. Dishes not scraped adequately	3. All large particles and "clinging" foods such as spinach, broccoli, etc. must be scraped.
4. Water too cool	4. Check temperature of hot water at outlet. Adjust if below 140° F.
5. Water too hard	5. Use rinsing additive. Install water softener as last resort.

Problem: Specks on dishes.

Possible cause	Repair
1. Caused by food	1. Clean filter screen; stack dishes properly; use proper amount of detergent; see to it that wash arm rotation is not blocked by utensil or dish; be sure wash arm holes are' not clogged by food particles.
2. Caused by detergent	2. Discard old detergent; if detergent is fresh, do not let it stand in dispenser — add just before washing.

Problem: Black marks on china.

Possible cause	Repair
1. Metal marks from knives or metal rims	1. Soak china in mild detergent.

Problem: Unit fails to fill.

Possible cause	Repair *
1. Water valve partially or fully closed	1. Check water valve on line leading to dishwasher and open fully.
2. Water pressure too low	2. Water pressure must be at least 15 pounds per square inch; call your local water company.
3. Clogged water inlet screen or damaged water valve	3. Most water valves are equipped with screens to trap deposits. Disassemble and clean screen. If parts are heavily calcified, replace entire water inlet valve assembly.
4. Defective water valve solenoid	4. Turn timer dial to "Fill" and check solenoid with tester. If voltage exists at solenoid, but water valve is not opening though free, solenoid is defective. Have repaired or replaced.
5. Faulty float switch	5. Some dishwashers are equipped with a float switch that controls the water valve. It will be in the tub. Test by picking up the float with your finger and letting it drop. You should hear a "click" and the float arm should fall squarely on the float switch. If not, replace the float assembly.

* Water valve servicing — usually called for when a dishwasher refuses to fill — should be done by an experienced technician with the proper tools.

Problem: Detergent dispenser cover stays closed.

Possible cause	Repair
1. Detergent has hardened from being left in dispenser too long or placed into a wet dispenser	1. Scrape out hardened detergent; add fresh. Dispenser should be dry when detergent is added. Add detergent just prior to washing dishes.
2. Dishes or utensils blocking dispenser cover	2. Position dishes and utensils so they do not block dispenser cover.
3. Calcium deposits on lid or on shaft	3. Clean calcium deposits from around dispenser mechanism with vinegar.
4. Defective detergent dispenser solenoid valve	4. Test. Replace if defective.
5. Defective timer	5. Advance timer to position where detergent dispenser cover should open. If cover fails to open, timer is probably defective. Replace.

Problem: Dishwasher leaks.

Possible cause	Repair
1. Loose or worn door gasket	1. Gasket should not be torn or flattened, and should be positioned tightly around door. Replace if necessary.
2. Broken door hinge	2. Replace.
3. Water inlet line fitting leaks or line is ruptured	3. Tighten compression nut. If line is damaged, replace.
4. Defective motor seal	4. If water leaks from around motor shaft, replace seal.
5. Loose hose clamp	5. Check all hose clamps for tightness.

Problem: Dishwasher does not operate.

Possible cause	Repair
1. Door not closed and latched	1. Door must be closed and latch locked.
2. Cycle selection button not fully engaged	2. Depress button all the way.
3. Blown fuse or tripped circuit breaker	3. Replace bad fuse or re-set circuit breaker. If fuse blows or circuit breaker trips again, there is an electrical defect. Call a serviceman immediately. Do not operate appliance.
4. Defective door switch	4. Open door fully and close slowly (or press switch button if visible). You should hear a "click." If not, door switch may be bad and should be replaced.
5. Defective timer	5. Turn timer dial by hand very slowly with door latched and Wash cycle button engaged. Timer should operate to turn appliance on. If not, timer is probably defective.

Problem: Refuses to turn off

Possible cause	Repair
1. Defective timer	1. "Fill" phase should last about 60 seconds. If timer does not move off "Fill," it is probably defective and should be replaced.
2. Water inlet valve stuck open	2. Have service technician disassemble and clean valve or replace.
3. Clogged water inlet valve bleed hole	3. Disassemble valve and clean out bleed hole.

Dishwashers

| 4. Defective float switch | 4. In those dishwashers equipped with a float, check switch for burned contacts. |

Problem: Dishwasher operates when door is open.

| Possible cause | Repair |
| 1. Faulty door interlock switch | 1. Replace. |

Problem: Dishes stay wet.

Possible cause	Repair
1. Water too cool	1. Check temperature of water at hot water outlet. Adjust if below 140°F.
2. Dishes incorrectly stacked	2. Stack so there is space around dishes. Avoid clutter and dishes resting against each other.
3. Water does not drain	3. See "Fails to Drain" below.
4. Calcium deposits on heater element	4. Clean heater element.
5. Loose connection at heater element	5. Tighten or repair.
6. Heater element burned out	6. Replace.
7. Inoperative fan motor (some models)	7. Replace.

Problem: Unit fails to drain.

Possible cause	Repair
1. Drain hose kinked or clogged	1. Remove drain hose, straighten, make sure hose is not clogged, and reinstall.
2. Damaged or defective pump	2. Remove and disassemble pump. Clean clogging material from around impeller. If impeller has suffered damage, replace.

3. Stuck timer	3. If timer does not advance by itself, it is probably defective. Replace.
4. Defective pump motor	4. Advance timer to "drain" phase. If motor hums, check impeller for obstructions. If impeller is free, pump motor wiring is probably defective. Replace pump motor.

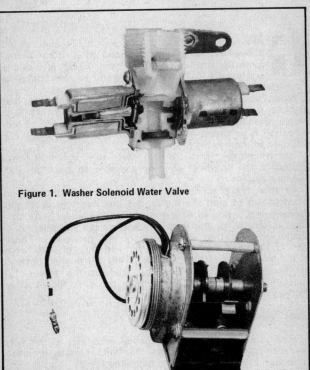

Figure 1. Washer Solenoid Water Valve

Figure 2. Washer Timer

Disposers

GARBAGE DISPOSAL begins with a flat plate called a flywheel that is spun around by a motor at the fantastic rate of speed of over 1700 revolutions per minute. This is equivalent to the speed of a car engine operating at almost 30 miles per hour.

When you stuff garbage through the sink drain into the disposer's canister (technically called a hopper), it falls on to the flywheel (see the disposer diagram). Free-wheeling lugs called impellers (there are usually two) are attached to the flywheel.

Free-wheeling? This means that the impellers are riveted to the flywheel so they are able to pivot as the flywheel rotates.

All this rotary action, which begins when you turn on the disposer to start the motor, has one aim: to dash garbage against a ring of elements called a shredder. As garbage is thrown by the impellers against the shredder, it is pulverized by cutters into relatively tiny particles. These bits of garbage are now able to slip through discharge holes in the body of the disposer. They are flushed through the holes into the drain line that leads to the sewer. A constant stream of cold water from the sink faucet does the flushing.

Classifying Garbage Disposers

GARBAGE DISPOSERS are classified according to the way in which garbage is fed into the unit. There are two methods: continuous-feed and batch-feed.

A continuous-feed garbage disposer allows you to deposit garbage into it as the appliance is running. This unit is turned on and off by a switch resembling an ordinary light

Disposers

switch on the wall near the sink. This type of unit should not be stuffed full of garbage; only a little should be fed in at a time.

A batch-feed garbage disposer pulverizes one load of garbage at a time. It operates only when the cover is placed over its opening and is turned to "lock" position. As soon as the cover is loosened, the unit shuts off. This type may be filled with garbage before it is turned on.

You can tell the difference between a continuous-feed and a batch-feed unit by looking into the opening. The opening of a continuous-feed disposer is normally equipped with a rubber baffle. The steel cover of a batch-feed model is constructed so it can be turned to trip the on-off switch located in the mouth of the appliance.

The cost of buying a batch-feed unit is somewhat more than that of a continuous-feed unit, but batch-feed units have advantages that make them worth your consideration, especially if you have youngsters in your home. Children have been known to stick their hands into operating continuous-feed models. A batch-feed unit makes this impossible since it will not operate unless the cover is locked in place.

Garbage disposers are also classified according to their ability to perform work. Less expensive models usually have low-capacity motors of only 1/3 horsepower that are not powerful enough to grind heavy food wastes, such as melon rinds, fruit skin, and corncobs. Units in this group are also limited to the amount of garbage they can handle at one time—about one quart.

More expensive models usually have heavy-duty 1/2-horsepower motors. They can grind heavy waste and handle up to two quarts of garbage at a time. Most also are equipped with extra features, such as noise reducing insulation and automatic unjamming.

Automatic reversing (unjamming) occurs each time the disposer is operated. Each start of rotation accomplishes a switching action that results in reverse direction on the next start, therefore direction-of-rotation alternates each time the disposer is turned on. If your unit does not have this feature, unjamming must be done manually, as we will discuss below.

Garbage Disposers and Septic Systems

WHO SAID you cannot have a garbage disposer in your home if you have a septic system? Nonsense.

Disposers

A garbage disposer that operates an average number of times a day uses about six gallons of water a day. This is the amount of water you would use in showering for 80 seconds.

According to the U.S. Public Health Service, you can use a garbage disposer without worry if your septic system falls within these limits:

The absorption field of the average home septic system is able to handle 50 gallons of water per day per person.

No. of Occupants in Home	Minimum Size of Septic System
4	750 gallons
6	900 gallons
8	1000 gallons
10	1250 gallons

Taking Care of a Garbage Disposer

THE LIFE of a garbage disposer can be extended many times over if the user observes the following simple precautions:

• Make sure that no forbidden waste material goes into the appliance. Not all disposers can grind the same kinds of waste; always consult the instruction manual which came with the unit when it was purchased. Most expensive models can dispose of bone, corncob and seafood shell, but some lightweight models will be damaged if forced into this heavy-duty work.

• *No* disposer can shred metal objects such as bottle tops and cans, or glass, crockery, rags, string, paper, cardboard, rubber, plastic, and cigarette filters. These materials will damage a disposer and clog the drain.

• Cold water must run constantly into the disposer the entire time the appliance is turned on and running, and for several seconds after the appliance has been turned off. Cold water flushes garbage particles into the sewer line, keeping the disposer free and helping reduce the chance of odor.

• Never allow hot water to run into a garbage disposer when it is operating. Hot water melts grease which will coat the sides of the drain pipe and eventually cause a stoppage. Cold water, on the other hand, causes grease to congeal into tiny globules that will easily flow through the drain and into the sewer.

• On occasion, fill the sink with several inches of cold water and allow it to drain through the disposer and drain pipe all at once. This flushes the drain pipe of waste and detergent scum. It also eliminates from the disposer caustic chemicals found in some detergents. These chemicals in time may damage the appliance.

• Never pour a chemical or solvent compound down the drain. It could damage the disposer. If a chemical drain cleaner is needed and the sink is a double-bowl unit, pour the chemical down the drain of the bowl not equipped with the garbage disposer.

• Never allow food scraps to remain in the garbage disposer for too long a period. Waste that is permitted to stand will begin to smell.

• If a dishwasher drains through the garbage disposer, run the disposer for several seconds and then turn it off before starting the dishwasher. This flushes away waste that may cause a backup of discharge water from the dishwasher. When the dishwasher has finished its cycle, run the disposer again for several seconds to flush away particles that may have been discharged into it by the dishwasher.

• To prevent objects from accidentally dropping into the disposer, keep the cover in place when the unit is not operating.

Repairs You Can Do Yourself

OVERBURDENING the motor with big loads of heavy waste, or jamming the motor with certain kinds of foods, causes the electrical overload device in the disposer to trip, disconnecting the electric power to the motor and thereby protecting it from damage. Pushing the red button on the side or bottom of the appliance *after the overload has been removed,* resets the overload device, allowing the disposer to be placed in operation again. This is seldom necessary in new, more expensive models equipped with automatic unjamming that reverses the direction of rotation each time the disposer is turned on.

In units that do not have this feature, several methods may be tried. Some models have a reverse action switch usually located on the outside of the hopper, near the bottom of the unit. Flipping it once may release the jam.

If a jam is stubborn and will not loosen with reverse action, or if your unit does not have such a switch, make

GARBAGE DISPOSER DIAGRAM

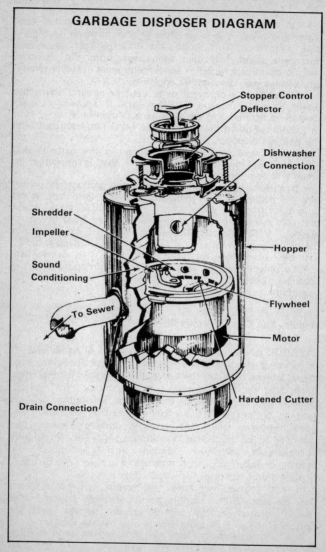

Stopper Control

Deflector

Dishwasher Connection

Shredder

Impeller

Sound Conditioning

To Sewer

Hopper

Flywheel

Motor

Drain Connection

Hardened Cutter

sure the appliance is turned off and try to pull out the object causing the jam with a pair of long-handled ice tongs.

Some disposers are equipped with an opening in the bottom that accepts a long handled wrench that can be manipulated back and forth to turn the motor and free its tightness, loosening the material that has caused the turntable to jam.

Never put your fingers inside a disposer for any reason.

Getting Rid of Odors

OVER A PERIOD of time, a garbage disposer may begin emitting an odor. To dissipate an offensive smell, follow this procedure:

1. Fill the hopper with ice cubes and run the disposer for about 15 seconds without the water running. Then run the water to flush the unit.

2. Grind up two halves of a lemon in the disposer without water running for about 30 seconds. Then turn on the water and run the disposer an additional 15 seconds.

3. Turn off the unit and fill the sink with water. Turn the disposer on, which will force-purge the sink of water.

Room Heaters

THE ELECTRIC ROOM HEATER, which is also referred to as a space heater, is a simple appliance. The working part is a heating coil (element) that is made of a special high resistance wire. Resistance refers to the fact that the coil wiring opposes the imposition of a steady electric current. This definition presents two interpretations, both of which are correct.

First of all, the special element wire draws only a certain amount of current.. Elements of different heaters differ. The greater the rating, the greater will be the amount of current drawn by the heater element, and the greater will be the amount of heat the current produces.

Another interpretation of resistance indicates that the special element wire can withstand tremendous current and heat. This, too, is true.

The amount of heat generated by an electric room heater (and, for that matter, other appliances that use heat to accomplish a task, such as an electric broiler) depends upon the amount of electric power the heating element assumes. Electric power (wattage) is the product of voltage and amperage—that is,

volts × amperes = watts.

Wall outlets supply most homes with 115 volts. This is a constant. If the heating element of a room heater allows only a five ampere flow of current through it, the output of the heater will be 575 watts—that is,

115 volts × 5 amperes = 575 watts.

Now, if another type of heater having a larger capacity (say, 10 amperes) is plugged into the same wall outlet, the output will be much greater. In fact, it will be 1150 watts (115 volts x 10 amperes = 1150 watts), which is double the amount of heat that the heater drawing five amperes can produce.

Incidentally, the wire used for the heating element of room heaters and other heat-producing appliances is a special nickel-chromium alloy called Nichrome. The metal has a very high melting point. The coil wire is attached to ceramic insulators; ceramic also has high resistance to heat.

PROBLEMS, CAUSES, REPAIRS

WHEN ROOM heaters fail, wires usually separate or burn apart. This is called an open circuit. However, no matter what the failure, testing and repairing of room heaters require the skills of a competent technician. Electric room heaters, if repaired improperly, present a potential for fire and also for electric shock.

ROOM HEATER

Porcelain or Ceramic Insulator

Blower Blade

Motor

Heating Element

Trash Compactor

THE TRASH COMPACTOR is a relatively new appliance that reduces trash to about one-quarter of its original volume and bags it for disposal. Most units also deodorize the garbage.

Frills aside, the heart of a trash compactor is a motor-and-drive assembly that provides the driving force for rams. The rams do the compressing.

The motor runs at a speed of approximately 1750 revolutions per minute. It drives the drive assembly by means of a gear-type belt which is similar to the drive belt of a snowmobile. Because of differences in drive belt pulley sizes (one on the motor and one on the drive assembly), the motor speed of 1750 revolutions per minute, or thereabouts, is reduced by approximately 75 percent. In other words, the speed at the drive assembly pulley is only about 450 revolutions per minute.

Decreased speed provides greater torque (turning or twisting force) that permits the drive assembly to drive ram screws with tremendous compressing force. This force is transferred from drive assembly to rams by means of a bicycle-type chain.

All in all, rams are driven with a force equal to approximately 2000 pounds to compress trash.

PROBLEMS, CAUSES, REPAIRS

Problem: Unit fails to start

Possible cause:

1. Power disconnected

Repairs:

1. See that power cord is in wall socket.

TRASH COMPACTOR DIAGRAM

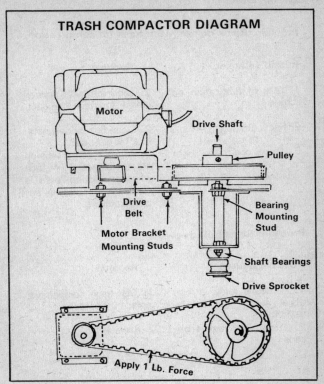

2. Blown fuse or tripped circuit breaker.

2. Replace fuse or reset circuit breaker. If trouble recurs, call an electrician.

3. Front door safety switch has failed

3. If switch has failed, motor will hum when start-switch is activated. Replace front door safety switch.

4. Rear drawer safety switch, safety lock switch, start switch, or relay has failed.

4. Test each part in turn for continuity; replace if necessary.

Problem: Rams do not reach trash for compression

Possible Causes:	Repairs:
1. Lack of lubrication on screws	1. Lubricate with special grease for trash compactors.
2. Rams binding	2. Clean out guide posts; look for bent parts.
3. Drive chain too tight	3. Adjust belt for tension not to exceed 1/4 inch when one-pound force is applied to belt midway between pulleys.

Problem: Rams fail to reverse

Possible Causes:	Repairs:
1. Defective relay, directional switch, or safety switch	1. Test each component; replace if necessary.
2. Defective ram stop pads	2. Replace

Water Heaters

WATER FOR your home is heated by electricity or by gas. In either case, the way in which the water circulates to and through a modern heater is the same. Cold water enters through a pipe in the top of the tank. This pipe, which extends almost to the bottom of the tank, is called a dip tube or drop tube.

As the cold water is discharged from this tube into the bottom of the tank, it is heated by electric elements or a gas burner. Hot water, being lighter in weight than cold water, rises to the top of the tank where it is drawn off through an outlet tube to faucets and appliances that use hot water.

Whether water is heated by electricity or gas, the temperature of the water is controlled by a thermostat that "senses" temperature. As water heat reaches a preset temperature, the thermostat responds by closing the switch that allowed the electric current to flow. When water falls below the preset temperature, the heating elements are turned back on.

About Electrically Operated Units

TWO TYPES of electrically-operated water heaters prevail: induction and immersion.

As the term indicates, an induction type heats water by inducting heat from an electric coil. The electric coil (or element) does not come into contact with the water. Instead, the element is strapped around the outside of the tank and is covered with heavy insulation, causing heat to pass through the wall of the tank (instead of dissipating into the air), and to "radiate" inward to the water.

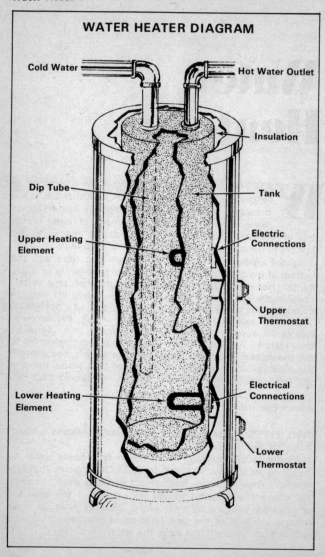

WATER HEATER DIAGRAM

Cold Water

Hot Water Outlet

Insulation

Dip Tube

Tank

Upper Heating Element

Electric Connections

Upper Thermostat

Lower Heating Element

Electrical Connections

Lower Thermostat

In contrast, an immersion water heater has the elements (there are usually two) in direct contact with the water. Elements pass right through the wall of the tank, with openings around them sealed tightly so the tank maintains its watertight integrity.

How Gas Operated Units Work

WATER HEATERS that use gas as the heating element have as their main parts a gas burner and pilot light. The burner is positioned outside the tank—never in contact with water. Its flame is directed against the bottom of the tank so cold water being discharged from the dip tube is heated.

The flow of gas to the main burner is controlled by a bimetal or bellows on-off valve that is controlled, in turn, by the thermostat. When the thermostat ''senses'' that water temperature has dropped below its preset level, it activates the bimetal or bellows, which causes the valve to open so that gas can be supplied to the burner. The burner is lit when gas is ignited by the pilot light.

Water Heaters

Situated in such a position as to be kept hot at all times by the pilot light is a flame sensor. If for some reason the pilot light goes out, the flame sensor cools, and in so doing cuts off the flow of gas to the burner.

A favorite type of flame sensor is the device known as a thermocouple. So long as it is heated by the pilot flame the thermocouple continuously generates a small amount of electricity. The thermocouple current is fed to a sensitive electric coil on a solenoid gas valve, to hold the valve open. If the pilot light goes out the thermocouple current ceases, the solenoid valve closes and the gas cannot get to the burner without a pilot flame to ignite it. Instructions on the gas hot water heater tell how to restore gas flow after relighting the pilot flame. Of course, no such device is required on electric water heaters.

Selecting a Water Heater

IF YOU ARE building a new home, remodeling an older home, or replacing a water heater that has failed, you will want to select a new heater that best meets your family's needs. The General Public Utilities Corporation has pro-

Water Heaters

vided a guide that may be used to make a selection:

No. of People in family		Without Automatic Clothes Washer and Dishwasher	With Automatic Clothes Washer and/or Dishwasher
Adults	Children	Tank Size	Tank Size
2	0	40 gallon	52 gallon
2	1	40 gallon	52 gallon
2	2	40 gallon	66 gallon
2	3	52 gallon	Two tanks of 40-gallon capacity*
2	4	82 gallon	Two tanks of 52-gallon capacity*

*Two tanks are suggested to handle this heavy load, because the installation will provide two times the recovery rate of a single tank.

Recovery rate is the time it takes a water heater to completely replenish a tankful. A minimum recovery rate is eight hours to heat a tankful of water from 50°F. to 150°F. At this rate, a water heater would heat a full load overnight, allowing a household to begin each day with a complete supply of hot water. Fortunately, most water heaters made by major manufacturers have a much faster recovery rate than this. Check this out before you buy.

Installing a Water Heater

WHEN YOU have a water heater installed in your home, it is a good idea to do some preliminary planning.

If you are building a home, place the unit near the area needing the hottest water—usually the kitchen-laundry area. Always avoid, if possible, long stretches of pipe where the hot water will stand, and cool. Ideally, the water should remain in the water heater until you need it. The more water stored in the heater, the more hot water you will conserve—as well as the energy needed to heat it.

Consider the advantages of installing two smaller water heaters rather than one large unit. It may prove less expensive in the long run since, by placing the two units wisely, you can reduce the length of piping, which will not only conserve energy but also cut down on plumbing costs.

Overall, it requires less fuel (electricity or gas) to heat two small tanks than one large one.

Make sure that the water heater (or heaters) you select is equipped with a pressure/temperature relief valve, which is installed in the cold water line just above the tank. This is very important, because the valve protects your home and water heater from the serious damage that can result if the thermostat fails and excessive pressure builds up inside the tank. The valve is set to give way when a certain pressure is reached (usually 125 pounds per square inch); pressure inside the tank to then is dissipated harmlessly. Explosions have resulted with tanks not equipped with pressure/temperature relief valves. In fact, so important is this valve that water heater installation will not pass local government inspection if the valve is not present.

Money-Saving Tips

EVERY HOUSEHOLD can conserve hot water by adopting some simple procedures. Conserving hot water saves money, energy, and frustration, since you help insure an ample supply of water. Consider the following ideas:

• Most clothes made of modern fabrics don't require hot water washing. (In fact, many fabrics are ruined by hot water.) Most clothes come clean in either warm or cold water. Hot water should be used only for washing white and colorfast cottons, and heavily soiled clothes. But when a load of laundry must be washed in hot water, you can still conserve by rinsing in cold water. Another benefit of cold water rinsing is that it reduces wrinkling in both permanent press and regular fabrics.

• Hot water in excess of the amount actually needed to wash a load of clothes is wasteful. Set the water level control of your washer for the proper intake (low, medium, or high). If there is no water level control on your washing machine, conserve hot water by avoiding small loads. Wait for full loads.

• Your automatic clothes washer may have other features that will help you conserve hot water if you use them. For example, a "suds saver" allows you to use hot or warm wash water for several loads, and a "soak" cycle removes stubborn dirt that might otherwise require a second washing.

• Surprisingly, a household normally uses less hot water if it has an automatic dishwasher. Hand washing of dishes almost always consumes more water. Homes with dish-

Water Heaters

washers use 11 to 16 gallons of water to wash a day's load of dishes. Washing and rinsing dishes by hand after each meal consumes 9 to 14 gallons of water each time (27 to 52 gallons per day). However, you should always make an automatic dishwasher do a full load of dishes. A half load uses as much hot water and electricity as a full load.

• With a modern dishwasher, you need not rinse dishes before placing them into the machine. The washing action of today's units does a thorough cleaning and sanitizing job. However, if you feel that you must rinse dishes, use cold or cool water.

• If you wash dishes by hand, use a dishpan or sink stopper. Washing and rinsing each dish under constantly running water wastes water and money.

• Never use hot water when operating a garbage disposer. Use cold water only. Hot water causes fat and grease to melt. As fat and grease pass through the drain pipe, they cool suddenly and settle along the pipe. In time, this will cause a clogging, which means a plumbing bill. Cold water, on the other hand, causes fat and grease to congeal. In a hardened state, they can be pulverized by the disposer and carried down the drain with the rest of the food waste.

• A tub bath consumes 10 to 15 gallons of hot water—a shower bath, 8 to 12 gallons.

• Good rules of thumb to follow are: don't use hot water when cold water will do, but if warmer water is needed, mix hot and cold so that no hot water is wasted.

• Set your water heater to provide a sensible temperature. Household needs are generally satisfied by water heated to 150° F. This also will lengthen the life of your plumbing.

• Finally, repair leaking water faucets promptly. A drip of one drop per second, which is considered a slow leak, wastes approximately 200 gallons of water per month. This is equivalent to five tankfuls if your home is equipped with a 40-gallon water heater.

Taking Care of a Water Heater

YOUR WATER HEATER requires no maintenance. However, the life of many units usually can be prolonged by periodic draining. This removes mineral deposits that may attack the inside surface. How often you need to do this depends on the amount and kind of minerals in the water, but draining cannot do any harm, even if you do it more often than necessary.

Some water heaters are equipped with a magnesium anode rod. Corrosive agents attack this rod rather than the tank's surface. When the rod becomes badly corroded, the hot water will darken, which indicates that the rod should be replaced.

Consult the owner's manual which came with the water heater, ask a dealer who sells your make of water heater, to determine if your unit needs to be drained. If your unit is an electric one, and complete draining is recommended, turn off the circuit to the heater by unscrewing the fuse or tripping the circuit breaker. If heating elements turn "on" as the tank is being emptied, they may be damaged, and should be checked by an electrician. Make sure the tank is filled before replacing the fuse or activating the circuit breaker.

Fixing a Water Heater

THERE IS little that the average homeowner can do to repair a faulty water heater. Your local gas company or electric company should be called when a problem affects the heat source. Other failures usually should be handled by competent professional water heater technicians.

However, so that you may know what you can handle, and also know what is going on even though you must call in an expert, CONSUMER GUIDE Magazine offers the following trouble-shooting charts:

PROBLEMS, CAUSES, REPAIR

Problem: No hot water

Possible cause	Repair
1. Blown fuse or tripped circuit breaker (electric heater)	1. Replace fuse or reset circuit breaker. If same thing happens, a short circuit exists. Call serviceperson. Do not activate circuit again.
2. Calcium buildup on heating element (electric heater, immersion type)	2. Have technician remove element and clean. (See chapter on Continuity Tester.)

3. Heating element burned out (electric heater)	3. Test with continuity tester. Replace if tester shows that element has failed.
4. Defective thermocouple (gas heater)	4. Clean pilot orifice and relight pilot. If pilot refuses to stay lit, replace thermocouple.
5. Defective thermostat (gas heater)	5. Replace.

Problem: Insufficient hot water

Possible cause	**Repair**
1. Thermostat setting too low	1. Normal setting is 140-150° F.
2. Tank too small for family's needs	2. As a family grows and/or the use of hot water appliances increases, the size of the water heater may have to be changed (see Selecting a Water Heater).
3. Lower heating element burned out (electric heater, immersion type)	3. Test with continuity tester. Replace if tester shows that element has failed.
4. Defective dip tube	4. The dip tube may have developed a hole, which is allowing cold water to dilute hot water near the top of the tank. The dip tube may have to be removed and replaced, but if the old tube is made of plastic, replace it with a tube made of copper. This is not an easy problem to spot; a technician probably would have to be called in.

Problem: Slow recovery

Possible cause	Repair
1. Top heating element burned out (electric heater, immersion type)	1. Test with continuity tester. Replace if tester shows that element has failed.

Problem: Steam in hot water

Possible cause	Repair
1. Thermostat contacts burned (electric heater)	1. Examine thermostat for shorted or burned terminals. Replace if necessary. (See the chapter on Thermostats.)
2. Thermostat does not cut off (gas heater)	2. If burner fails to go off when thermostat is set lower, replace thermostat.
3. Thermostat setting too high	3. Normal setting is 140-150° F.

Problem: Water beneath tank

Possible cause	Repair
1. Leaky thermostat	1. Replace thermostat gasket.
2. Leaky plumbing connections	2. Make necessary repairs.
3. Condensation	3. Not much you can do, but this is not serious.
4. Hole in tank	4. Replacement of tank is indicated.

Clothes Dryers

THE CLOTHES DRYER is a simple machine. A rotating drum tumbles damp clothes in an atmosphere of warm air, and the clothes become dry. The drum is rotated by an electric motor. A drive belt connecting the electric motor and the drum allows the two to turn in tandem.

The heat source is either electric or gas. A dryer which uses electricity as a heat source contains one or two heating elements that become red hot when an electric current flows through them. A dryer using gas as a heat source warms the air by means of a pilot-light-operated burner that is similar to that of a gas stove.

Important: CONSUMER GUIDE Magazine's information on dryers is for owners of both electric and gas units *except* when referring to repairs of the heat source; the information then is for owners of electric units only.

Repairing an electric clothes dryer is possible, but you should never attempt to repair a problem with the heat source function of a gas dryer. Call your local gas company's service department. They respond promptly and most service is free to homeowners.

Once the heat source in a clothes dryer is generating heat and the drum is rotating, a fan blows hot air through and around the clothes as they tumble. Moist air is expelled to the outside through an exhaust flue.

Only two controls are needed to operate a clothes dryer. One is a clock timer (synchronous motor) that controls the amount of time of the drying cycle. (A detailed explanation of how these timers work is in the chapter on clothes washers.)

The second control in a clothes dryer is a thermostat—

actually a safety device, although in some dryers a second one is included to control temperature. The thermostat automatically turns off the dryer if the temperature goes higher than a safe limit, usually set around 200° F.

When a thermostat is used to control temperature, it functions during the drying cycle in response to the particular setting you choose for drying different types of fabrics—permanent press, sheers, cottons, wools, knits, and so on. As the air in the dryer reaches the peak temperature for the setting you selected, the thermostat reduces the amount of electric current or gas going to the heating element. This is the same type of control used by temperature-controlled ovens and ranges; it is explained in the chapter on thermostats.

Caring for Your Clothes Dryer

ONLY ONE preventive maintenance task is required by a clothes dryer, but it is of utmost importance. Every dryer includes a filter that traps lint (shaken loose from the clothes) carried by the warm, moist air as it is expelled through the exhaust flue. If the filter is not cleaned, lint builds up and blocks the passage of air. This reduces the efficiency of the dryer, and eventually could cause a fire.

Clean the filter after every use.

Consult the instruction manual which came with the dryer; it will show you where the filter is located and the best way to remove and clean it.

PROBLEMS, CAUSES, REPAIRS

THE CLOTHES DRYER usually is simple to repair. A problem shows itself most often in one of four ways:
1. The basket will not rotate, although the motor operates.
2. Little or no heat is generated.
3. Clothes remain damp.
4. The motor does not go on.

You should observe two important safety precautions when working on a clothes dryer. First, pull the power cord from the wall socket. Make repairs or connect a test light, as necessary. Only then reconnect the power cord to check on your repair or to test a component. *Never work on the appliance with electricity connected.*

The second precaution involves a gas dryer. If you must move the dryer, use extreme caution to prevent breaking a gas line connection.

1. Basket will not rotate although motor operates. In most cases, a stretched or broken drive belt causes this malfunction. Most dryers use one belt, called a belly band, that goes completely around the drum and is driven by the motor. The band extends from the motor pulley around another, called an idler pulley (its job is simply to support the extended length), and around the drum.

Other dryers use two belts. One of these extends between the motor and an idler pulley. The second belt extends from the idler pulley to the drum drive pulley. If either of these belts breaks or loosens to a point where it slips, the drum will not rotate or will rotate sluggishly.

A few dryers use three belts. Two of these are connected in the same way as a two-belt setup. The third belt drives the fan.

To check a drive belt (or belts), pull the power cord from the wall, then remove the rear panel of the dryer. If a belt has broken (this will be readily visible), replace it with a new one.

It is best to order a new drive belt from a dealer who sells those for your brand. Order by brand and model number to make sure you get the correct belt.

Each belt on a dryer must be tight, though not too tight. It should have a play of ½ inch when pressure is applied with your thumb to the mid-point. If a belt needs tightening, loosen the drive and exert pressure against the belt by pulling on the drive. Retighten the drive when tension is correct.

If you do not find a break in the belt or belts, then the reason for a drum not rotating, or rotating sluggishly even though the motor runs, is either a buildup of lint around the drum or a frozen drum bearing. You can determine which problem exists by removing the drive belt and rotating the drum by hand. If the drum turns, but catches intermittently, look for lint trapped between the drum and dryer housing. The drum has vanes which usually are removable. Through the openings you should be able to clean out the lint.

If the drum will not turn at all, but feels as if it is binding constantly, the drum bearing is frozen and should be replaced. To do this, the drum will have to be removed from the dryer, a job for the service technician.

2. Little or no heat is generated. As was mentioned before, this section refers only to electric dryers. If you have

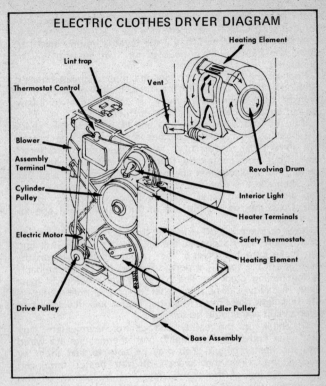

ELECTRIC CLOTHES DRYER DIAGRAM

Heating Element

Lint trap

Thermostat Control

Vent

Blower

Assembly
Terminal

Revolving Drum

Cylinder
Pulley

Interior Light

Heater Terminals

Electric Motor

Safety Thermostats

Heating Element

Drive Pulley

Idler Pulley

Base Assembly

a problem with the heat source of a gas dryer, call your local gas company.

The first thing to do when you discover your electric dryer is not giving off heat is to check the fuse or circuit breaker in the main electric panel. Dryers are serviced by two 30 ampere fuses or two circuit breakers. If one of these fuses is bad, or if one of the circuit breakers has tripped, it is possible that the dryer will run, but the heating element will not operate. In other words, if one fuse is out the motor will run; if the other is out the motor will not run. In neither case will the element heat up.

Clothes Dryers

In other words, an electric clothes dryer operates on a total of 220 volts. The motor requires 110 volts, the heating element 220 volts. Thus if the dryer is getting only 110 volts, the motor will continue to run, but no heat will be generated.

Replace the bad fuse or reset the tripped circuit breaker. Start the dryer again. If the fuse blows or the circuit breaker trips soon after, there is an electrical problem. Do not operate the dryer. Call an electrician.

If fuses and circuit breakers are in good shape, check the heater. Most electric clothes dryers have one heater, but some older models have two. Dryers open in different ways, but one commonly found uses the following procedure: First disconnect the power cord from the wall outlet, then slip a screwdriver in the joint formed by the unit's top and its front panel, and pry upward, popping up the top. Open the top. At the rear of the unit you will see the heater terminals.

Now connect a 220-volt test light across the terminals (See Figure 1). Reconnect the power cord to the wall outlet, make sure the dryer's door is closed and turn on the machine. If the test light does not glow, the heater probably is functioning properly. The cause of the problem is most likely a faulty safety thermostat or control thermostat. If the test light does glow, then the heater has developed an open circuit and should be replaced.

To check on the safety and control thermostats, you first must find them. Generally, both thermostats are wired into the heater circuit. You may be able to find them by tracing the wires that branch off the heater terminals.

The location of the thermostats may be shown on the schematic wiring diagram that should be glued inside the cabinet of the machine.

Check each thermostat by connecting the 220-volt test light across its terminals. If the light glows when the dryer is turned on, an open circuit exists in that thermostat and the part should be replaced.

One other part can cause the problem of little or no heat: the timer. To test the timer, make sure that no electricity is getting to the appliance (disconnect the wall plug) and remove the control knobs and control panel. Knobs are probably held by small Allen screws (you will need an Allen head wrench).

First examine the contacts of the timer closely. If contacts are burned, the timer is bad and should be replaced.

Clothes Dryers

Notice that the timer has two terminals on its output side and one terminal on its input end. Connect a test light between one of the terminals on the output side and the terminal on the input end. Reconnect current to the dryer, see that the door is closed, and turn the timer dial. If the light glows, the timer is bad. If the light does not glow, test the other input terminal of the timer.

3. Clothes remain damp. If the heat source is generating heat and the basket is revolving, but clothes remain damp, then the reason is either a vent that is clogged with lint or a malfunctioning blower fan. Bet on a buildup of lint, since blower fans seldom go bad.

As indicated before, lint is the main enemy of a clothes dryer. If it has been allowed to accumulate so that drying is affected, you will have to disassemble and clean out vent pipes as well as the lint trap. You can check for excessive lint buildup by putting your hand on the top of the dryer—if it seems unusually hot to the touch, you have a lint problem.

If a blower fan does go bad in those machines where the fan is a part of the motor, the fan can be replaced without replacing the entire motor. Incidentally, an indication of a defective blower fan is a racket coming from the motor. When the fan is no longer in balance, the motor will begin vibrating.

Dryers with three belts have a blower fan which is independent of the main motor. If clothes remain damp, inspect the belt that extends from the main motor to the blower. If the belt has broken or is slipping, the blower cannot operate efficiently.

4. Motor does not operate. The problem could spring from a variety of malfunctions: the timer, motor starter switch, motor bearings, door switch, or bad fuses or circuit breakers. It may be as simple as a cord accidentally pulled from the wall receptacle. In checking fuses, be aware that many machines have a fuse in the dryer itself which serves as protection against a motor overload. If this fuse blows, the machine will not run.

To check on the door switch, loosen the top of the dryer as explained above. The door switch is immediately in back of the small pushbutton which is visible when the door of the dryer is open. The function of the door switch is to shut the dryer off when the door is open.

Disconnect the power cord from the wall outlet, disconnect the two wires connected to the door switch, tie the

Clothes Dryers

two ends of the wire together, and reconnect the dryer. Turn on power. Even with the door open, the dryer will start running if the cause of the problem is a bad door switch. Do not use this bypass method to run the dryer for general use; it is dangerous. Buy and install a new switch.

The final cause of a motor not operating is a burned out motor. You will know this is the problem if you smell an odor of scorched insulation. A burned-out motor must be replaced.

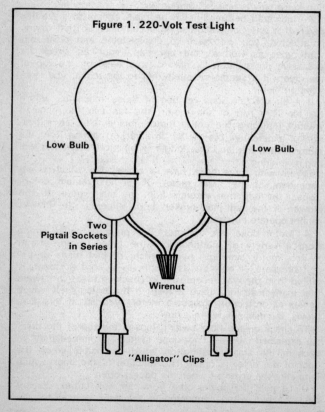

Figure 1. 220-Volt Test Light

Low Bulb

Low Bulb

Two Pigtail Sockets in Series

Wirenut

"Alligator" Clips

Clothes Washers

A CLOTHES WASHER becomes automatic — doing all the jobs it is meant to do without manual control by the owner — because of its timer. Actually, the timer is an assembly of cam-operated switches driven by a synchronous motor. The same motor is found on the timer of other automatic appliances, including clothes dryers and dishwashers.

A synchronous motor runs at a set speed at all times, never speeding up or slowing down (unless it malfunctions) its speed is controlled by house current, which is set to deliver exactly 60 cycles per second. Since the speed of current never varies (unless there is a utility malfunction), the operating speed of a washer's synchronous motor never varies.

Along the shaft of the synchronous motor are several discs called cams. Each cam is lined up facing, and in touch with, a switch. As the motor shaft rotates, the cams rotate so that their high and low points push or release (activate or deactivate) the switches at different times. A spring-loaded trip gear in the reduction gear train allows the synchronous motor to drive the timer cams in spurts so that instead of gradually opening and closing, which might cause arcing, the timer switch opens and closes with a snap action. As each switch is activated or deactivated, a different function of the washing machine is started or stopped automatically. The machine fills with water, the tub agitates, water is drained and spun out, rinse water fills the tub, and a final draining and spinning end the cycle.

Clothes Washers

Putting it simply — the timer controls the functions of the washer and the duration of the cycles you set at the beginning — a short, cool water cycle for permanent press clothes, a longer, hot water cycle for bed linens, and so on.

How a Washing Machine Works

IF YOU FOLLOW a typical agitator-type washing machine through several of its functions, you will get a good idea of how the synchronous timer motor performs its job, as well as how other parts function:

1. When you turn on the machine, water begins filling the basket. The water can be hot or cold, or a mixture of the two (warm). It depends on the water valves — whether one or the other, or both, open.

Attached to the valves — one valve for cold water and one for hot water — are hoses that connect to a cold water pipe and a hot water pipe. The flow of water through the pipes is controlled by an electric device called a solenoid, which allows the valves to open or close.

Each pipe has its own solenoid (coil) which operates a stem (armature). When the stem is down, water pressure seals off the valve intake so that water cannot enter the washing machine. When the stem is up, the intake passage is clear and water pours in.

The solenoid valve stem lifts electrically; it closes by spring pressure. There is not enough power in the stem movement to control the water flow. Therefore the valve is designed so that it is the water pressure which opens and closes the valve. All the solenoid stem or plunger does is control passageways that determine where the water pressure flows to activate the valve.

Most washing machines have a water temperature switch that permits you to select cold, hot or warm water. By setting the switch, you determine which solenoid will be activated. For warm water, both solenoids open both the hot and cold pipe valves and the two waters come together and mix. This is why the water intake valve is frequently called the water mixing valve.

Once the solenoid has opened the valve, and water is rushing into the tub of the washing machine, the length of time the water continues to flow is determined by one of those cams on the shaft of the timer. There are ususally several water-fill times possible on a machine — the tub can be filled to a "low" or a "high" level for wash and rinse cycles, and during the rinse cycle additional water flows in as soapy water is spun out. These time periods are set at the factory.

Other washers — not on a "time-fill" system — have a float-like device that allows water to rinse to a predetermined level. The float then trips a switch that turns operation back to the timer and shuts off the water flow.

2. As soon as the water flow is shut off by the valve when the preset time period has run out, another switch is turned on by one of the cams on the synchronous motor. This switch controls the agitator shaft in the center of the tub. Either through a belt or coupling, the split phase motor drives a train of reduction gears terminating in an oscillating arm that converts the rotation from the gear train into a reciprocating movement for the agitator.

This is the real working phase of a washing cycle. Water, detergent, and the agitation of the clothes combine to rub, soak, and wash out dirt and stains. The agitation, preset at the factory, lasts for varying periods of time, depending on the type of washing you select at the beginning (permanent press, blankets, bed linens, and so on).

3. When the preset washing time has elapsed, the timer does several things: it switches off the agitator drive, it turns on the pump, and it operates the drain valve. A solenoid provides the movement to open the drain line.

As the drain valve opens and the pump begins operating, the basket, or tub, starts spinning, first slowly, then faster and faster until the clothes are flung by centrifugal force to the sides of the basket and held there as long as the spinning continues. This spinning "wrings" the cloths of most of their water so that they are damp when removed. (For some cycles, such as those for permanent press clothes, the spin cycle is slower than normal so that creases do not form in the clothes as they are pressed tightly against the sides of the basket.)

In most washers, the basket is spun by the same motor that controlled the agitator in the wash cycle. Whether the agitator will move back and forth in short spurts, or the tube will spin

CLOTHES WASHER

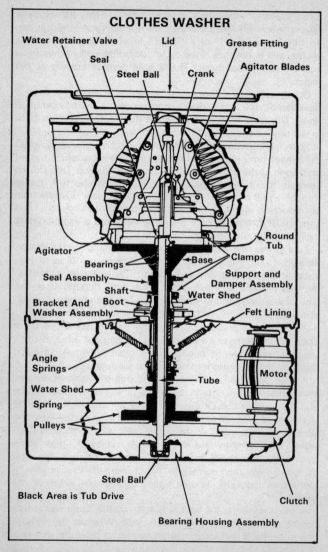

Water Retainer Valve
Lid
Grease Fitting
Seal
Steel Ball
Crank
Agitator Blades
Agitator
Round Tub
Bearings
Base
Clamps
Seal Assembly
Support and Damper Assembly
Shaft
Water Shed
Bracket And Washer Assembly
Boot
Felt Lining
Angle Springs
Motor
Water Shed
Tube
Spring
Pulleys
Steel Ball
Clutch
Black Area is Tub Drive
Bearing Housing Assembly

(that is, whether the motor will cause rotation from side to side or in one direction for the spin) is determined by the transmission.

There are many different kinds of transmissions and drive mechanisms used in automatic clothes washers. One type employs two motors — one with a low-speed drive for agitation and the other with a high-speed drive for spinning. The motors interlock so that both cannot operate at the same time.

Another type of drive mechanism uses two pulleys on one shaft that is equipped with a clutch. One pulley is for low speed; the other is for high. The clutch simply engages one or the other to initiate agitation or spin. In this type, the motor reverses; one direction for agitate, the other for spin.

How to Take Care of a Clothes Washer

YOUR MODERN AUTOMATIC clothes washer is a strong machine that should give many years of service even if you never have it checked. However, by practicing these simple maintenance procedures you will extend its life and assure yourself of the best possible washing results:

1. Read and follow the instruction booklet that came with your washing machine. If you have lost this valuable document, write the manufacturer for another. This guide tells you everything you need to know about preparing clothes for washing, loading the machine, pretreating the wash, selecting the correct cycle and washing aids (soaps, detergents, bleach, fabric softeners), removing stains, and how to wash special items.

2. After each wash has been completed, disconnect the power cord from the wall socket and wipe the outside and inside of the machine with a clean damp cloth. Also wipe off the agitator. Leave the door of the machine open so the interior can dry thoroughly.

3. Occasionally wax the exterior surface to provide extra protection. Use one of the special appliance waxes sold in hardware stores.

4. If you spill bleach on the surface of the machine, wipe it up immediately. Bleach is highly corrosive.

5. At the end of each wash day, turn off the valves on the

Clothes Washers .

pipes leading to the washing machine to relieve water pressure on the water valve inside the machine. This is a safeguard. A water valve can fail, if one does, and the pipe valves are open, water can drip into the tub, or even pour in, causing a flood.

How to Repair a Washing Machine

THERE ARE many reasons for clothes washer failure, but a malfunction usually affects one of four functions: filling, washing (agitation), draining, spinning.

Many times the cause of a problem is easily corrected. The troubleshooting charts below begin with minor, easy-to-fix problems and go on to more serious and complex ones. You may be able to fix the simpler problems yourself before calling a repair person for adjustments or repairs you feel are beyond your ability.

When you work on an automatic clothes washer, or for that matter on any electric appliance, it is imperative that you take these precautions:

1. Make sure that electricity is turned off before handling components. Remove the fuse or trip the circuit breaker servicing the appliance, or pull the power cord from the wall outlet. Don't take chances of getting a fatal electric shock.

2. Turn off water at the main intake when working on a water-handling component, such as a water valve.

3. Do not go to the expense of replacing an electrical component that you think has gone bad before checking to make sure that the trouble is not caused by a loose wire connection that can be corrected easily.

4. After replacing an electrical component, make certain all wire connections are tight.

5. Do not restore electrical service to the appliance (reinsert the plug or replace the fuse or circuit breaker) until you are sure that ground wires are reattached firmly.

6. To prevent water leaks, see to it that water connections are tight.

7. If a replacement part is needed, use one that meets the specifications. You cannot go wrong using parts made by the manufacturer of your appliance.

PROBLEMS, CAUSES, REPAIRS

Problem: Washer does not fill with water

Possible Causes	Repairs*
1. Water valves on pipes closed.	1. Open valves.
2. Water inlet hoses kinked or knotted.	2. Straighten out hoses.
3. Clogged water intake screens	3. Screens are located in hose connections at water faucets and at those connections of the water intake valve. Remove screens and clean out sediment.
4. Defective water valve solenoid	4. Remove leads from valve and connect a 115-volt test light across terminals. (See the chapter on Continuity Tester.) Turn off electricity and move control knob (timer dial) to "Fill" position. If test light does not light, the water valve solenoid should be replaced.
5. Defective water valve	5. Disassemble water valve and inspect parts for damage. Replace a bad part with a new one, if possible. If not, replace the entire valve.

---

*Pull power cord from wall outlet first. After each repair is made, reconnect electric power and test operation. If the action fails to remedy the condition and further action has to be taken, be sure to pull the power cord from the wall outlet again before continuing.

6. Defective timer

6. Test according to manufacturer's recommended procedure and replace if faulty. Be sure to try the lead wires for correct replacement.

7. Defective water temperature switch or water level pressure switch

7. Test according to manufacturer's recommended procedure and replace if faulty.

8. Open circuit in timer, in water solenoid valve coil, or in connecting wires.

8. To test timer, use continuity tester to check for complete circuit from line cord plug prong to solenoid, make continuity check between two solenoid terminals (See Figure 1). There should be continuity from ''source to load''—from the line cord plug to the motor lead wire—when the timer is set to WASH.

Problem: Washer does not wash (agitate)

Possible Causes

Repair*

1. Broken drive belt
2. Drive belt is too loose and slipping.

1. Replace with new belt.
2. Tighten. The correct belt tension is attained when the belt can be deflected 1/2 inch.

*Pull power cord from wall outlet first. After each repair is made, reconnect electric power and test operation. If the action fails to remedy the condition and further action has to be taken, be sure to pull the power cord from the wall outlet again before continuing.

3. Defective drive clutch	3. Replace control knob (timer) in "Wash" position. Remove the drive belt and turn the clutch by hand. If there is no strong resistance, the clutch is bad and should be replaced.
4. Defective transmission	4. Place control knob (timer) in "Wash" position. Remove the drive belt and turn the transmission pulley by hand in the direction of agitation, which is generally clockwise. If the agitator is not driven by this action, the transmission is probably bad and should be overhauled or replaced.
5. Defective timer or water level pressure switch	5. Test according to manufacturer's recommended procedure and replace if faulty.
6. Open circuit	6. With control knob (timer) at "Wash" position, probe each wire connection with a test light to determine if there is a defective wire or loose connection.

---

*Pull power cord from wall outlet first. After each repair is made, reconnect electric power and test operation. If the action fails to remedy the condition and further action has to be taken, be sure to pull the power cord from the wall outlet again before continuing.

Clothes Washers

Problem: Water drains from machine during wash and rinse cycles instead of at the end of the cycle.

Possible Cause	Repair *
1. Drain hose may be positioned lower than the water level in basket. This creates a vacuum and water will siphon out.	1. Reposition drain hose so that it is higher than the highest water level in the basket.

Problem: Machine does not spin or does not spin at correct speed

Possible Cause	Repair*
1. Broken drive belt	1. Replace with new belt.
2. Slipping drive belt	2. Tighten belt. The correct belt tension is attained when the belt can be deflected 1/2 inch.
3. Loosen motor drive pulley	3. Tighten pulley, set screw.
4. Defective drive clutch	4. With dryer unplugged, pull control knob (timer) in "Spin" position. Remove the drive belt and turn the clutch by hand. If there is a strong resistance, the clutch is bad and should be replaced.

*Pull power cord from wall outlet first. After each repair is made, reconnect electric power and test operation. If the action fails to remedy the condition and further action has to be taken, be sure to pull the power cord from the wall outlet again before continuing.

5. Spin brake does not release or transmission is frozen

5. The spin brake and transmission are attached and checked as one unit. Place control knob (timer) in "Spin" position. Remove drive belt. Turn brake stator. It should move freely. If the brake stator binds, the brake assembly or transmission is defective. Have one or both, repaired.

6. Defective timer

6. Test according to manufacturer's recommended procedure and replace if faulty.

7. Open circuit

7. Use continuity tester to check for complete circuit from line cord to solenoid terminals.

Problem: Motor does not operate

Probable Cause

Repair*

1. Power cord disconnected

1. Make sure that power cord is plugged into wall outlet.

2. Blown fuse or tripped circuit breaker

2. Replace fuse or reset circuit breaker. If fuse blows or circuit breaker trips again, disconnect appliance. Do not operate. A malfunction exists that

---

*Pull power cord from wall outlet first. After each repair is made, reconnect electric power and test operation. If the action fails to remedy the condition and further action has to be taken, be sure to pull the power cord from the wall outlet again before continuing.

3. Defective lid switch

4. Defective timer

5. Defective motor

may cause fire. Consult an electrician or appliance serviceman.

3. Most newer washing machines have a safety switch which is activated by the lid; the machine turns off automatically when the lid is raised during operation. Test this switch by connecting a test light across its terminals. With the control knob at "Wash" position, the light should light. If not, replace the lid switch.

4. Test according to manufacturer's recommended procedure and replace if faulty.

5. Most washing machines are protected by an internal overload circuit breaker which turns the appliance off if the motor overheats. If the motor cannot be started 30 minutes after this protective part turns the machine off, one of the following conditions exist:
(a) If the motor has switched off as the washing machine went into the "Spin" position, the rea-

---

*Pull power cord from wall outlet first. After each repair is made, reconnect electric power and test operation. If the action fails to remedy the condition and further action has to be taken, be sure to pull the power cord from the wall outlet again before continuing.

son for the problem may not be the motor, but the clutch, transmission or brake. To determine if this is the case, remove the drive belts, set the control knob at "Spin" position and turn on the machine. If the motor operates, there is no motor problem. Isolate the failure to the clutch, transmission or brake.

(b) If the motor operates in "Spin" position, but not in "Wash" position, or vice versa, the cause of the problem may be a bad timer or defective lid switch. Check these two components before blaming the motor.

Problem: Water does not drain out of washer

Possible Cause	Repair*
1. Kinked or knotted drain hose	1. Straighten out hose.
2. Broken drive belt	2. Replace with new belt.
3. Slipping drive belt	3. Tighten belt. The correct belt tension is attained when the belt can be deflected 1/2 inch.

---

*Pull power cord from wall outlet first. After each repair is made, reconnect electric power and test operation. If the action fails to remedy the condition and further action has to be taken, be sure to pull the power cord from the wall outlet again before continuing.

4. Clogged drain	4. Free drain.
5. Defective water pump	5. Either disassemble pump, clean out sediment and replace bad parts; or replace entire pump.
6. Defective timer	6. Test according to manufacturer's recommended procedure and replace if faulty.
7. Open circuit	7. With control knob at "Drain" position, probe each wire connection with a test light to determine if there is a defective wire or loose connection.

Fig. 1 WASHING MACHINE SOLENOID WATER VALVE

When the coil pulls the plunger tip out of the small hole in the washer, water pressure unseats the washer and water pours through. When spring pushes plunger into hole, water pressure unequalizes and forces washer to closed position.

*Pull power cord from wall outlet first. After each repair is made, reconnect electric power and test operation. If the action fails to remedy the condition and further action has to be taken, be sure to pull the power cord from the wall outlet again before continuing.

CONSUMER GUIDE

Vacuum Cleaners

VACUUM CLEANERS and electric brooms are almost as basic today as once were the ordinary broom and dustpan. With or without their special attachments, these cleaners can handle hardwood floors, walls, carpets, furniture, and draperies, and are an important factor in the maintenance of appliances such as window air conditioners and refrigerators.

Although vacuum cleaners are available in a variety of sizes and shapes (the two major categories are tank or canister and upright), they all work on the same principle. As for electric brooms, they are in fact lightweight, upright vacuum cleaners with the same working parts.

At the heart of a vacuum cleaner is an electric motor housed in a compartment. The motor drives a shaft which causes a fan to whir. The fan pulls air through the housing and forces it out through the outlet end of the cleaner.

All this occurs at a very high rate of speed. Vacuum cleaner motors operate at approximately **3000** to **10,000 +** revolutions per minute, depending upon design. With this speed, a great quantity of air is moved at once, creating suction.

As the fan draws air through the compartment, it creates suction at the inlet end of the housing—the end with the pick-up attachment. In canister-type vacuum cleaners, the pickup is a long hose equipped with a nozzle (or brush or wand, or other cleaning attachment). In upright units, the pickup is a brush-equipped roller mechanism (sometimes with a beater bar) that sweeps along the floor or rug.

The high-speed fan sucks air through the pickup attachment and into the inner compartment. As it does so, it creates a vacuum—an empty space from which all air has

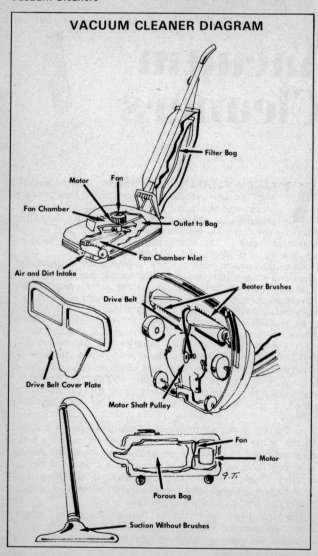

VACUUM CLEANER DIAGRAM

Filter Bag

Motor

Fan

Fan Chamber

Outlet to Bag

Fan Chamber Inlet

Air and Dirt Intake

Beater Brushes

Drive Belt

Drive Belt Cover Plate

Motor Shaft Pulley

Fan

Motor

Porous Bag

Suction Without Brushes

been removed. The crucial point of a vacuum is that air around it always rushes in to fill the empty space. In other words, an area of high pressure always rushes toward an area of low pressure.

In a vacuum cleaner, the air that surges in to fill the vacuum carries with it dust, dirt, and lint particles, thus literally "vacuum cleaning."

The air that flows in to fill the vacuum flows on into a container or bag. (One brand of electric broom uses a plastic cup; others, and vacuum cleaners, use a bag.) Vacuum cleaner bags are made of a special paper or cloth that is porous enough to permit a free flow of air, tight enough to trap most of the dust and dirt, and tough enough to withstand the pressure without tearing. The cloth bags can be cleaned and re-used. Paper bags are discarded when full and replaced with new ones.

Beyond the bag is a filter that permits air to flow through but which captures finer dust and dirt that was not trapped by the bag. The air—relatively clean by now—passes next over the vacuum cleaner motor, cooling it, and then on out through the outlet.

How to Repair a Vacuum Cleaner

THE CHIEF COMPLAINT of those who use vacuum cleaners and electric brooms is lack of suction—"It won't pick up." Sometimes the complaint is based on a real problem; other times, the solution can be a simple one.

You can check to see if your cleaner is creating sufficient vacuum by scattering some sawdust over the floor. If some of the sawdust remains after you have swept the vacuum cleaner over it, the suction is not sufficient. The unit needs servicing.

The most common cause of insufficient suction is a full dust bag or a dirt-clogged filter. Dirt-clogged nozzles, hoses and passages also reduce suction—in fact, anything that cuts down on the free movement of air cuts down on the efficiency of a vacuum cleaner.

If you are having problems with suction, check first to see if the dust bag or filter are clogged. Remove both. Place the cleaner in a position where it will not pick up dirt, then switch it on. (Never operate a vacuum cleaner or electric broom in the cleaning position without a dust bag, pickup

Vacuum Cleaners

receptacle or filter. Dust will be pulled into the motor, where it can clog air passages, causing the motor to overheat and burn out.) Hold your hand over the pickup end of the clean-

ELECTRIC BROOM DIAGRAM

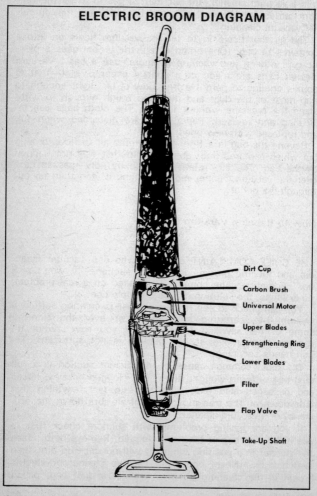

Dirt Cup

Carbon Brush

Universal Motor

Upper Blades

Strengthening Ring

Lower Blades

Filter

Flap Valve

Take-Up Shaft

er to check the suction. If it seems stronger without the dust bag and filter, replace them.

If removing the dust bag and filter does not increase the vacuum (suction), all hoses, nozzles and passages should be inspected for dirt buildup. Pull the power cord from the wall outlet, then clean all parts of the unit. Make sure, too, that hoses are not torn or otherwise damaged. Check gaskets for tears. A bad hose will create an air leak, which will result in reduced vacuum and weaker suction.

Other common problems with vacuum cleaners are listed in the chart below.

PROBLEMS, CAUSES, REPAIRS

Problem: Motor will not run

Possible Causes	Repairs
1. Damaged power cord	1. Reconnect wires and retape
2. Worn motor brushes	2. Replace
3. Bad on-off switch	3. Have repaired or replaced
4. Loose wiring	4. Tighten
5. Damaged motor	5. Have repaired or replaced

Problem: Shock felt when motor is started

Possible Causes	Repair
1. Wire has come loose and is grounded against unit's case	1. Unplug unit; check wires; if in doubt, have professionally checked before using again.

Problem: Hard to push (upright)

Possible Causes	Repair
1. Machine set too low (too close to floor)	1. Adjust
2. Worn out brushes	2. Replace
3. Brush spindles need lubrication	3. Follow diagram and lubricate

Floor Polishers

AN ELECTRIC floor polisher works on the same mechanical and electrical principles as smaller motor-driven appliances, such as drills, saws and electric knives. The object of the machine is to drive two brushes against a floor to polish it.

A point to remember is this: polishing brushes rotate in opposite directions from each other. This opposing action is accomplished in several ways depending on the type of floor polisher.

In the design and construction of a standard floor polisher, gears and bearings that drive the brush drive shafts are positioned in the lower part of the appliance housing. The motor is located on top of the gear box, while the motor itself is mounted in a vertical position.

The handle is hinged to the housing to make it easier for the user to keep the brushes flat on the floor while moving the machine back and forth. The line cord enters the hollow handle from the top, is tapped into an on-off switch, and extends down and is connected to the electric motor.

The operation of the machine is quite simple. The motor is turned on by switching on the on-off switch. The motor revolves and drives a gear. This gear, in turn, drives a small pinion which is attached to one of the two main gears. The two main gears are meshed, but are positioned in such a way that if one turns to the right, the other turns to the left. In other words, driving of the one main gear by the pinion causes the other main gear to be driven in the opposite direction.

A pinion beneath each main gear drives the final-drive gear that drives the drive shaft to which the brushes are attached.

Another method used to operate a floor polisher is called

FLOOR POLISHER DIAGRAM

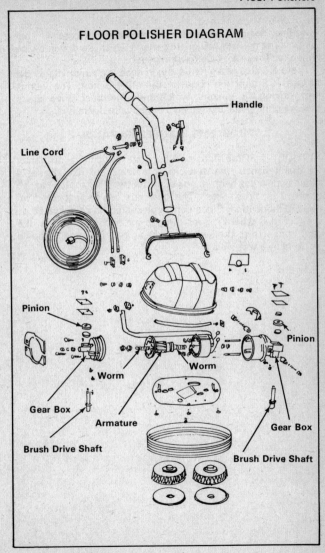

Handle

Line Cord

Pinion

Pinion

Worm

Worm

Gear Box

Gear Box

Armature

Brush Drive Shaft

Brush Drive Shaft

Floor Polishers

the double-worm method.

In this design, the motor is mounted horizontally, but controls not one but two geared shafts which are driven by the armature. These are called worm gears.

There are also two gear boxes. In each is a pinion that is cut to turn in a direction opposite the other pinion. The worms turn, driving the pinions, which drive the brush drive shafts that drive the polishing brushes in opposite directions.

PROBLEMS, CAUSES, REPAIRS

ALTHOUGH SOME floor polishers are difficult to dismantle for maintenance, the servicing problems are like those of other appliances with a universal motor. The motor can be checked for brush wear. The gear box can be inspected for need of lubrication. Since cord replacement is complicated by the fact that, where it goes through the appliance handle, the cord connects to the switch, perhaps its replacement should be done by a technician.

Freezers/ Refrigerators

ALL HOME FREEZERS and refrigerators have essentially the same components and work on the same principle as air conditioners. The cooling medium used in all refrigeration appliances is called dichlorodifluoromethane—Freon, for short.

Freon is odorless, nonpoisonous and nonflammable. It is handled in different ways to provide a boiling point suitable for the particular system in which it is being used. For example, Freon in some home freezers has a greater volume than Freon in a comparative refrigerator. The greater the Freon charge, the greater will be its ability to lower the temperature.

The Cooling System

IN A freezer, refrigerant in a gaseous state is pumped throughout the sealed refrigeration system. Refrigerant is laden with heat and is in vapor form on the low pressure side of the refrigeration system. It is cool and in liquid form on the high pressure side.

The compressor draws in the heat-laden vapor from the low pressure side and squeezes it into a smaller area. The purpose of compression is to raise the temperature of the vapor above the temperature of the air outside the refrigerator.

Keep in mind that warm always flows to cool. As its temperature rises above the temperature of the surrounding air, the refrigerant vapor gives off its heat. This lowers the boiling point of the vapor, which causes it to revert to

Freezers/Refrigerators

liquid form for another cycle through the refrigeration system.

Don't be misled into thinking that heat transfer takes place in the compressor. It doesn't. Heat is transferred in the condensor. As refrigerant leaves the compressor, it flows into the zigzag tubing of the condensor. This tubing is enclosed in cooling fins which resemble the radiator core used in automobiles.

The compressed vapor enters the condensor and wends its way through the tubing. As it comes into contact with the cooler outside air (tubing is exposed to the outside), it gives up its heat, so by the time the refrigerant leaves the condensor, it does so in a cooled, liquified state.

As the liquid refrigerant leaves the condensor, it flows into a capillary tube, a very small line with a tiny hole. The tube restricts the flow of refrigerant and meters out the correct amount of refrigerant to the evaporator, which is positioned in the refrigerator cabinet.

The evaporator consists of a series of coils made of tubing which is larger in diameter than the capillary tube. As the refrigerant comes out of the restricted capillary tube into the larger-diameter evaporator tube, its pressure drops. At the same time, it absorbs heat from inside the refrigerator cabinet.

Reduced pressure and heat cause liquid refrigerant to start boiling, and it changes back to vapor. The suction action of the compressor draws the heat-laden refrigerant back into the low pressure side of the system and the cycle continues.

Let's elaborate a bit on the refrigerant. As you know, all liquids vaporize at different temperatures and pressure levels. For example, water boils and vaporizes at 212° F. at sea level. But if pressure on water is increased, it does not begin boiling until it reaches a higher temperature. Conversely, if pressure on water is reduced, it would begin boiling at a temperature lower than 212° F.

Refrigerant boils and vaporizes at a comparatively low temperature, but this can be controlled by increasing or decreasing pressure. In your refrigerator, for example, the evaporator probably functions at about 0° F. In order for refrigerant to vaporize at 0° F., the evaporator has to exert a pressure on it of about 10 pounds.

As liquid refrigerant boils and vaporizes, it absorbs

heat. To get rid of heat, it is necessary only to increase pressure on the refrigerant so its boiling point rises.

Another component which all refrigerators have in common is a thermostat to control the temperature inside the cabinet. The thermostat responds to slight changes in temperature and turns the compressor on or off to maintain even coolness. A knob on the thermostat control allows you to select the desired temperature.

The "Frost-Free" Refrigerator

MOST NEW refrigerators are "frost-free," which is a misnomer, because frost develops in all refrigerators. A more accurate term would be "self-defrosting."

In a self-defrosting refrigerator, frost that accumulates on the evaporator coil and panels of the box is automatically and periodically dissipated. In most cases, an automatic timer sets off defrosting action every 24 hours. The actual defrosting device is either a built-in small electric heater or a "hot" gas system.

At the appropriate time, a small electric heating coil heats up quickly, for a brief period, to melt ice from the evaporator coils and panels. With a "hot" gas system, the timer mechanism switches on the compressor unit and opens a solenoid valve on the high pressure side of the system. This allows hot refrigerant vapors to flow quickly into the evaporator, melting away frost.

To prevent water (melted frost) from running onto the floor, most self-defrosting refrigerators have a drain pan at the base of the unit. A drain tube diverts water to the pan, where it is made to evaporate by a small heater or fan.

The Importance of the Refrigerant Charge in Freezers

HOME FREEZERS are highly reliable units that give service for many, many years. But a problem may arise now and then. These problems, which are outlined for you below in chart form, are covered only briefly because they occur infrequently. However, we have reserved for special mention here the one problem that occurs most often: low refrigerant charge.

Every freezer is designed to accept a specific amount of Freon. When a freezer develops a refrigerant problem, it does so usually because it does not have sufficient refrigerant. The system is undercharged.

Undercharging may occur from failure of the factory to charge the system to capacity. Most times, though, under-charging results when Freon is lost because of a leak.

The following will occur if your freezer loses Freon:

• The compartment will lack normal frost accumulation on its sides.

• The evaporator coil in the compartment will lack normal frost accumulation buildup.

• The temperature inside the compartment will rise.

• Depending upon severity of refrigerant loss, food may soften.

• The compressor will run continually or for extremely long periods.

• The evaporator will feel warm (during normal operation, the evaporator feels cold).

• The condensor will feel warmer (during normal operation, the condensor feels warm).

Important: When a loss of refrigerant is indicated, the entire system must be examined for leaks, and leaks must be repaired before the system is recharged. Failure to do this will result in further refrigerant loss.

To be sure, any repairs involving the refrigeration system require the services of a qualified refrigeration expert. However, if you wish to examine the unit for leaks, these are the steps to take:

Make a closer examination by brushing soapy water on joints on the system's so-called high pressure side while the freezer is running. The high pressure side includes the compressor, condensor and capillary.

The system's low pressure side must also be checked, but with the freezer not running. The low pressure side includes the evaporator and suction line (this is the line from the evaporator to the compressor).

Bubbling of the solution points to a leak!

PROBLEMS, CAUSES, REPAIRS

FOLLOWING are some of the more common problems that afflict home freezers and refrigerators. One standard maintenance procedure always should be followed:

Cleanliness is essential to good operation. Clean dirt

and dust from around and beneath the unit often. In particular, vacuum dirt and dust from the condensor regularly.

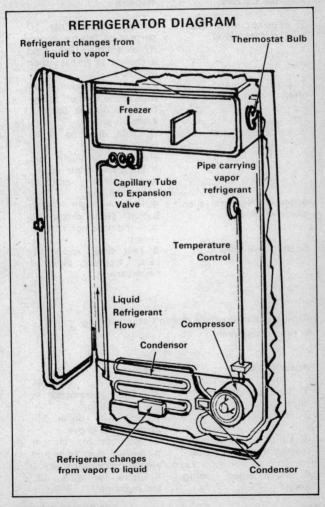

REFRIGERATOR DIAGRAM

Refrigerant changes from liquid to vapor

Thermostat Bulb

Freezer

Pipe carrying vapor refrigerant

Capillary Tube to Expansion Valve

Temperature Control

Liquid Refrigerant Flow

Compressor

Condensor

Refrigerant changes from vapor to liquid

Condensor

Freezers/Refrigerators

Problem: Freezer compartment is too warm

Possible Causes	Repairs
1. Freezer overloaded with unfrozen food.	1. Add no more than 10 percent of freezer capacity at a time. Give food a chance to freeze; then add more.
2. Door opened too often	2. Limit the number of trips to the freezer. Everytime the door is opened, warm air enters.
3. Ineffective door seal	3. Close door on dollar bill and pull. There should be a slight tug. If bill pulls loose easily, door liner probably needs adjusting.
4. Interior light stays on, giving off heat	4. Push in light switch button. Light should go out—if it does not, replace switch.
5. Defective timer	5. Test timer for continuity. Replace timer if necessary.

Problem: Compressor doesn't stop running, or runs excessively

Possible Causes	Repairs
1. Thermostat set too high	1. Adjust thermostat to warmer setting.
2. Poor door seal	2. Test with dollar bill as explained above.
3. Clogged condensor, restricting air circulation	3. Use vacuum cleaner to remove dust from and around condenser coil.
4. Undercharged refrigerant	4. Check for leaks; fix, and recharge.

Problem: Compressor does not operate

Possible Causes:	Repairs
1. Blown fuse or tripped circuit breaker	1. Replace fuse or reset circuit breaker.
2. Defective thermostat	2. Test for continuity and replace if faulty.
3. Defective timer	3. Test for continuity and replace if faulty.
4. Defective relay	4. Test and replace if necessary.
5. Defective compressor	5. Test and replace if it has failed.

Problem: Freezer too noisy when running

Possible Causes:	Repairs
1. Unit not level	1. Check with carpenter's level and adjust if necessary.
2. Loose compressor	2. Tighten compressor mountings.
3. Tubing hitting against cabinet	3. Adjust tubing so it does not rub against cabinet.

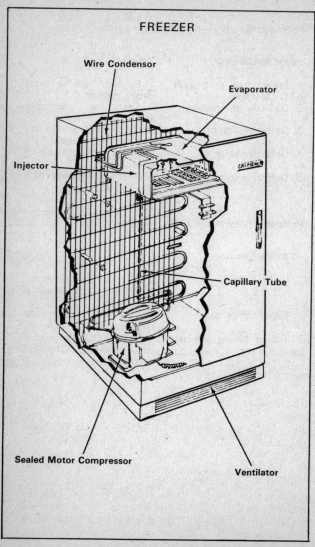

FREEZER

Wire Condensor

Evaporator

Injector

Capillary Tube

Sealed Motor Compressor

Ventilator

Electric Ranges

AS IN ALL heat-producing electrical appliances, the electric range changes electricity into heat by means of a nichrome heating element. The elements are quite durably built; actually, each element is a nichrome wire embedded in an insulating powder and hermetically sealed inside a stainless steel tube. The elements for the surface units are coil-shaped in order to fit in a space and size suitable for a cooking utensil to sit on. In the oven part, the elements are in the long bent tubular shape that distributes the heat fairly evenly in the oven space. Most ranges operate from 240-volts alternating current. This higher voltage gives quick heat, and a great deal of it, to make the range respond to virtually any cooking or baking situation.

Although all surface units look somewhat alike, there are two types of electrical elements: the single element and the double element. The double-element type actually is two elements — a small spiral coiled inside a larger spiral — as you can see from Figure 1. Three wires go to the elements, supplying both 120 volts and 240-volts. So, with two voltages and two elements, the heat selector switch or push-button set can select voltage and element combinations for a variety of temperatures from just warm to very hot.

But even five switch settings often are not considered enough for the modern housewife. In the single-element surface unit, the switch (called an infinite heat selector) cycles the element on and off, increasing the length of the on time as the switch is advanced — thus allowing a wide range of heat selections. Some units even have a thermostat sensor positioned in the very center of the element where it "feels" the bottom of the cooking pan and holds some set temperature at that point.

Three "troubles" can keep the range surface unit from heating: a burned-out element, a bad switch, or a blown fuse. Another possible cause, defective wiring, is rather rare; it usually occurs right at the element, and is caused by a poor attachment between wire and heating element.

Before investigating any trouble in a range, always disconnect the power by pulling the fuses or tripping the circuit breakers. Usually the surface unit element can be lifted or hinged outward after removing the snap ring. Use the test lamp described in the Continuity Tester chapter to determine if the element or elements are burned out. The continuity test lamp also can be used on the switch to see if pushing the button actually closes the switch contacts. Both replacement elements and replacement switches are available, but be sure to tag wires before disconnecting them to make sure of correct reattachment.

Thermostats

OVEN UNITS are thermostatically controlled, but the oven thermostat is different from the bimetallic kind described in the chapter on Thermostats. The same thermostat handles both the broil (upper) and bake (lower) elements. Notice in Figure 2 the slender tube called the thermostat bulb. The bulb contains a fluid that expands when heated and, in expanding, presses against a bellows. Movement of the bellows trips a switch. Alteration of the temperature control knob changes the space between bellows and switch contacts, which changes the cycling and therefore the oven temperature.

There is an adjustment on the thermostat. In many ovens, pulling off the temperature knob reveals the adjusting screw (Figure 3). Turn the oven on and place a thermometer on the racks (Figure 4). After the thermometer temperature rises, allow it to settle; then change the adjustment until the pointer on the knob agrees with the oven thermometer.

One of the special features offered in many electric ranges is a timer. On an electric range, you set the timer for a specific start time, and you set the oven control to the

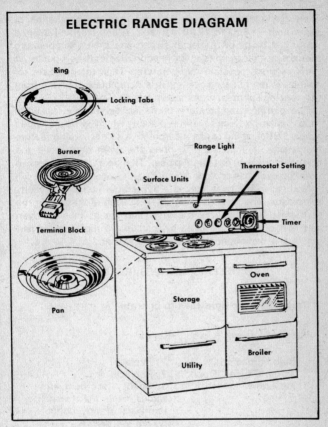

ELECTRIC RANGE DIAGRAM

temperature you want. At the preset time, a cam — which has been rotating on the motor shaft — hits a switch that automatically turns the element on. Food is cooked for the desired time, and the range automatically switches off (although most ranges have a provision for keeping the element at low temperature to keep food warm).

Another feature found on some ranges is a self-cleaning

oven. Self-cleaning is nothing more than the generation of super heat — 800 to 1200 degrees. A self-cleaning oven is controlled by its own special switch and a high temperature thermostat that permits oven heating elements to operate at their highest possible temperature. This temperature, of course, is too hot for cooking; it is completely separate from the cooking controls, with its own switch.

The extreme temperature burns up spilled and baked-in foods, charring them to a fine powder which is easily wiped away. Self-cleaning ovens incorporate a safety locking feature that makes it impossible to open the oven door while the cleaning process is taking place. The door remains locked until the oven has cooled.

No heat in the oven means a burned-out element, a faulty thermostat, or a defective switch. Test each of these with the test lamp. No light from the test lamp means that the oven part is bad. Repair the oven by installing a replacement part that is an exact duplicate of the defective part.

PROBLEMS, CAUSES, REPAIRS

Problem: Oven light fails to operate.

Possible Causes	Repair
1. Bulb burned out.	1. Replace.
2. 15 amp fuse "Open."	2. Replace.
3. Inoperative switch.	3. Check for continuity across oven light switch terminals. If no continuity, replace switch.

Problem: Convenience outlet inoperative.

Possible Causes	Repair
1. 15 amp fuse "Open."	1. Replace fuse.
2. Clock-Timer not "Set."	2. Set clock for automatic operation.

Figure I

Heating Element

Figure 2

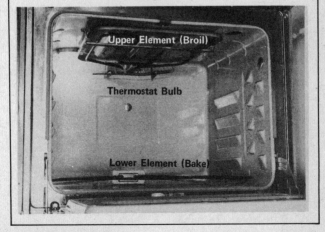

Upper Element (Broil)

Thermostat Bulb

Lower Element (Bake)

3. Defective Clock-Timer switch.	3. Check continuity. If no continuity, replace Clock-Timer.

Problem: Fluorescent light doesn't light at all.

Possible Causes	Repair
1. Burned out bulb.	1. Replace. Hold switch longer in start position.
2. Open ballast.	2. Check continuity across ballast. If no continuity, replace ballast.
3. Inoperative switch.	3. Check continuity across terminals. If no continuity, replace switch.
4. Lamp not making contact with lamp holder.	4. Replace lamp holder or adjust holders to make contact.

Problem: Fluorescent light lights on ends only and/or flickers.

Possible Causes	Repair
1. Defective indicator light.	1. Replace.
2. Defective Cook-Clean Switch.	2. Replace.
3. Defective Oven Thermostat.	3. Replace.

Problem: Single surface elements inoperative.

Possible Causes	Repair
1. Burned out elements.	1. Check continuity; if open replace.
2. Defective Terminal Block.	2. Replace.

3. Loose wires	3. Connect wires.
4. Defective infinite switch	4. Replace.

Problem: Surface element overheats.

Possible Causes	Repair
1. Defective Infinite Switch.	1. Replace.

Problem: Oven will not bake with selector set on "Bake."

Possible Causes	Repair
1. Defective thermostat.	1. Have replaced.
2. Loose connection.	2. Have repaired.
3. Defective selector switch.	3. Have replaced.
4. Defective bake relay.	4. Have replaced.

Problem: Oven will not operate manually.

Possible Causes	Repair
1. Timer not set for "manual."	1. Set for manual operation.

Problem: Oven will not bake with selector switch set on "Timed Bake."

Possible Causes	Repair
1. If oven comes on when selector switch is set on "Bake," there is a possibility of defective selector switch.	1. Check for continuity across appropriate terminals. If no continuity, replace selector switch.

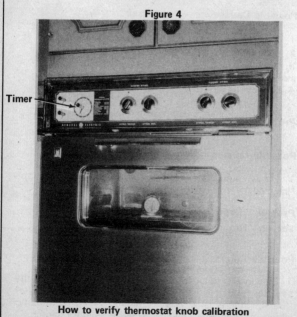

Figure 3

Thermostat Adjustment

Figure 4

Timer

How to verify thermostat knob calibration

2. Defective Clock-Timer.

2. If no continuity between appropriate terminals on Clock-Timer Switch, replace Clock-Timer.

Problem: Oven does not Broil.

Possible Causes

Repair

1. Defective Broil Relay.
2. Defective Selector Switch.

1. Have replaced.
2. Check continuity between appropiate terminals. If none, replace.

Problem: Oven door will not open.

Possible Causes

Repair

1. Cook Clean Switch must be turned to "Off."

1. Cook Clean Switch defective; replace. Microswitch on electromechanical linkage inoperative—replace. If the "Cook Clean" Switch is turned back to bake before one minute has elapsed, the oven door will not open.

2. Main circuit breaker or fuse "Open".
3. Door latch motor defective.

2. Reset circuit breaker or replace fuse.
3. Check continuity of motor. If open, replace motor.

4. Check for one or more of the following switches being defective: Motor limit switch, Door switch Cook Clean Switch, Oven Thermostat.

4. Check continuity of switches. If open, replace the switch in question.

Electric Ranges

5. Broken or loose wires or terminals.

5. Check for broken or loose wires and repair same.

6. Cool down period not complete.

6. Wait until lock light goes out.

Problem: Oven overheats or "runaway."

Possible Causes

Repair

1. Defective thermostat.
2. Relay sticking.
3. Defective or miswired Clean Limit Switch.
4. Thermostat bulb not in oven.

1. Adjust or replace.
2. Replace.
3. Replace switch or correct wiring.
4. Replace.

Humidifiers

THE PURPOSE of a humidifier is to add moisture to dry household air, especially in cold weather. Modern heating systems, particularly forced air types, dry the air, and pull (evaporate) moisture from the structure and furnishings. Dry air is a direct cause of cracked walls, squeaking floors, loose doors and windows, cracked paint, peeling veneer, and excessive rug wear.

Dry air is also a suspected cause of human ailments. Doctors find a direct relationship between dry air in the home and respiratory infections, frequent colds, and dry, itchy skin.

Furthermore, dry air worsens the energy shortage and wastes money. The comfort level in a home is increased one degree for every eight percent of humidity in the air. To raise the heat in your home above the 70° level, heating costs rise about 3 percent for each degree.

By increasing humidity, instead of heat, you save the cost of turning your thermostat higher and making your furnace work longer and harder.

There is a percentage of relative humidity that should not be exceeded, since excessive moisture in the air can do as much damage in a home as lack of moisture (see the section on dehumidifiers). This level is around 70 percent at 70°.

The ideal relative humidity for maximum comfort, and protection of health and property, in a home is 30 to 40 percent with the temperature at 70 degrees. Yet the fact is that in many homes in the United States today the relative humidity is only about 13 percent during the heating season.

You can achieve the ideal relative humidity in your home with a humidifier. There are two general types: those that fit

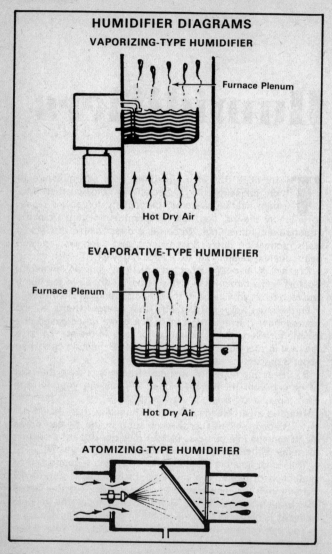

HUMIDIFIER DIAGRAMS
VAPORIZING-TYPE HUMIDIFIER

Furnace Plenum

Hot Dry Air

EVAPORATIVE-TYPE HUMIDIFIER

Furnace Plenum

Hot Dry Air

ATOMIZING-TYPE HUMIDIFIER

in a furnace, and separate room units. Several models of each kind are available.

How Humidifiers Work

THE LEAST EXPENSIVE and most common type of humidifier is the evaporative-plate model, installed in the furnace plenum. A water line leads into the humidifier pan from a main water pipe. Plates mounted in the pan absorb the water by capillary action; this moisture is picked up off the plates by the movement of air in the furnace and circulated through the house.

There are no moving parts in an evaporative humidifier with the exception of the float assembly which is used to control the water level. This assembly is similar in action to the float assembly in a water closet. When the water level drops, the float drops and pulls a small valve off the water inlet seat. With the valve open, water can flow into the pan. When the water rises, the float rises and drops the valve against the water inlet seat, shutting off the flow.

Another kind of humidifier is the vaporizer model. Some types can be mounted in the furnace; larger units are made for placement in a room. These are the vaporizers mothers are familiar with for use in a youngster's room to ease the pain of breathing and coughing in a dry atmosphere.

Vaporizers generally use an electric immersion heater that heats water to form steam. This steam is sprayed out, much like the steam that comes from the spout of a tea kettle. In a furnace model, the steam is absorbed directly into the duct and is circulated through the house with heated air.

Another type of humidifier is the atomizing model. It is installed either in the furnace plenum or cold air return, depending upon the model. Water from the humidifier pan is atomized (sprayed) by a rotating motor-driven pick-up mechanism into the plenum or cold air return where moving furnace air picks it up for circulation.

The most popular type of room humidifier works on the atomizing principle. It is simply a large-diameter wheel mounted on two small drive pulleys which are driven by a motor. The motor also drives fan blades. The wheel holds a fiberglass-type pad that extends around its entire circum-

Humidifiers

ference. Beneath the wheel is a large reservoir which holds many gallons of water.

As the wheel slowly turns, the pad becomes saturated with water. The fan blows this moisture off the pad and into the room air.

PROBLEMS, CAUSES, REPAIRS

NO MATTER what type of humidifier you have in your home, it needs periodic maintenance. Without it, the unit may soon become clogged, especially in hard water areas, making it doubly difficult to clean. Furthermore, the unit may start emitting an odor from stale water if parts are not kept clean.

Most humidifiers should receive care about once every six weeks during the heating season. Clean water pans with detergent. Scrape away calcium deposits with steel wool. You can cut down on the amount of these tenacious deposits with water-treatment solutions sold in hardware stores.

Motors of some humidifiers may require lubrication. Consult the instruction guide for your unit to determine its needs. Only a drop or two of household appliance motor oil is needed.

Plates of evaporative humidifiers usually have to be replaced every three years. Be sure that the parts of the float assembly are kept free of deposits.

Dehumidifier

TOO MUCH MOISTURE in household air occurs most often in summer when warm, moist air contacts cool surfaces — like basement floors — and the moisture in the air condenses. (Too little moisture, which is just as damaging, occurs primarily during winter — see the chapter on humidifiers). Excessive moisture causes mold and mildew on home furnishings; rusting of household metal components; warping of furniture and wooden structural elements, such as doors and windows; and an unpleasant musty smell.

A dehumidifier is an appliance that draws moisture from the air to prevent these problems, especially in homes not equipped with air conditioning. Air conditioners, when operating, not only cool the air, but dehumidify it as well.

The ideal relative humidity in a home during the summer is 30 to 50 percent. If moisture seems excessive and is causing some of the problems listed above, a dehumidifier may be necessary.

How Dehumidifiers Work

THE CONTROL of the unit is a component called a humidistat, much like a thermostat. When moisture in the air reaches an undesirable level, contacts close to let current flow. This turns the dehumidifier on, and it pulls moisture from household air.

Odd though it may seem, the dehumidifier does this through the principles of refrigeration. Since refrigerating (cooling) air also removes moisture from it, the design of a dehumidifier follows closely the design of all appliances

DEHUMIDIFIER DIAGRAM

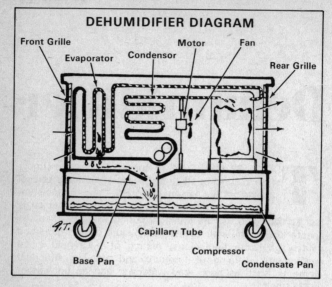

Front Grille

Evaporator   Condensor   Motor   Fan

Rear Grille

Capillary Tube

Base Pan   Compressor

Condensate Pan

based on refrigeration, including refrigerators, home freezers, and air conditioners.

Refrigerant (usually Freon 12) is circulated through the system by means of a compressor driven by a split phase motor. Both compressor and motor are closed up in a hermetically-sealed unit. Freon is pumped by the compressor from the evaporator into the condenser, where it liquifies and gets hot. The Freon then seeps through a long thin capillary tube into the evaporator where it vaporizes and gets cold.

A fan pulls room air through both the condenser and the evaporator coils. Since it is both warmed by the condenser and cooled by the evaporator, the air temperature is not much changed; probably it is a little bit warmer. The big happening is that airborne moisture forms like dew on the cold evaporator coil. So the air that comes out is drier than the air that entered the dehumidifier. The moisture drips off the evaporator coil either into a pail or through a plastic tube into a sewer drain.

The whole refrigeration system is designed to be balanced so that the "dew" drips off as moisture instead of freezing up and forming ice on the cold evaporator coil. In fact, coil frosting generally indicates that some Freon has leaked out of the system.

Located in the entering air stream is the humidistat. Its humidity sensor is a nylon strip that stretches when moist and shrinks when dry (nylon naturally does this). When the entering air is sufficiently dry, causing the sensor strip to shrink, and shrinkage pulls against a switch lever, turning off the compressor motor.

Maintaining a Dehumidifier

REMOVE THE POWER cord from the wall outlet. Remove the outer shell, then clean the unit thoroughly. Do this at least once a year. Wipe evaporator coils with a clean rag, and vacuum out the dust and lint from condensor coils and from other areas inside the unit.

Consult manufacturer instructions to see if the fan motor needs lubrication, or, after unplugging the unit, examine the motor to see if it has oil ports. Apply a few drops of heavy-weight household motor oil (comparable to 20-weight oil) to the ports.

Once each month during the period that the unit is operating, clean out slimy deposits that form on the bottom of the drain pan. Use a scrub brush. These are mold and algae deposits and, to keep your home a healthy one, they should not be allowed to accumulate.

PROBLEMS, CAUSES, REPAIRS

Problem: Unit will not run

Possible Cause	Repair
1. Humidistat set too high	1. Lower setting.
2. Overflow switch reads "on."	2. Make sure water level is not at peak. Empty drain pan.
3. Bad fuse or tripped circuit breaker	3. Replace fuse or reset circuit breaker. If problem

Dehumidifiers

4. Defective power cord; problem with internal wiring.

5. Humidistat is not working

6. Bad overflow switch

recurs, call an electrician — there is an electrical problem.

4. Test continuity with meter. Replace faulty wiring.

5. Test switch; replace if defective. Inspect sensor strip. If defective, replace entire humidistat.

6. Check switch and float linkage. Replace bad switch or fix bent linkage.

Problem: Fan does not operate; refrigeration system is all right.

Possible Cause

1. Fan motor binds

2. Fan motor electrically defective

Repair

1. Disassemble motor, and clean and lubricate bearings. If trouble continues, replace motor.

2. Check continuity with meter or test lamp. Replace motor if necessary.

Problem: Unit operates, but dehumidifying action is not adequate.

Possible Cause

1. Area being treated is subjected to continuous moist, warm air flow.

2. Air flow through unit is obstructed.

3. Size of unit is not adequate for area being treated.

4. Low refrigerant charge as indicated by evaporator coil freezeup, or total lack of moisture accumulation.

Repair

1. Close doors and windows; isolate area.

2. Be sure grilles are not blocked — keep unit away from wall. Clean evaporator and condensor coils.

3. Get larger unit, or a second unit of the same size.

4. Have unit checked for leaks; have leaks repaired by technician. Have unit recharged.

Mixers

A FOOD MIXER is nothing more than an old-fashioned egg beater that has been equipped with a small electric motor, which relieves you of providing the drive energy. Mixers are either portable handheld units or stand appliances in which the bowl holding the food fits on a base plate and the two beaters, locked into an upper arm, hang down into the bowl.

Whether portable or fixed, mixers operate pretty much in the same way. The small electric motor is positioned horizontally in the mixer housing. The front of the motor has a shaft, the end of which is cut out in gear fashion. This is called the worm.

As the electric motor revolves, the worm also revolves. The worm, in turn, drives two small gears called pinions. These pinions are located on opposite sides of the worm so that when the worm turns the pinions rotate in opposite directions—one clockwise, the other counterclockwise. Locked into the pinions are the beaters, also rotating in opposite directions as the pinions rotate.

Other important components of a food mixer include a fan on the other end of the motor which cools the parts to prevent overheating and deterioration, and an off-on variable speed switch. The switch not only turns the unit on and off, it also permits you to adjust the motor speed from low to high to meet mixing requirements. By means of the switch, you reduce or increase electric power to the motor, driving it slowly or at higher speeds.

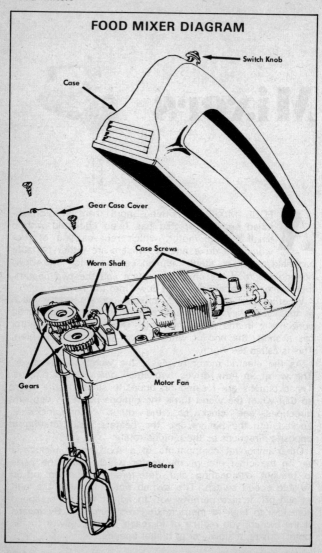

FOOD MIXER DIAGRAM

Switch Knob

Case

Gear Case Cover

Case Screws

Worm Shaft

Gears

Motor Fan

Beaters

PROBLEMS, CAUSES, REPAIRS

FOOD MIXERS fail as a result of an electrical breakdown or mechanical malfunction.

Electrical failure can be minor or major. Minor failures are those that can be repaired relatively easily and inexpensively. They are discussed below.

Major failures, particularly complete breakdown of the electric motor, are expensive to repair. It is important for you to determine the cost of a major repair before you make a commitment to have the work done. Often, the cost of repair will equal or exceed the cost of a new mixer.

Minor problems include the following:

1. Damaged power cord. Try a new cord. Frequently, wires in the cord are pulled apart. When this happens, electric power cannot get through to the motor. To reach the motor end of the cord, you must partially disassemble the mixer. Follow the diagram, and use the manufacturer's information that accompanies the appliance.

Important: To prevent damaging a power cord, pull only on the heavy plug end. Never pull on the cord itself to disconnect it from a wall outlet.

2. Worn brushes.

Appliances equipped with the kind of motor that has an armature—called a universal motor—have two brushes. When you remove the screw caps located on the side of the appliance, you can take out the brushes to check them. Mixer motor brushes should be about 3/4-inch long. The springs fastened to the brushes should have good tension. Brushes worn too short, or with weak springs, should be replaced. For true fit, be sure to use exact replacement brushes from the manufacturer or a dealer who stocks parts for your brand of mixer.

Also check wires leading to brushes to see that they are not broken or disconnected.

3. Bad switch.

The mixer switch, which is usually combined with a governor-type of speed controller, is not easily replaced; even when replaced, it often needs adjustment requiring the know-how of an experienced technician. This is a major problem—not one for the layman to tackle.

A mechanical problem with a mixer involves stripped

gears, usually one of the pinions. The worm gear on the motor shaft is made of hard steel, so it seldom will be damaged. However, pinions are made of soft brass, plastic, or nylon. Damaged gears can be replaced at little cost.

Sometimes the problem with a food beater is the simplest kind: bent or damaged beaters or a "dry" bearing under the bowl platform. One part of mixing food is pushing the batter down from the sides of the bowl into the center where the beaters can mix it thoroughly. If the utensil used to push down the batter touches, or gets caught in, the beaters, the beater blades will bend or twist. Once this happens, they will not turn properly. Nor can they be repaired. They are easily replaced, though you must make sure that you buy only beaters made for your blender.

The revolving platter beneath the bowl of the mixer (found on almost all mixers) works on a simple bearing. If the bearing dries out, lubricating it with household oil will permit it to spin freely which, in turn, permits your bowl to turn as the beaters revolve.

With a mixer, as with all appliances, it is best to check out the simple things first, before getting involved in intricate repairs inside a unit.

Roaster/ Rotisseries

AROASTER OVEN is a large steel case insulated with heavy rockwool to retain heat. Heat for roasting and baking comes from elements built into the sides and bottom of the case. Broiler-ovens have heating elements in the top and bottom, to permit roasting, baking, and broiling.

Cooking temperature is determined by the amount of electricity allowed to pass through the heating elements and also by the number of elements that may be in use at any one time. You control the temperature by means of a dial on the outside of the unit; the higher you set the dial (which uses the same degree settings as an oven) the more electricity flows through the elements, and the more elements come into use.

The case of a roaster-oven normally opens at the top (the lid is removable) and food is placed on a rack. The heavy lid is then placed back in position, and the roaster is turned on. Roasters are usually large enough to cook large roasts and good size turkeys. Broiler-ovens open at the front; the door—usually made of glass—pulls down and rests on the table while food is put in or removed.

A rotisserie is similar to a broiler-oven, but with a heat element only in the top, and a spit for turning the food as it cooks. The door of a rotisserie also opens downward to rest on the table while the spit is being put into place. The component that distinguishes roasters from rotisseries is an electric motor used by rotisseries to drive the gear train that rotates the spit.

The cooking time of both roasters (roaster ovens and broiler ovens) and rotisseries is controlled by a clock mechanism. This may be a mechanically spring-wound motor or

Roasters/Rotisseries

a small electric motor. In either case, an operating rod starts moving when the timer is set. At the end of the pre-set cooking period, the rod comes in contact with a small block of insulation on the end of a thermostat blade. This pushes the blade, which in turn pushes open a set of con-tact points, breaking the flow of current to the appliance and shutting off heat.

In the rotisserie food is threaded onto a large skewer or spit. One end of the spit rests in a curved area which allows it to turn freely. The other end is set into a notch which is the output end of the gear train.

The gear setup contains a small pinion gear on the elec-tric motor shaft. A pinion is a gear that drives a larger gear. The pinion turns the first gear; the first gear has its own small pinion on its shaft. This pinion drives the large second gear.

It is the second gear that has the notch cut into its center to hold the square end of the spit. Thus, as the second gear rotates, the spit held by the notch also rotates.

Roaster and Rotisserie Problems

ALTHOUGH ROASTERS and rotisseries usually last for years without problems, when trouble does occur it comes in one of three ways: the unit does not go on, it gets too hot, or it does not get hot enough.

When a unit fails to go on, the problem in most cases is either a bad on-off switch or a heating element that has an open wire. The switch or element then must be replaced.

If the unit gets too hot or does not get hot enough, the trouble most likely is with the thermostat that controls heat. The thermostat includes the blade and contact points controlled by the clock mechanism. Replacing the thermo-stat usually solves the problem since points must make contact (or break it) cleanly for electricity to flow to heat the unit to the temperature you desire.

The gears of a rotisserie electric motor can lose grease because of screws that come loose and allow the grease to seep out. When this happens, the gears bind, or freeze, and will not turn. If this happens, remove the gears, clean them, replace any that may be bent or otherwise damaged, and relubricate them with light oil.

ROASTER AND ROTISSERIE DIAGRAM

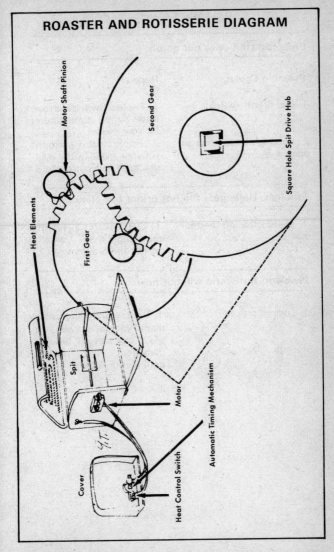

Motor Shaft Pinion

Second Gear

Square Hole Spit Drive Hub

Heat Elements

First Gear

Spit

Motor

Automatic Timing Mechanism

Cover

Heat Control Switch

PROBLEMS, CAUSES, REPAIR

Problem: Unit does not go on

Possible Cause:	Repair:
1. Bad on-off switch	1. Replace switch with one made by the manufacturer for your model.
2. Heating element has an open wire	2. Replace the element with one made by the manufacturer for your model.

Problem: Units gets too hot or not hot enough

1. Malfunctioning thermostat	1. Check contact points; replacing them usually solves the problem.

Problem: Rotisserie will not turn

1. Loss of grease	1. Remove the gears, clean them with a solvent, replace any that are bent or damaged, and relubricate with a light oil.

Can Openers

T HERE IS NOTHING very complicated about the way in which an electric can opener works. When you place the can into position between the cutting knife and serrated drive wheel, and press the starting lever, several things happen: you lock the can in place, you drive the cutting knife into the can, and you cause a small electric motor to start.

The motor drives a train of reduction gears, which turns the serrated drive wheel. As the drive wheel turns, it slowly moves the can in a circular motion. This allows the sharp cutting knife to do its work of cutting off the lid. When the cutting knife comes full circle to the "open space" between the cut lid and the side of the can, pressure is relaxed on the starting lever. (On some models, the user must release pressure when the cutter comes full circle.) This causes the lever to switch off the electric motor.

Repairing Electric Can Openers

A FREQUENT CAUSE of failure in an electric can opener is failure of the cutting knife. This leads to a skipping of the knife: instead of cutting off lids cleanly, it leaves uncut gaps that you must try to catch on a second or third time around. A cutting knife fails because of dirt and food build-up. Keeping it clean, then, is the first requirement for smooth operation.

You must remove the cutting wheel and knife assembly to clean them properly. *First, pull the power cord from the wall outlet.* Then loosen and remove the screw that holds the assembly in place. Observe the shoulder location on the

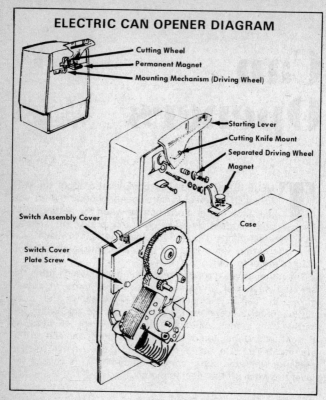

ELECTRIC CAN OPENER DIAGRAM

Cutting Wheel

Permanent Magnet

Mounting Mechanism (Driving Wheel)

Starting Lever

Cutting Knife Mount

Separated Driving Wheel

Magnet

Switch Assembly Cover

Case

Switch Cover
Plate Screw

cutting wheel to be sure you put it back the right way after cleaning. With the cutter out of the way, it is easy to scrape out the accumulated dirt between the teeth on the serrated drive wheel. If an inspection shows that the cutting wheel is no longer sharp, obtain a replacement cutting wheel. Soak the assembly in soapy water. After cleaning and drying the cutter wheel, place a few drops of household oil on the shaft the wheel fits on, then reattach the wheel.. It is important that the wheel rotate while cutting, and if put back in place dry, the cutter might "freeze" on the shaft and fail to turn.

If an electric can opener refuses to turn on, the problem probably is either a faulty cord or a defective OFF/ON switch. A power cord fault occurs when wires are damaged by owners pulling the cord. When removing the power cord from the wall outlet, pull only on the thick plug.

If the switch is bad, it can be reached only by disassembling the appliance. The diagram shows the location.

The can opener may refuse to turn on because of a worn drive wheel or gears. To replace defective parts, it is necessary to dismantle the appliance. Remove the screws that hold the case on, then remove the case. Examination will usually reveal the way to remove and replace the cord, switch, motor or gears. If a grinding wheel is mounted on the motor shaft, observe its condition and, if it is worn, replace it with a new wheel. If gears are replaced, make sure they are properly lubricated. Broken or defective parts can be replaced with duplicates obtained either from the parts department of an appliance dealer selling your particular brand, or by writing to the manufacturer.

Motor burn-out is quite rare, since the shaded pole motor in a can opener can carry current indefinitely with the rotor locked and not burn out. But occasionally a motor must be replaced because of bearing wear. In this case, check the cost before committing yourself to a repair. Often repair runs as high as, or higher than, the cost of a new unit.

PROBLEMS, CAUSES, REPAIRS

Problem: Cutting knife skips instead of cutting

Possible cause:	Repairs:
1. Dirt in knives	1. Remove cutting assembly and soak in hot soapy water until dirt floats away.

Problem: Unit will not turn on

Possible cause:	Repair:
1. Damaged power cord	1. Replace cord

Can Openers

| 2. Burned out motor | 2. Replace: but check cost first; it may be less expensive to buy a new unit. |

Problem: Motor hums but knife will not turn

| Possible cause: | Repair: |

| 1. Broken or damaged gear | 1. Replace gear with duplicate made for your brand of can opener. |

Problem: Excessive noise

| Possible cause: | Repair: |

| 1. Broken or damaged gear | 1. Replace as above |

Coffee Makers

A N ELECTRIC coffee maker is either a percolator or brewer that makes from two to eleven cups of coffee. Larger urns which have a 25 to 50 cup capacity also are available. Whether small or large, percolator or brewer, all coffee makers work in much the same way. Let's discuss percolators first.

The working parts of the unit consist of a heating element, thermostat and connecting wires, located in the base of the appliance. The base is usually made of plastic so the percolator can be placed on a counter or table without burning the surface. The pot itself may be made of aluminum, stainless steel, glass, plastic, or ceramic.

The object of a percolator is to force water repeatedly upward, so it seeps down through the coffee grounds. Cold water is poured into the pot, the basket is filled to the proper level with ground coffee, and the electric cord is plugged into a wall outlet. The water soon begins boiling vigorously.

This forces water beneath the small dome-shaped disk of the stem and up the tube in a gush so that it hits against the glass cap in the lid. This allows water to spray out over the basket that holds the coffee. The water seeps through the coffee and through the holes in the basket back into the pot. As water continues to filter through the ground coffee, it picks up more flavor. The sequence keeps occurring until the coffee has reached the desired strength.

Most electric coffee makers are equipped with a control that allows you to vary the strength of the coffee to your taste. This control is nothing more than a thermostat which cuts off power at a predetermined point in the percolating cycle. In many electric percolators, a small in-

ELECTRIC COFFEE PERCOLATOR DIAGRAM

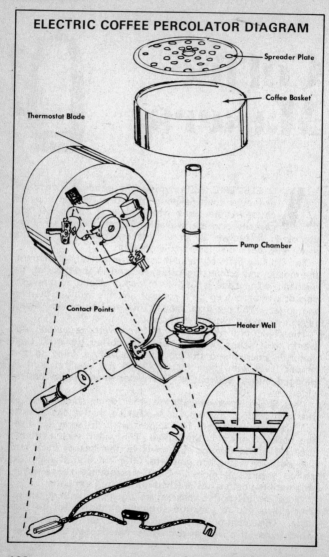

Spreader Plate

Coffee Basket

Thermostat Blade

Pump Chamber

Contact Points

Heater Well

dependently-operating element of very low voltage remains on as long as the power cord is connected to keep coffee hot.

Some electric coffee percolators do not have thermostats that can be set. Their thermostats are built-in and set for you at the factory. Coffee is made to one strength which can be varied only according to the amount of coffee you put into the basket.

Electric coffee brewers work in a similar fashion. Cold water is put into the lower bowl and coffee is placed in the upper bowl on top of a filter that is made of paper or cloth. The two bowls are attached.

Power is turned on, and water begins to boil vigorously. Steam pressure forces the boiling water up through a center tube until the bottom bowl is practically empty. After water passes into the upper bowl, a thermostat shuts off the heat.

The hot water overspreads the coffee. Then, as the lower bowl begins to cool down, a vacuum develops that literally pulls the water from the upper bowl into the lower bowl, picking up flavor as it filters through the ground coffee. The coffee passes between the two bowls, but the grounds are kept in the upper bowl by the filter. A low voltage heating element then turns on automatically to keep the coffee hot.

PROBLEMS, CAUSES, REPAIRS

COFFEE PERCOLATORS and brewers are simple appliances that seldom give trouble. When they do, the problem is often easily fixed.

Percolators

Problem: Unit does not heat up

Possible Cause:	Repair:
1. Faulty power cord connection	1. Be sure power cord is firmly connected at terminal prongs and in wall socket.
2. Bad power cord	2. With cord plugged in, bend it back and forth over its length. If appliance turns on, cord is bad. Replace.

Coffeemakers

| 3. Open heating element | 3. Have percolator tested for continuity. Repair or replace if element is bad. |

Problem: Unit does not maintain heat

Possible Cause: **Repair:**

| 1. Incorrect thermostat setting | 1. Readjust and test by placing a thermometer in percolator after making coffee and with basket and tube removed. With thermostat set at "medium" setting, temperature should be about 212°. |
| 2. Faulty thermostat | 2. Replace. |

Problem: Unit does not pump water

Possible Cause: **Repair:**

| 1. Clogged tube or well | 1. Clean out sediment. |
| 2. Bad washer in base of tube (washer assists in pumping water up tube) | 2. Replace. |

Problem: Bad tasting coffee

Possible Cause: **Repair:**

| 1. Dirty pot | 1. Buy electric percolator cleaner at hardware store and use as directed. |

Note: Many of the problems afflicting a percolator can also trouble a coffee brewer, so where applicable refer to the chart above. But here are some troubles that belong to brewers alone.

Brewers

Problem: Water doesn't get to top bowl

Possible Cause:	Repair:
1. Improper thermostat adjustment	1. Readjust.
2. Inoperative main heating element	2. Test continuity and replace.

Problem: Coffee boils over

Possible Cause:	Repair:
1. Improperly positioned filter.	1. Position filter correctly.
2. Leaky gasket	2. Replace gasket.

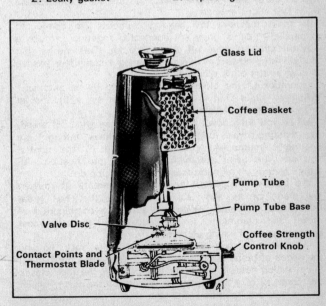

Glass Lid

Coffee Basket

Pump Tube

Pump Tube Base

Valve Disc

Coffee Strength Control Knob

Contact Points and Thermostat Blade

Toasters

TOASTERS have been with us since shortly after the invention of the electric light. Basically, a toaster is simply a few heating elements that produce radiant heat to toast (brown) slices of bread. Most toasters have three heating elements so that two slices of bread may be toasted at the same time. Some toast four slices at once.

In most toasters, the heating elements are connected in parallel—that is, they are connected together in such a way that they operate off one conductor. This means that electricity going to one element from the conductor passes through to the other elements.

Operation of the elements is controlled by an automatic switch—a timer that is controlled either by a thermostat or by a clock mechanism.

When you push down the rack holding the slices of bread, the toasting cycle begins—electricity flows through the heating elements. At a time determined by the control you set, the timer automatically causes the heating elements to turn off, and the toasted bread to pop up.

To be more specific, the heating elements of toasters are made of an alloy called Nichrome that has great resistance. Nichrome, which is made of a combination of nickel and chromium, is the substance used in most appliances with heating elements.

In a modern pop-up toaster, when the rack holding the slices of bread is pushed down, it engages a mechanical latch, which holds it down. In this position the rack closes the contacts of a switch at the bottom of the case, which allows current to flow, and the Nichrome elements to become red hot. Closing of the contacts also activates the automatic timer.

The length of the toasting time is set by the adjustment of the automatic timer. Two basic types of timers are used:

1. One kind of timer is a thermostat that bends when it is heated. The bending releases a set of points that in turn trips the mechanical latch which was holding down the rack. When the rack is freed, it pops up. Besides tripping the latch, the released points also break the circuit which allows current to flow to the heating elements. By setting an adjustment mechanism on the outside of the toaster case for darker or lighter toast, you place more or less tension on the bimetal thermostat.

2. The other type of timer is a clocking mechanism that is a spring-wound device. When the rack is pushed down, the pressure causes a spring to wind tightly; at the same time, a circuit is closed which allows current to flow. The electric current starts a clocking device. As the clock runs, it moves a small gear toward a trigger. At the end of a preset time (which you determine by setting the toast control), the gear activates the trigger to release the rack.

Some toasters use a combination thermostat and clocking mechanism. With this combination, the clocking mechanism depends on the thermostat. When the thermostat bimetal reaches a preset temperature, the clocking mechanism begins ticking off toasting time. This dual mechanism provides better control over the desired degree of toasting (light, medium, or dark) than either the simple thermostat or clocking mechanism.

PROBLEMS, CAUSES, REPAIRS

SINCE THE average toaster operates for only a few minutes each time it is used, the appliance seldom fails electrically. The strong wire elements give years and years of service. Therefore, most toaster problems are mechanical.

Crumbs that drop into the unit can clog the release latch and other moving parts. The best way to avoid this is to clean your toaster often.

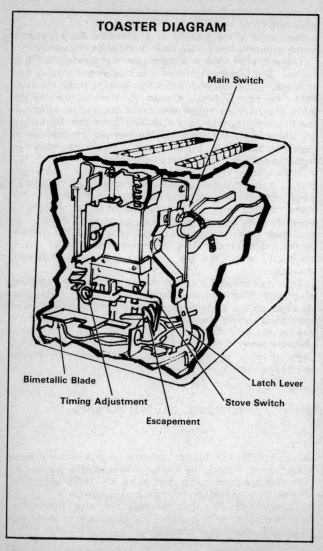

TOASTER DIAGRAM

Main Switch

Bimetallic Blade

Timing Adjustment

Escapement

Latch Lever

Stove Switch

Many models have clean-out trap doors in the bottom of the case. Pull the power cord from the wall outlet, open the trap, and brush out the crumbs. A new one-inch paint brush or pastry brush makes an ideal cleaning tool.

Toasters lacking trap doors must be turned upside down and shaken vigorously to clean out crumbs.

Caution: If a slice of toast becomes stuck in the toaster, do not dig inside with a knife, fork or any other implement without first pulling the power cord from the wall outlet. The toaster's wire elements are loaded with electricity, and silverware is a conductor. If you rupture the element with the utensil, which is a good possibility since the opening is narrow, you could be seriously injured or killed.

If a toaster fails and has to be disassembled for replacement of parts, be sure to find out first how much repair will cost. The cost of repairing a toaster frequently equals or exceeds the price of a new toaster.

Waffle Irons

Waffle Irons

WAFFLES must cook quickly or they become tough. Waffle irons, then, must be made of a material that transfers heat readily. Such a material is aluminum and today all waffle iron grids, both top and bottom, are made of heavy cast aluminum. Increasingly, the aluminum grids are coated with a non-stick material such as Teflon, which just about eliminates the cleaning and scraping once required to keep the grids clean.

Behind the two grids, in the top and bottom casings of the appliance, are the heating elements (wires that heat the grids). These elements are thermostatically controlled.

A thermostat is a device that cuts off the flow of electricity when the temperature reaches a selected level and turns electricity back on again when the temperature goes down. Thermostats in waffle irons are made of a set of contact points. When the points are touching, the circuit is complete and current flows. When the points separate, the circuit is broken and current no longer reaches the elements. (See the chapter on thermostats.)

It is the construction of the points that, with temperature, determines their position. The points are made of a metal that bends when heated and straightens when cool. The points are together when they are straight.

When you first take out the waffle iron for use, the thermostat is cold and the switch is closed. As soon as you plug the power cord of the unit into a wall outlet, and turn the appliance on, current flows through the circuit wires; the current can flow because the points are together, completing

146   CONSUMER GUIDE

WAFFLE IRON DIAGRAM

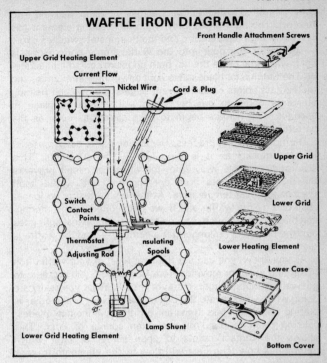

Front Handle Attachment Screws

Upper Grid Heating Element

Current Flow

Nickel Wire

Cord & Plug

Upper Grid

Lower Grid

Switch Contact Points

Thermostat

Insulating Spools

Adjusting Rod

Lower Heating Element

Lower Case

Lamp Shunt

Lower Grid Heating Element

Bottom Cover

the circuit. The current flows to the elements, and the waffle iron heats up. As the temperature increases, the bimetallic thermostat blade begins to bend. When the desired temperature is reached, the blade has bent sufficiently to cause points to pull away from each other. This breaks the circuit, shutting off electricity to the elements.

At the moment the proper temperature is reached and the electric current is stopped, an indicator light goes on to signal that the waffle iron is at the right temperature to cook batter. The indicator light is a small bulb in a socket that is wired into the thermostat circuit; when the points are open, the bulb receives electricity and glows. In closing, the thermostati-

Waffle Irons

cally-controlled switch jumpers across the lamp, causing it to turn off. The light glows only when the heating element has reached a high temperature and the thermostat switches off.

The batter you pour into the waffle iron's bottom grid is cold; when you close the lid, both grids are cooled immediately. The thermostat blades also cool down; they straighten, and the contact points close. Current begins to flow, and heating elements begin to get hot again. All this takes place in seconds. The waffles begin to bake almost as soon as the batter is poured.

During the baking process, the cooler waffle batter absorbs heat as quickly as it is produced by the elements. This absorption of heat away from the electrical circuit prevents the thermostat points from opening until the waffle itself reaches a preset temperature. At this point, heat is no longer absorbed by the waffle and flows uninhibited to the thermostat blades, which bend. The points open, the signal light goes out, the elements no longer get electricity — and the waffle is reading for eating.

As you know, you can set the heat level of your waffle iron by turning a dial or moving a rod. In this way, you are able to get waffles that are light, medium or dark. What you really are doing when you activate the dial or rod one way or the other is putting more or less tension on the thermostat blades, causing them to bend or straighten sooner or later. This allows the contact points to open earlier or later which determines how long heat will flow to the elements to cook the waffle.

Troubleshooting Waffle Irons

THE FOLLOWING CHART lists the most common waffle iron problems and what must be done to correct them. If you consult an appliance serviceman, be sure to establish the cost of repair before allowing him to make repairs. Frequently, with small appliances, the cost of repair is equal to, or in excess of, the cost of a new appliance.

PROBLEMS, CAUSES, REPAIRS

Problem: Waffle iron doesn't heat

Possible Cause	Repairs
1. Open circuit	1. Test power cord for continuity. Replace if defective. 2. Test elements for continuity. Replace if element wire is broken. 3. Check thermostat for dirty contact points, bent blades, broken wires. Repair if possible; replace thermostat if not possible to repair.

Problem: Waffle iron gets too hot

Possible Cause	Repairs
1. Contact points welded together, causing elements to stay on all the time	1. Pry contacts apart and clean them. If this isn't possible, install a new thermostat.

Problem: Waffle iron doesn't get hot enough

Possible Cause	Repairs
1. Misadjusted thermostat	1. Readjust

Electric Knives

THE TWO TYPES of electric knives are the cordless and the cord type. The cordless operates from batteries built into the handle; the cord type plugs directly into the base or wall receptacle. A charger in the base on which the cordless knife rests keeps the batteries charged.

Cutting action is obtained by an electric motor that drives a gear set. The cord type contains a universal motor, the cordless has a miniature DC motor designed to operate from batteries.

The main part of the reciprocating gear set is an eccentric — a wheel with a shaft attached. This wheel, however, does not rotate in one direction. Instead, it moves a limited distance in one direction, and then swings back and moves in the other direction. This is made possible by the fact that the shaft is not attached to the center of the wheel, but in an off-center position.

This limited back-and-forth motion of the eccentric drives the knife blades (there are two blades) about 1/2 inch in a back-and-forth motion; that is, blades move forward 1/2 inch and then move back 1/2 inch. However, blades are reciprocating — that is, both of them do not move in the same direction at the same time, but in opposite directions.

The end of the motor shaft is a worm gear. The worm drives a reduction gear. On either side of the reduction gear is an eccentric — pins or wheels off-center relative to the gear. As the gear rotates, the eccentric turns with an oscillating motion. Levers on the eccentric change the oscillating motion to a back-and-forth motion which is transmitted to the knife blade.

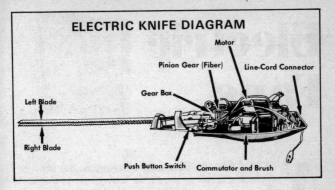

ELECTRIC KNIFE DIAGRAM

Motor

Pinion Gear (Fiber)   Line-Cord Connector

Gear Box

Left Blade

Right Blade

Push Button Switch   Commutator and Brush

Troubleshooting Electric Knives

THE MOST common problems associated with electric knives are the following:

1. Damaged power cord. If the cord has been pulled so that wires have been damaged, no electricity will get through to the appliance motor, and the unit will not run. Pull only on the cord's heavy plug end when disengaging the cord.

2. Worn brushes. Electricity flows through the armature by way of two carbon brushes on each side of the motor. Brushes must remain in contact with the commutator end of the motor in order for the motor to revolve. Brushes wear in use, however, and a gap eventually will develop between them and the commutator. Therefore, check brushes and replace them if they are worn shorter than 1/2 inch.

3. Damaged motor. Check all wires for looseness. If the commutator end of the motor has become rough and developed pitmarks, it often can be restored to use by polishing it with a strip of fine sandpaper. Sanding the commutator is done either with the motor running or with the armature in a lathe — both actions best performed by an experienced technician. If you do decide to tackle the job yourself, be sure to use sandpaper, not emery paper. Any other motor damage, such as a broken armature wire, usually necessitates replacement of the motor. Check on the price of a repair of this sort before allowing it to be made.

Electric Fans

A SET OF BALANCED blades mounted on the shaft of an electric motor to create air movement is the sum total of an electric room fan. The blades can blow air into a room or pull (exhaust) air from a room. The air movement depends on the shape of the blades and the direction in which the motor shaft rotates.

Room fans come in various shapes and sizes. Small fans sit on a table or mount on the wall. Some fans rest on pedestals which are equipped with wheels, so the unit can be rolled from one spot to another. Large, heavy floor fans are intended for stationary emplacement, while others are permanently mounted in attics.

There are fans that remain stationary as they move air: the motor stays still; the blades revolve. By contrast, other fans have gears which drive an arm-and-link assembly so the entire motor assembly can move from side to side. These are called oscillating fans.

No matter what kind of fan you have, its main parts are blades and a motor. The operation is simple to understand. All that must occur is for the motor to work so the blades revolve.

Desk fans and floor fans contain a shaded pole motor. Window units may contain either a shaded pole motor or a split phase motor. See the chapter on Types of Motors for a discussion of these motors.

When electricity is applied to the field coils, a magnetic force is established between the field and rotor or armature. This causes the rotor or armature to begin spinning at a comparatively high rate of speed. The blades spin and air in the room begins to move. This is the stationary fan in which the motor stays still while the fan revolves.

Electric Fans

If the unit is an oscillating fan, a small gear box on the back of the motor makes the motor, and hence the blades, turn slowly from side to side to distribute airflow through a greater angle.

A clutch, operated by a knob on top of the oscillator gear box, connects the pinion (first reduction gear) to the eccentric arm gear. Tightening the knob causes the fan to oscillate. Loosening the knob allows the second reduction gear to slip on its shaft, stopping the oscillating action.

Bent Blades

BLADES BECOME unbalanced when one or more leaf is bent forward or backward, usually when the fan gets knocked over. Balance as follows: 1. Remove the blade. Place on a flat surface. If one leaf is seen to be misaligned, carefully bend by hand back to the same plane as others; or,

2. Firmly hold a screwdriver where the tip will touch the back edge of one leaf. Slowly turn the blade. All leaves should touch the screwdriver tip.

Carefully bend back into shape any leaf that is misaligned. BUT DO NOT BEAT IT WITH A HAMMER. Unless obviously damaged beyond repair (one leaf missing, for example), it is not too difficult to bend the leaf by hand back to its original shape closely enough to make any residual unbalance scarcely noticeable in fan operation.

Preventive Maintenance

DISCONNECT the power cord from the wall outlet whenever you service the fan.

Check the fan motor carefully (or consult manufacturer data or the instruction book) to see if it has oil ports. If it does, lubricate the motor at the beginning of the warm season with a few drops of heavyweight household motor oil.

Keep the fan clean at all times. Dirt and dust on the motor will impede the cooling power of the motor.

PROBLEMS, CAUSES, REPAIRS

Problem: Fan motor does not run.

Electric Fans

Possible Cause

1. Damaged power cord

2. Burned out motor

Repair

1. Check with continuity test lamp to see if wires are broken. Replace cord if defective.

2. Discard unit if motor has burned out; it does not pay to install a new one.

Problem: Blades rotate sluggishly.

Possible Cause

1. Blades bent

2. Lack of oil in motor

Repair

1. Try to bend blades back to shape. If not possible and if fan has replaceable blades, replace blade unit. Otherwise replace entire fan.

2. Lubricate.

Problem: Noisy operation

Possible Cause

1. Loose part
2. Loose blade hub
3. Blades out of balance

Repair

1. Tighten.
2. Tighten if possible.
3. Put up with noise; replace blade unit if fan has replaceable blades; or replace entire fan.

Problem: Oscillating fan turns sluggishly.

Possible Cause

1. Lack of lubricant in gear box, on eccentric arm, or link assembly
2. Bent eccentric arm and/or link

Repair

1. Disassemble parts and lubricate.

2. Replace assembly.

Blenders

F OOD BLENDERS and food mixers are virtually the same, except for the working end of the appliance. A food mixer uses beaters; a blender uses cutter blades that whirl at high speed in the bottom of a container to mix, chop, and liquefy foods.

Like the food mixer, a blender is driven by an electric motor. There are no gears; the parts of an electric food blender that provide power are the motor, line cord and switch.

Electricity is delivered to the motor, which is the same universal type used in many appliances and tools, mixers, and drills.

As the motor spins, it causes the cutter blades to revolve. Simple revolving is not enough, however; a chef must have a way to control the speed for various operations — slow for chopping nuts, for example; high for making mayonnaise. The method used for speed reduction is a multi-speed switch.

This category of switches is a simple one. Most use resistors in series with the motor to control speed. In other words, special devices (resistors) that limit the amount of current going to the motor are activated when you press certain buttons; as they come into use, they reduce speed. These resistors, called dropping resistors, have varying degrees of resistance. With them, you are able to set up to 14 or 16 speeds in your electric food blender. Most present-day blenders, however, contain a solid state controller with push-button speed selector. As illustrated, the controller is a

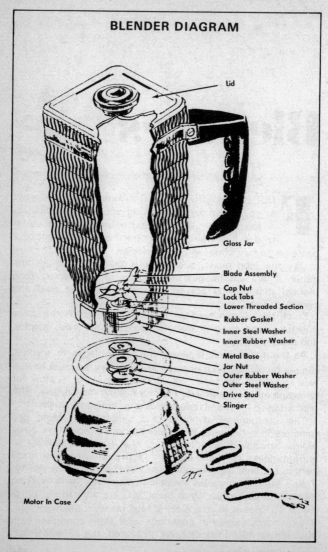

BLENDER DIAGRAM

Lid

Glass Jar

Blade Assembly
Cap Nut
Lock Tabs
Lower Threaded Section
Rubber Gasket
Inner Steel Washer
Inner Rubber Washer

Metal Base
Jar Nut
Outer Rubber Washer
Outer Steel Washer
Drive Stud
Slinger

Motor In Case

modular replaceable unit. Operating the push button switches connects one or more of a string of resistors into the phase shift circuit of the controller or provide the various blender motor speeds.

PROBLEMS, CAUSES, REPAIRS

MOST ELECTRIC blender malfunctions occur in the motor and associated components, such as seal leakage allowing food to enter the motor, and damage or wear to the speed controller. A common problem is with the line cord and switch. As with practically all other electric appliances, line cord failure predominates and results primarily from misuse. Do not pull on the cord to disconnect it from the wall socket. Use the plug only.

In time, a switch can go bad, usually from a resistor that has failed, staying totally open. The blender then will run at only one speed. Testing a resistor requires an ohmmeter; this, like the test for the motor and seal leakage, requires proper tools and the training of a service technician.

After long service, the motor bearing or bowl seal may wear out. The motor revolves on a bearing; a seal is used in the base of the bowl to prevent leakage. Both parts usually can be replaced without replacing a major component.

Another malfunction that may occur in time is damaged cutter blades. This generally happens when a foreign substance that cannot be blended finds its way into the container. Cutter blades generally can be replaced by removing the nut and lockwasher holding the blades to the blade shaft, and inserting a new blade. It always is wise to use only replacement parts made for your blender.

Hair Dryers

WHETHER THEY are professional beauty or barber shop models, or smaller home models, hair dryers (and stylers) are built pretty much the same way and work on the same principle. We will drop the term "styler" for the remainder of this section, because a styler is nothing more than a hand-held dryer, which works the same way as the dryer described here. The only difference is the working end of the appliance. A dryer dries while a styler dries and styles simultaneously.

Simply put, the working parts of a hair dryer consist of a heater assembly (made of the same type of coil wire as a toaster) and a fan or impeller. The heater gets hot and the fan moves the warm air through a nozzle or air duct into a bonnet, or shoots it out of a barrel.

Hair dryers have a minimum of three selector switch positions: Off, Cold (which turns on the motor only, so that cold air is blown), and Warm, which turns on the motor and the heating unit so that warm air is blown.

More elaborate hair dryers have a selector switch that provides as many as five positions: Off, Cold, Warm, Medium, and Hot. These units contain two heating elements: a high-heat element and a low-heat element. The two are connected so that at maximum heat, both of them are working.

So you can get some idea of how you can get all these varying settings from one little hair dryer, see the illustrations accompanying this section. They show the following:

• Figure 1 shows the Off position. Nothing is engaged, so nothing is working.

• Figure 2 shows the Cold position. The fan motor is

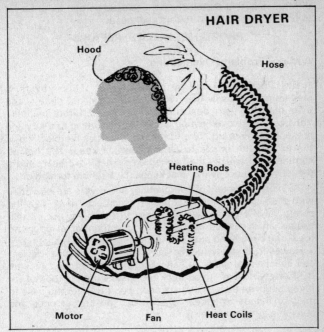

HAIR DRYER

Hood

Hose

Heating Rods

Motor   Fan   Heat Coils

engaged, so the fan is on, but the heating elements are not engaged — they are off.

• Figure 3 shows the Warm position. The fan and low-heat element are both engaged, and warm air is coming out of the end of the tube.

• Figure 4 shows the Medium position. The fan and high-heat element are both engaged, so air that is warmer than in the Warm setting is coming out of the end of the tube.

• Figure 5 shows the Hot position. The fan, low-heat, and high-heat elements are all engaged, and the air coming out of the tube is the hottest you can get.

The fan (also called impeller or blower unit) used in hair dryers is basically a simple, small electric fan. The major difference is that the blades are enclosed so that air is blown in one direction only — toward your head.

PROBLEMS, CAUSES, REPAIRS

A Major Problem: Overheating

A BIG PROBLEM faced by manufacturers of hair dryers is preventing excessive heat, which would damage, distort, and even melt the thermoplastic case. Several different malfunctions can cause overheating, which may also lead to injury and present a fire hazard. Two of the more serious are blocking of the end of the nozzle or air duct, which keeps the hot air confined and causes the heating element to overheat; and a defective selector switch that keeps the fan from turning on.

To avert the hazard of overheating, hair dryers are equipped with a so-called safety thermostat which acts much like the safety valve on a hot water heater. If a problem occurs that causes an excessive heat build-up, the thermostat opens to break the circuit and stop the heating element from heating.

However, a safety thermostat is only a mechanical device, and mechanical devices fail. For this reason *you* are the best safety device. If you think the case is getting too hot, or if you begin smelling a strange odor, don't wait for the case to melt or flames to appear. Disconnect the unit at once and consult a service technician.

Other Problems Affecting Hair Dryers

UNLIKE MANY other small appliances, a hair dryer includes a comparatively great variety of components. The more components an appliance has, the greater is the chance of failure. The following outlines some of the major problems that may occur and generally what can cause them:

● Erratic heating. Switch to Warm, Medium and Hot positions. Hold your hand over the output end. If the three heating positions are working properly, you will feel a distinct temperature difference between them. If not, then the switch has gone bad, wiring is faulty or a heating element has burned out.

Before having a major repair made, compare the price to repair to the price of a new unit. Particularly in the case of hand-held models, it is almost always more economical to get a new unit.

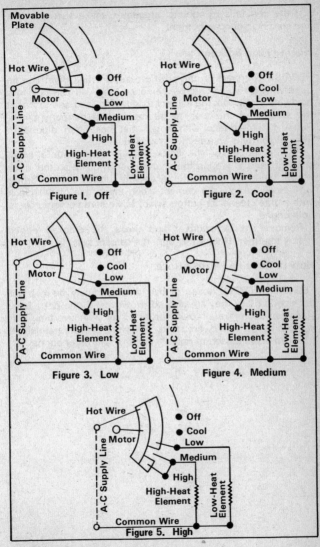

Figure 1. Off

Figure 2. Cool

Figure 3. Low

Figure 4. Medium

Figure 5. High

Hair Dryers

If the unit fails to operate altogether, make sure that the line cord is in good condition.

How to Fix a Broken Case

REPAIRING a crack in the plastic case of a hair dryer can be done with a two-part epoxy cement which you can buy in a hardware store. Mix the cement as directed, and see to it that the surface of the area to be repaired is perfectly clean. Rubbing the surface with a rag that has been dipped in mineral spirits is an effective way of cleaning.

Pry the edges of the crack slightly apart with a small screwdriver and wedge the screwdriver in place so the crack is kept open. Do this gently; once split, plastic cracks further very easily. Apply the cement along the edges of the crack with a pipe cleaner or cotton swab. Make sure cement covers both edges.

Remove the screwdriver and press the cracked edges tightly together. Hold firmly until the cement sets.

How to Repair a Flexible Hose

FLEXIBLE NOZZLE hoses of hair dryers usually do not get damaged unless they are abused. However, if one does tear, you often can make a repair with soft vinyl adhesive tape that you can buy in a hardware store. This same pressure-sensitive tape can also be used to repair a tear in a hair dryer bonnet.

Electric Irons

THE MODERN electric clothes-pressing iron may seem like a complicated appliance, but it is really very simple. Basically, an iron consists of a heating element mounted in a thick metal soleplate and a temperature controller. The heating element is connected by means of terminals and a line cord to an electric wall outlet. With the iron connected, the heating element heats up and brings the soleplate to temperatures over 600°.

Since different types of materials respond best to pressing at particular temperatures, some means of controlling heat is necessary. Excessive heat will ruin fabric, while heat that is too low will not give effective pressing. The component used to control heat is an adjustable thermostat.

(The first electric irons did not have thermostats. Temperature was controlled by pulling the line cord from the iron when it got too hot, then plugging it in again to reheat it when it became too cool.)

Thermostat operation is simple. The device is bimetallic (see the chapter on Thermostats for a complete explanation of this device) and opens and closes according to temperature. When you turn a knob or dial to the temperature setting you want (sometimes indicated by a fabric name such as "cotton," "linen," or "silk"), you are putting a certain amount of tension on the thermostat blades. When the temperature reaches the desired range, the heat causes a thermostat blade to bend back away from its mating blade. The thermostat opens, breaking the flow of current to the heating element. As temperature cools down (and more heat is needed), the thermostat blade returns to its original position, again making

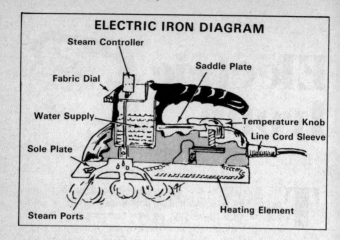

ELECTRIC IRON DIAGRAM

contact with its mating blade. The circuit is then complete and the flow of current begins again.

Although manufacturers use various methods by which you may select a heat range for pressing different fabrics, the principle in all cases is essentially the same, and an extremely versatile one. A modern-day electric pressing iron allows you to select temperatures over a greater range than most small cooking appliances. For example, you can select an ironing temperature for rayon, which is about 200°, and an ironing temperature for linen, which is about 550°.

Almost every electric iron made today may be used interchangeably as a dry or a steam iron. For steam, a reservoir in the iron is filled with water. As the iron heats, the water boils and steam is emitted through vent holes in the soleplate. In some irons, steam flows continually. In most others, you control the bursts of steam by pushing a small button in the handle.

What Can Go Wrong

THE ELECTRIC IRON probably gets more use than any other small appliance in the home, and is usually one of the most reliable of all home appliances. A heating element may "open," which will prevent the soleplate from getting hot; a thermostat may go bad, affecting operation. However, these problems rarely arise, and an electric iron used with some care often will be discarded after many, many years of use, only because the owner wishes a new one.

Ninety-nine percent of all electric iron failures are caused by abuse to the line cord. Some stress is placed on the cord normally as the iron is moved back and forth. The cord is pulled, flexed and stretched.

But this normal use usually does not cause damage. Most problems are caused by pulling on the cord to disconnect it from the wall socket. This pulls strands apart inside the insulation.

Pull only on the heavy plug when disconnecting a line cord. Many plugs have indentations for your fingers to make the task even easier.

Another potential problem to watch for is overextending the cord's reach. It is safer and less damaging to move the ironing board closer to the wall plug, so the cord remains slack, than to stretch the cord and put constant pressure on the inner wire strands.

Besides the visible fraying of insulation, one indication of a damaged line cord is erratic heating: the iron becomes hot one time you use it but not the next. When the cord has deteriorated to this point, arcing and sparking usually occur. A damaged line cord should be replaced.

In replacing an iron cord, use one of the heat-resistant types (HPD or HPN) only. In type HPD the wires are covered with asbestos over rubber; the entire cord assembly has a woven cloth outer cover. To prepare the ends, cut the cover back 3 or 4 inches. Remove all insulation from about 1-inch from the end. Wrap thread around the loose asbestos at the end.

Type HPN looks like heavy lamp cord, but is different; its insulation is heat resistant thermoplastic. The best bet is to replace the cord with whatever kind was formerly on the iron. Cord manufacturers offer "cord sets" custom-made to an appliance, complete with strain grommet and snap-on terminal lugs. Using such an exact replacement simplifies installation of the new cord in the iron.

Electric Irons

PROBLEMS, CAUSES, REPAIR

EXAMINE the soleplate frequently. If it looks corroded, scratched or tarnished, polish it with a stitched-rag buffing wheel. This is available from hardware store dealers; it is an attachment to an electric drill or electric motor, but you should use it with your hand for this job. (Do not use abrasive tools or compounds on irons with a Teflon shoe.)

Buff the soleplate lightly and wipe it off. Then polish it carefully with a very fine grade of buffing compound. Tell the hardware store dealer what you need the product for. He will see that you get the correct buffing compound for the job.

Steam irons demand special attention. Many require the use of distilled or filtered water to prevent mineral deposits from creating scale inside the iron. Others can be used with tap water. All, sooner or later, will probably require cleaning. As soon as you hear a rattling sound inside the iron, stop using it and clean it out with a special chemical made to dissolve mineral scale in steam irons. Again, ask your hardware store dealer for help; he will know what you need. Use as directed. If the iron is badly clogged, more than one treatment will be required.

One way to prolong the life of a steam iron without special chemicals is to pour out the water while it is still hot. When water sits for hours or overnight, it deposits extra minerals that cause extra problems.

Shavers

THE MOST popular of all powered personal care appliances is the electric razor. And with refinements in design and performance, its popularity continues to grow.

Three kinds of motors are used in electric shavers. Some contain a tiny universal motor, others contain a vibrator type motor. Cordless razors contain NiCad cells, miniature DC motor, and charging components all within the shaver unit. A scraper (razor) or series of scrapers attached to the motor moves in reciprocating fashion — that is, in a back-and-forth, straight line way.

Reciprocating motion is established by means of a small pinion. Essentially, the pinion and scraper are connected by a stud set in an offset position in the pinion. Thus, the scraper is prevented from making a full 360° turn as the motor revolves; its travel is limited to the size (distance) of the razor head.

There are variations in the way different makes of electric razors are built, but the principle just described applies to all, with the exception of those that employ rotary heads.

Electric razors generally use very thin perforated shields to enclose the whiskers as skin is pressed against the shields. The rapidly moving scraper shears off the hairs extending through the surface of the shield.

The power source to operate an electric shaver's motor may come from a wall outlet by means of a line cord or through a

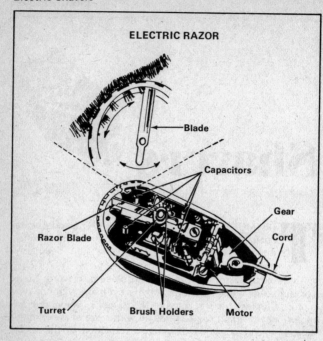

ELECTRIC RAZOR

Blade

Capacitors

Gear

Cord

Razor Blade

Turret

Brush Holders

Motor

tiny nickel-cadmium battery in cordless electric razors. Batteries of cordless electric razors have to be recharged periodically by being connected to a wall outlet through use of a line cord.

PROBLEMS, CAUSES, REPAIRS

THE ELECTRIC RAZOR is one appliance that owners — even those with technical ability — cannot repair. Replacement parts are not usually available, not even to professional appliance technicians. The shaver must be returned to the factory when a problem occurs.

The key word to keep in mind regarding caring for your electric razor is "clean." The razor should be brushed clean of hair after every use to maintain its effectiveness and extend its life.

INSIDE A "CORDLESS" RAZOR

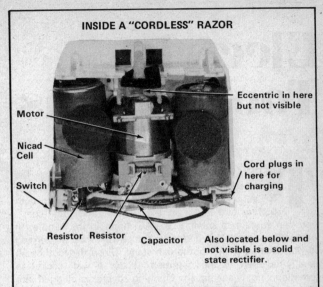

Eccentric in here but not visible

Motor

Nicad Cell

Switch

Cord plugs in here for charging

Resistor   Resistor   Capacitor

Also located below and not visible is a solid state rectifier.

INSIDE A VIBRATOR TYPE RAZOR

Each AC Cycle
These teeth align due to magnetism, then separate due to a heavy internal spring.

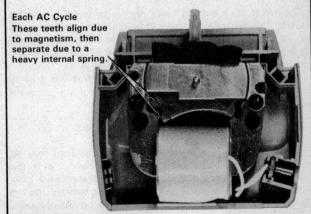

Resulting vibrating action drives razor comb and cutter

Electric Toothbrushs

THERE ARE two types of electric toothbrushes: the "cordless" type that operates from a battery of NiCad cells that power a small DC motor, with both battery and motor in the handle, and the "cord" type that contains a small 115 VAC motor in the handle. In the cordless type, the batteries are powered by a charging adapter located in the toothbrush stand. Since the toothbrush usually is used in the bathroom where a wall socket is sometimes not available, the charging adapter is plugged into the electric shaver receptacle on the medicine cabinet lamp fixture.

The motor of an electric toothbrush is encased in a sealed housing that cannot be opened. It is a low-power motor since the job does not require much power. The motor will operate for a total of about 1/2-hour before the NiCad battery will need recharging.

The motor turns a small pinion gear which drives a bevel gear on the switch position. This is one of the simplest motors in the appliance field.

PROBLEMS, CAUSES, REPAIRS

IF THE TOOTHBRUSH develops a defect, the fault may be either in the parts (battery and motor) in the handle, or in the charger base. If the batteries run down immediately after charging, the fault is in the toothbrush; if the batteries do not charge up at all, the fault is, most likely, in the charger base. Neither the toothbrush nor the charger base can be repaired, but instead must be replaced.

ELECTRIC TOOTHBRUSH DIAGRAM

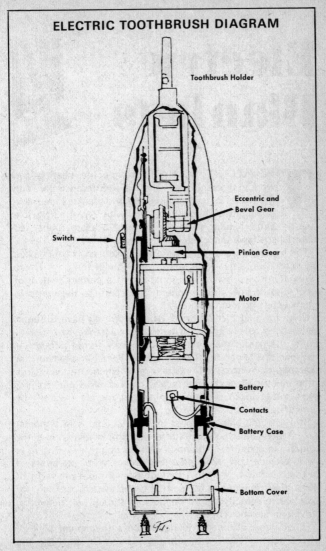

Toothbrush Holder

Eccentric and Bevel Gear

Switch

Pinion Gear

Motor

Battery

Contacts

Battery Case

Bottom Cover

Electric Blankets

THE ELECTRIC BLANKET and electric heating pad work in the same way. The major difference between the two is in construction: electric blankets are made of a lightweight cloth material with very thin, flexible heating wires; heating pads are made of a heavy rubberized material and have thick, molded-in wires.

The heating wires in both electric blankets and heating pads are laid out in a neat grid pattern throughout the unit. These wires are of a particular value that allows a certain amount of electricity to flow through them. This permits the wires to reach a specific temperature.

Keep in mind that different types of wiring have different resistances to electricity. The more resistance in a set of wires, the harder the electricity must work to get through — and thus, the lower the heat generated. Wires in a toaster, for example, have much less resistance to electricity than wires in an electric blanket. That is why toaster wires get red hot, while wires in an electric blanket get merely ''warm'' by comparison.

Still, electric blankets must provide variations in temperature to please sleepers with different comfort levels. In some models, temperature is controlled by a simple switch that is set to provide Low, Medium or High heat. Wires are arranged so that electricity will flow through one or more networks of wires, depending upon the setting of the switch. At High, for example, electricity would be flowing through all networks, providing maximum heat.

Other types of electric blankets use a thermostat control, with a separate switch to turn the blanket On and Off. The thermostat is made of strips of metal that bend and straighten in response to the amount of heat being generated. This causes the electric circuit to break (when the strips bend) or remain intact. When metal strips are cool, they are straight and the circuit is closed, allowing electricity to flow to the blanket's wire elements. As heat reaches the level you set, the metal strips get warm enough to bend, pulling thermostat points apart and breaking the circuit. The flow of electricity is halted until the temperature drops enough for the strips to straighten again and repeat the heating cycle.

With these blankets, you control the degree of heat by setting the thermostat. You turn a dial to indicate a position of relative heat. By so doing, you put more or less tension on the metal strips. This causes the circuit to open or close to reach and maintain the desired temperature.

PROBLEMS, CAUSES, REPAIRS

Problem: Blanket will not heat

Possible cause:	Repair:
1. Points in the control have gone bad	1. Remove the points and solder in new ones. If points are too tightly welded, replace the entire control, unless the control for your blanket is no longer in stock. In that case, you must buy a new blanket.
2. Wires bent or broken	2. Buy a new blanket; this cannot be repaired.

Turntables and Tone Arms

IN A HI-FI system, these elements perform basic functions. Whether you own an automatic record player (in which several records can be stacked for continuous playing) or a separate manual-play turntable/tone-arm combination, the sole function of the rotating platter (turntable) is to *rotate*—at constant speed.

Any mechanical system with moving parts generates vibrations, inconsistencies of motion or speed which can cause unevenness of musical pitch in the record (called "wow" and "flutter") and the induction of low-frequency noise in the electronic reproducing system (via the pick-up cartridge) called "rumble." The drive motor in a hi-fi turntable system ideally should meet these criteria: constant rotational speed, constant speed with voltage variation, vibration-free operation, adequate rotational torque, and long-term, continuous operation without change in characteristics.

Two types of motors are generally used in turntables and record changers. The induction motor, whose speed varies with load and with changes in applied voltage, is used in less expensive models. The synchronous, or hysteresis synchronous, motor, which depends on the *frequency* of the incoming power for speed accuracy, is generally freer from vibration and noise and is therefore found in top-priced turntables and changer mechanisms. Recently, slow-speed servo-controlled DC and AC motors have been used with good results as well.

Drive Systems

BOTH INDUCTION and synchronous motors generally

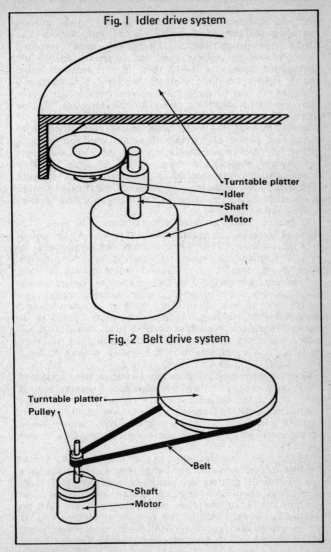

Fig. I Idler drive system

Turntable platter
Idler
Shaft
Motor

Fig. 2 Belt drive system

Turntable platter
Pulley
Belt
Shaft
Motor

Turntables

run at much higher speeds than the 33-1/3 or 45 rpm required for record playing. (In the pre-LP days, 78 rpm was standard record rotation speed, though modern machines seldom include this; nor do they include the 16-2/3 rpm speed intended for "talking book" records.) Two methods are widely used for "stepping down" the high speed (generally 1800 rpm) to the required lower speed. In the rim-drive system, illustrated diagramatically in Figure 1, one or more idler wheels transfer the power from the motor shaft or pulley to the turntable via the friction of their rubber rims.

In this method, the motor shaft is usually equipped with a stepped pulley of varying diameters and the idler is moved up and down, engaging the different diameters and thereby altering the speed of the turntable which it drives. Usually, the step-down ratio from motor to idler is about 8-to-1, with the remainder of the required step-down accomplished because of the diameter ratios of idler to inner rim of turntable.

A second common drive system, shown in Figure 2, employs a rubber or plastic belt to convey motor power to the turntable. This system lends itself primarily to manual turntable arrangements, and speed changes are made by guiding the belt around motor pulley sections of differing diameters. The belt serves to isolate motor vibrations from the turntable, thus reducing noise and rumble. In precision turntables, the belt is often ground or honed after molding, to be as free from bumps or irregularities as possible. Resistance to heat, changes in humidity and even contamination by lubricating oil all must be taken into consideration in the choice of belt material and design.

More recently, some high-quality turntables have appeared which are directly driven by slow-speed motors which rotate at exactly the required 33-1/3 or 45 rpm. These motors are often electronically driven and controlled; because of their slow speed of rotation, they transmit lower vibration and very low wow and flutter components to the turntable.

While many manufacturers of turntables maintain that the heavier the turntable the better, this is not universally true. Turntable platters are made of pressed steel plate or die-cast aluminum alloys. A quality turntable will be carefully machined and even custom-balanced just like an automobile wheel, and for the very same reasons—so as not to induce once-per-revolution speed variations or jitter. As for weight of the turntable, the important thing is that

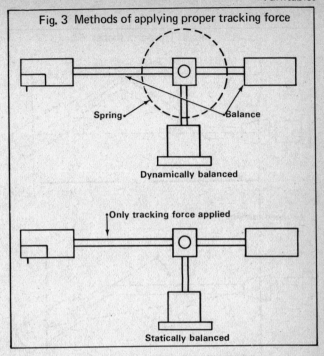

Fig. 3 Methods of applying proper tracking force

Spring

Balance

Dynamically balanced

Only tracking force applied

Statically balanced

the weight and flywheel action be properly matched to the torque characteristics of the motor that drives the platter.

Tone Arms

MAJOR EFFORTS in the design of hi-fi record playing equipment have concentrated on the pickup system, i.e. the tone arm and phono cartridge. A good phono cartridge can deliver best performance only if it is mounted in a tone arm of proper design and quality. The tone arm's main function is to keep the cartridge (or more properly the stylus or needle) in the record groove while it travels across the record, and to apply the proper downward tracking force while compensating for other, un-

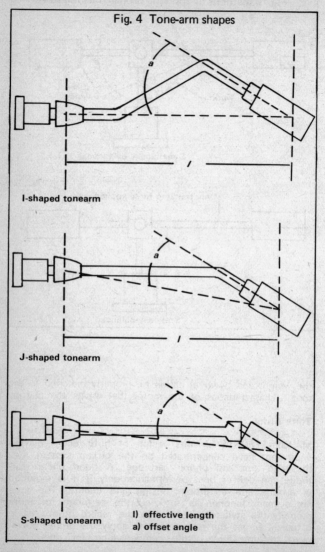

Fig. 4 Tone-arm shapes

I-shaped tonearm

J-shaped tonearm

S-shaped tonearm

l) effective length
a) offset angle

wanted forces. High quality tone arms are often made of a light metal alloy to reduce weight and increase stability.

Several shapes of tone arms are shown in Figure 4. In each shape, the shell-cartridge section is at an angle designed to minimize the arm's tracking error. Tracking error is the angle that the cartridge axis deviates from tangency to the record groove—and the smaller it is the better. On low-priced changers, the cartridge shell is an integral part of the tone arm, while on better equipment the cartridge-shell is a plug-in type facilitating rapid interchange of different cartridges.

Since different cartridges work best at different tracking forces, tone arms provide a means for adjusting this force. Adjustment is made either by spring action or by counterweights and sliding weights.

An additional adjustment often provided on better tone arms is called anti-skate adjustment. Because of the geometry of the tone arm, there exists an inward force which tends to pull the arm inward when the record is rotating. Uncompensated for, this force would push the stylus against the inner groove wall of a record, causing increased record wear and unbalanced reproduction. Anti-skate adjustment provides the necessary counter-force and is made adjustable on most tone arms equipped with this feature. Since skating force varies with tracking force and even with shape of stylus tip (conical or elliptical), the anti-skate adjustment should be made when a new cartridge is installed.

Automatic Record Changers

AUTOMATIC RECORD changers incorporate all the elements already discussed and, in addition, are capable of continuously playing six or more records in a row. Usually, the same motor that drives the turntable is used to actuate a series of mechanical linkages which both drop the successive records from their spindle support and cause the tone arm to swing back and forth between records. They normally are equipped with an automatic shut-off feature which causes them to turn off after the last record has been played.

Preventive Maintenance

DUST is the chief evil when it comes to the preservation

of records. In addition to keeping all your records clean and in their protective jackets, it is important that the turntable and its surface, and the tone arm and cartridge be kept free of dust at all times. If your record player is not equipped with a dust cover, by all means purchase one that fits over the entire mechanism and keep it in place whenever the player is not in use.

Some turntables require periodic lubrication of the main center-bearing of the platter, while others are permanently lubricated. Consult your owner's manual for frequency and type of lubrication required and follow those instructions. Motors used in modern turntables rarely if ever require lubrication and, in fact, attempts to lubricate them often result in the inadvertent spilling of oil on the rubber idler wheel or belt which quickly causes these components to deteriorate.

If your tone arm's tracking force adjustment involves a spring or springs, check actual tracking force every few months to make certain that spring tension has not changed. This is best done using an inexpensive tracking-force gram scale available from most hi-fi equipment dealers. Such an external scale will also help you check accuracy of tone-arm calibrated scales of tracking force. Inspect the underside of your platter and idlers or motor shafts periodically, using a soft lint-free rag to clean oil or moisture from all surfaces that rotate and are involved in the drive chain.

If the power cord of your record player is connected to a convenience receptacle on your receiver or amplifier, never turn off the entire system before the last record has played through and cycled the changer to the OFF position. While turning off the system in this way also may turn off power to the changer, the idler wheel will then be pressing against both the motor shaft and the turntable inner rim and, since it is not free to rotate, permanent depressions or deformations of the idler will result. This will almost always result in severe audible "wow" or a thump-thump sound which can only be cured by replacement of the idler wheel itself.

If you must leave the system before the last record has played, simply cycle through the remaining records manually, so that the changer comes to a complete stop before you turn off all power to the system. Some amplifiers and receivers are equipped with "unswitched" convenience receptacles which continue to supply power even when they are turned off. If such a receptacle is used, it is safe to turn off the amplifier or receiver, since the record player will continue to rotate (though, of course, no sound will be heard) until the last record has cycled and the changer has come to a complete stop.

PROBLEMS, CAUSES, REPAIRS

Problem: Unit fails to turn on when switch is activated

Possible cause	Repair
1. Power cord disconnected	1. Connect other appliance to receptacle to make sure it is live.
2. Faulty switch	2. Check continuity of motor leads after first disconnecting power cord.
3. Power cord connected to other equipment which is not turned on	3. Replace motor if open.
4. Burned out motor	4. Replace changer switch if faulty

Problem: Motor turns but platter does not

Possible cause	Repair
1. Idler wheel slipping or not engaging motor shaft or platter	1. Remove turntable and examine idler and motor shaft. Clean if oily.
2. Belt has slipped off motor pulley	2. Check for loose springs which may have slipped out of anchor points.
3. Belt is torn	3. Check condition of belt, replace if necessary.
4. Speed selector is in neutral position	4. Check action of speed selector knob with turntable removed.

Problem: Motor turns at wrong speed

Possible cause	Repair
1. Slipping drive system	1. Check for slippage as above.

PROBLEMS, CAUSES, REPAIRS

2. Displaced idler wheel (vertically)

2. Check step positions of idler wheel against motor pulley for each available speed—adjust vertical position as required.

3. Mis-oriented, loose selector knob

3. Check orientation; tighten.

Problem: Increase in audible wow and flutter

Possible cause

Repair

1. Flat spot has developed on idler, slipping belt, eccentric center hole in record being played

1. Examine idler or belt for defects noted. Replace if defective. Try playing a different record. Rotate table by hand, feeling for any rough spots per revolution. Check table bearing, lubricate if required.

Problem: Stylus hops from record groove to record groove

Possible cause

Repair

1. Defective stylus

1. Have stylus condition checked with microscope.

2. High tonearm pivot-bearing friction

2. Move tone arm through its arc by hand to detect friction point, if any.

3. Jammed linkage under changer

3. Examine underside of changer for possible tone-arm restricting forces.

4. Excessive record warp

4. Discard record.

Problem: Tone arm sets down at wrong point of record start

Possible cause

Repair

1. Indexing adjustment has altered with use

1. Adjust indexing per owner's manual. Check

PROBLEMS, CAUSES, REPAIRS

2. Records mounted on changer spindle improperly
3. On manually selected size types, wrong selection was made

other items enumerated.
2. Remount.

3. Change type selector.

Problem: Record fails to drop during change cycle, or multiple records drop.

Possible cause	Repair
1. Variation in center hole size on some records	1. Try variety of records and check other points.
2. Worn or improperly seated changer spindle	2. Replace center spindle, if found defective.

Problem: Platter jams or stops during change cycle.

Possible cause	Repair
1. Motor losing torque with age	1. Rotate table manually through cycle to determine force required for changer cycle.
2. Lubrication of changing linkages required; undue friction has developed in moving parts due to rust, etc.	2. Lubricate changer mechanism parts only if owner's manual so instructs. Otherwise, refer to qualified service personnel.

Problem: Changer does not cycle at end of record.

Possible cause	Repair
1. Automatic trip mechanism mis-adjusted	1. Adjust trip mechanism per instructions supplied.
2. Tone arm repeating last musical groove	2. Try several records before servicing.

Tuners Receivers

A "RECEIVER" in the high fidelity component sense contains all the elements of what would commonly be called a "radio" except for the loudspeakers which must be connected externally. In addition, stereo receivers usually have connection facilities for a record player, any one of several forms of tape-playing mechanisms, and one or more other sound signal sources such as the sound portion of a TV set, and so on.

As shown in the block diagram of Figure 1, there are three basic sections which make up a receiver: the tuner or radio signal receiving section, the preamplifier control section, and the power amplifier section. In very elaborate hi fi systems these three sections actually may be purchased as separate units, for increased flexibility and control or as a means of assembling the system in stages using the "building block" approach.

Modern receivers are solid state devices—that is, they use transistors, rather than vacuum tubes. Transistors have, in theory at least, almost infinite life, although transistor failure (particularly in the power amplifier section) is an occasional occurrence caused either by improper use of the equipment or by random failure of components.

The Tuner Section

THE TUNER SECTION may be equipped to receive only FM signals or both AM and FM signals. Since it is possible to broadcast stereo (two channel) sound via FM, most hi fi receivers have circuitry for decoding the complex composite received signal into separate "left and right" channel signals.

The front end of the tuner section selects the particular

signal desired from the hundreds of radio signals present in the atmosphere. As you tune the dial, resonant or tuned circuits are changed so as to be responsive to a single frequency. In the case of FM signals, tuning is adjustable from 88 mHz (millions of alternations/second of the radio wave) to 108 mHz. Since each FM station occupies a space of 0.2 mHz, that means a theoretical maximum of 100 stations is possible in one geographical area. Actually fewer stations are assigned in any one area, so that one station's signal will not cause audible interference with an adjacent station. In the case of AM, stations broadcast at frequencies ranging from 540 kHz to 1605 kHz (1 kHz = 1000 alternations per second) and selection of desired stations is similar to the technique used in FM.

The signal is amplified by the front end and mixed with a locally generated signal in the receiver to produce a difference frequency known as the IF signal (Intermediate Frequency). In the case of AM, the IF frequency is generally 455 kHz. In the case of FM radio, the IF frequency is 10.7 mHz. The process is known as superheterodyne and since the local signal and received signal are always a fixed amount apart, the succeeding IF amplifiers need not be variably tuned but can be designed simply to amplify 455 kHz (for AM) or 10.7 mHz (for FM).

Difference Between FM and AM

IN AM RADIO the amplitude of the radio wave is varied in accordance with the audio information to be broadcast. Hence the name AMPLITUDE MODULATION. In FM it is the radio frequency that is varied based on audio signals. It is this feature that makes FM relatively noise free since noise or static is an amplitude phenomenon. If noise accompanies the FM signals the noise can be sliced off by circuits called limiters without impairing the frequency-changing nature of the FM signal.

While the circuits themselves differ, the amplified IF signals are then applied to a detector circuit which strips off the original audio information. In FM, the detector is called a ratio detector. The output of either the AM detector or the FM detector is an audio signal suitable for application to and further processing by the "preamplifier control" section of the receiver.

In the case of stereo FM the recovered audio signal must

be further processed or "unscrambled" to recover the separate "left" and "right" audio channels. This is accomplished by the multiplex decoder circuits.

Preamplifier Control Section

THIS SECTION of a receiver is the "nerve center" of a high fidelity system. It contains selector switches for choosing audio program sources, tone control circuits for modifying the tonal emphasis of the audio signal, a volume control for setting the levels of loudness of signals to be fed to the power amplifier section, and the early stages of amplification needed to raise the electrical signal strength to a point suitable for application to the power amplifier section. Note that the phonograph input undergoes more amplification than do either the radio or tape input signals. That is because the output of a magnetic phonograph cartridge is minute compared to those other program signals. In addition, recordings are made with deliberate attenuation of the low bass frequencies (to prevent overcutting of the record grooves) and accentuation of the higher frequencies (to overcome or override high frequency record surface noise). The phonograph equalizer stages have a response which is the converse of the recording response characteristic, as shown in Figure 1. Thus, the equalizer restores flat response or proper tonal balance.

The Power Amplifier

THE FINAL section of a receiver handles any of the program source signals fed to it from the preamplifier section, amplifying them further, until they are powerful enough to drive externally connected loudspeakers. Power amplifier sections in receivers may vary in power capability from just a few watts per channel to as high as 100 watts or more per channel. The most conservative kind of rating is that which specifies continuous, or RMS watts, though several other means of specifying power output are used by manufacturers. The greater the power output rating, the louder the sound capability of the amplifier section. If an amplifier is driven beyond its power capability, severe distortion usually results and the sound becomes unpleasant to listen to. Since some loudspeakers require considerably more power than others to produce a given amount of sound power output, it is almost impossible to generalize as to how

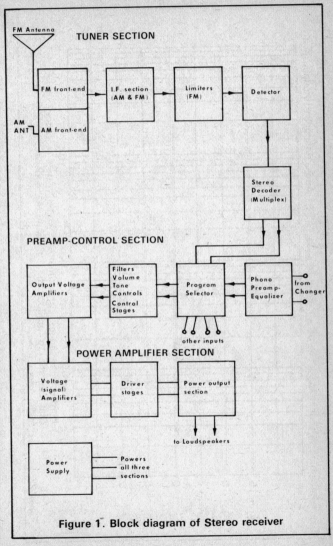

Figure 1. Block diagram of Stereo receiver

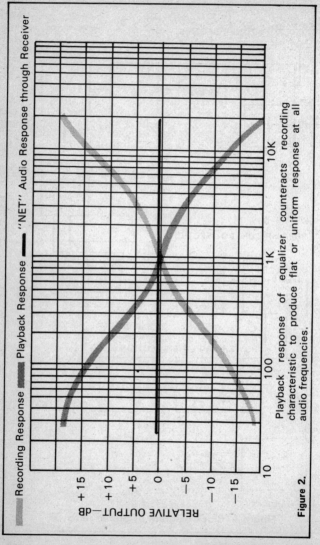

Figure 2.

Recording Response ▬ Playback Response ▬ "NET" Audio Response through Receiver

Playback response of equalizer counteracts recording characteristic to produce flat or uniform response at all audio frequencies.

RELATIVE OUTPUT—dB

+15 +10 +5 0 −5 −10 −15

10 100 1K 10K

much power output one needs in a power amplifier to produce realistic, loud, clean sound.

Many receivers make provision for connecting more than one pair of stereo speaker systems. When multiple pairs of speaker systems are used and listened to simultaneously (as in two different rooms), power necessarily divides between the sets of speakers. Solid state amplifier sections operate well with speakers of impedance ranging from 4 ohms to 16 ohms, but if lower impedances are used (as in the case of paralleling two or more sets of speakers), power output sections may overheat because of excessive current drain. Unless protective circuits or fuses are incorporated, severe damage to the amplifier can result.

While transistors produce less heat than vacuum tubes did, they do produce some, and adequate ventilation should be provided around the receiver cabinet, to permit air flow and proper heat dissipation.

Preventive Maintenance

THERE IS little or no maintenance required with today's modern solid state receivers. If supplied in a wooden enclosure or cabinet, make certain that the holes or ventilating slots above the cabinet are left exposed, with at least three or four inches of air space above them. If the receiver is to be installed in your own furniture cabinet, allow at least as much air space around the unit as was afforded by its own enclosure. From time to time, use a small hand vacuum cleaner to remove dust from the chassis and components, always disconnecting the power cord from the wall outlet before cleaning. Although some receivers use parts which require no alignment, others must be aligned periodically. Approximately every year or two, the receiver should be brought to a qualified service center for realignment of the FM and AM tuner sections. This will insure optimum sensitivity and station-pulling ability as parts age over the years.

If your receiver was not supplied with a full service manual and schematic diagram when purchased, it is a good idea to write to the manufacturer and obtain such material, even if there is a small charge involved. In that way, if, years from now, the unit requires major servicing, you will be able to supply the service technician with adequate information which might no longer be available from the manufacturer. Good service technicians often can find the source of trouble without such aids, but having a manual and schematic cuts down the trouble-shooting time considerably

Tuners/Receivers
and reduces servicing costs.

If trouble develops and cannot be corrected by trying the steps outlined below, DO NOT attempt to go beyond the simple remedies listed. A receiver is a complex piece of electronic equipment, and by attempting to unsolder parts and replace them yourself, you may overheat and damage nearby parts, especially if they are installed in printed circuit boards or modules. Of course, if you still own a tube-type receiver, it is perfectly all right to remove tubes and have them checked at your nearest TV or radio repair shop. Make certain, however, that you note their location on the chassis before removing them, since not all receiver chassis are marked with tube notations.

In many cases, a tube that reads marginally acceptable in a tube tester socket should be replaced, since in a high quality stereo receiver it is expected to operate at optimum levels. If any of the "front-end" or IF section tubes are replaced, it is generally advisable to have the radio section completely realigned, since new tubes can change the alignment characteristics of the FM or AM section of the receiver.

PROBLEMS, CAUSES, REPAIRS

Problem: No sound or panel illumination when power is switched on

Possible cause:	Repair:
1. AC plug not connected	1. Connect plug.
2. Home fuse or circuit breaker needs replacing or tripping	2. Replace fuse. If fuse continues to blow, refer to qualified technician.

Problem: Set lights up, but no sound

Possible cause:	Repair:
1. Speaker fuse blown	1. Check speaker fuses.
2. Tape Monitor switch on	2. Set Tape Monitor to Source or Normal.
3. Open speaker cables	3. Check speaker cable connections and speaker selector switch settings.
4. Selector switch improperly set	4. Check FM muting switch (turn off) and tuning meter if on FM or AM.

CONSUMER GUIDE

Problem: Hum is heard on phono

Possible cause:	Repair:
1. Poor or no ground from record player to receiver chassis	1. Connect ground wire from changer to set.
2. Open audio cable from player to receiver	2. Replace changer audio cables. Check that selector switch is set to appropriate phono setting.

Problem: Howling feedback sound when volume is turned up

Possible cause:	Repair:
1. Record player too close to speakers	1. Reposition record changer.
2. Bass control set too high	2. Turn down bass control.
3. Loudness on	3. Turn off loudness control when listening at loud levels.

Problem: Rough, scratchy or distorted high-frequency sounds

Possible cause:	Repair:
1. Worn stylus, worn record	1. Check stylus condition, test with known good record or on FM.
2. Treble control set too high	2. Use high-filter setting if required.

Problem: Buzzing on AM

Possible cause:	Repair:
1. Nearby fluorescent lights or other nearby electrical appliances operating	1. Change orientation of AM bar antenna; eliminate local source of interference; install outdoor AM antenna.

Speakers

A S SIMPLE as loudspeakers are in theory, new loudspeaker systems continue to appear on the market every year—each claiming to be superior to all its predecessors. The fact is that loudspeakers, or more properly loudspeaker systems (which may contain many "loudspeakers" in a single enclosure or cabinet), are the least perfect element of a high fidelity component system. Whereas electrical and electronic circuits can be built to amplify and process audio signals with virtually no distortion or alteration, loudspeakers are a class of components known as transducers—devices that transform electrical energy back to mechanical energy (or vice versa), and as such they are subject to all the limitations imposed upon purely mechanical devices.

Figure 1 represents a simplified cross-sectional view of a conventional dynamic loudspeaker. Current flowing through the voice coil causes it, and the mechanically-connected cone or diaphragm, to move back and forth, repelled or attracted to the fixed, permanent magnet structure at the left. The entire voice-coil/diaphragm structure is suspended (but free to move) at the voice coil area and at the forward portion of the cone.

The generation of sound depends upon alternate compressions and rarefactions (partial vacuums) of the air projected into the listening room. If a "raw" loudspeaker such as that shown in Figure 1 is the sound source, each compression of air in front of the speaker is accompanied by a rarefaction of air at the rear of the cone. Unbaffled, compressed air waves from the front rush around to equalize the partial vacuum at the rear thereby cancelling some of the sound you would normally hear—particularly at low bass frequencies.

At higher frequencies, the air does not have time to rush around from front to back since the speaker cone is moving so rapidly back and forth. It is for this reason that a variety of speaker enclosures was developed to prevent the cancellation effect or, in some cases, to use the "back-wave" to actually reinforce the forward-emanating sound waves.

Two-way, Three-way and Four-way Systems

JUST AS IT would be difficult for a single human voice to handle bass, baritone, tenor and soprano vocal efforts musically, so is it difficult for a single speaker element to handle all the audio frequency range from lowest bass to highest treble. Accordingly, many hi-fi speaker systems utilize two, three and even four separate speaker driver elements, each designed to handle a particular fairly narrow range of audio frequencies. Based upon the number of sections into which the audio spectrum is divided, such systems are called two-way, three-way or four-way. The number of speaker elements in a speaker system is not always the same as the number of "ways" because often, the high frequency elements (called "tweeters") are doubled to provide better angular sonic dispersion or for other design reasons.

Auxiliary parts in a multiple speaker element system include crossover networks and one or more level controls. The crossover network is an electronic circuit which splits up the sound spectrum into the required segments—lows, middles and highs in a three-way system for example. The border frequencies between one range and another are called "crossover frequencies." Level controls for the mid-range and high-frequency elements are often included to permit the user to adjust overall speaker response to suit personal taste or the acoustic characteristics of the listening room.

Speaker Enclosures

AS PREVIOUSLY mentioned, speaker systems include enclosures which are an integral part of the total design

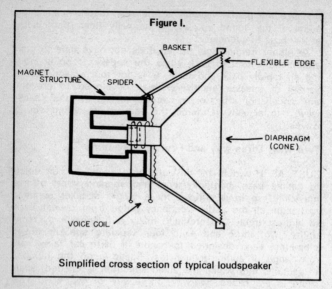

Figure I.

BASKET

MAGNET STRUCTURE

SPIDER

FLEXIBLE EDGE

DIAPHRAGM (CONE)

VOICE COIL

Simplified cross section of typical loudspeaker

and help to reinforce bass reproduction. Enclosures can be roughly divided into three types: closed boxes, ported or bass-reflex types, and horn-loaded types. The closed boxtype is hermetically sealed so that sound emanating from the rear of the speaker element is absorbed inside the box (which is usually lined with absorbent material). While closed boxes usually excel in sound quality, they require rather large dimensions to obtain satisfactory bass response. A modern variety of the closed box is the air suspension (or acoustic suspension) type, often used as compact bookshelf speaker systems, in which the woofer (low frequency driver) is mounted with a soft cone suspension so that it can make greater piston movements for better bass response. Such designs are, however, rather inefficient and require greater amplifier power for equivalent sound levels compared to the more efficient bass-reflex and horn types of designs.

The bass reflex design, on the other hand, boosts bass sound by rechanneling part of the rear sound back to the

194

front via a duct, or port, as shown in Figures 2 and 3. The port or opening must be optimally ''tuned'' to the woofer with which it is used and such designs are widely used because of their smaller volume (compared to the infinite baffle closed box types), and higher efficiency (compared to air suspension designs). Their drawback is that the bass sometimes sounds a little boomy, tending to emphasize a narrow band of frequencies rather than the entire bass region.

Outdoor speaker systems and, for that matter, a great many movie theater sound systems, employ speaker systems designed as ''horn enclosures.'' A true horn design, with a constant rate of flare, provides a proper match

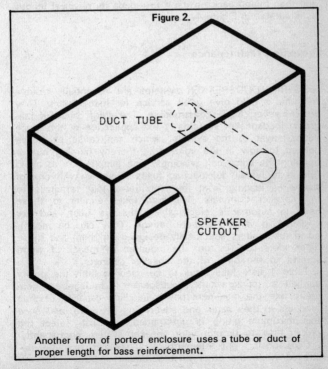

Figure 2.

DUCT TUBE

SPEAKER CUTOUT

Another form of ported enclosure uses a tube or duct of proper length for bass reinforcement.

Speakers

between the cone of the driver loudspeaker and the air to which the sound energy must be coupled. To be effective, horns must be designed to a length determined by the lowest cut-off frequency desired. For example, a horn capable of 32 Hz reproduction would have to be about 9 feet long! Obviously, the average sized living room would not easily accommodate one of these monsters. Nevertheless, horn designs provide by far the greatest speaker efficiency attainable and are often used in high-frequency (tweeter) arrays in multi-element home speaker systems.

For use at lower frequencies many manufacturers have developed variations of the horn principle called "folded horn" designs. The enclosure is first designed as a "horn" and then folded back on itself to reduce its physical length, as illustrated in Figure 4.

Preventive Maintenance

MODERN LOUDSPEAKER systems are essentially trouble free and should give good service for many years. They are, however, NOT indestructible. The chief cause of failure in loudspeaker systems is the application of too much audio power to the system, which can cause excessive current to flow in the voice coil, thereby burning out or opening the voice coil windings. One simple way to avoid this is to install quick-acting fuses in series with one of the wires leading from the amplifier output terminals to the speaker terminals. Miniature fuses similar to those used in automobile electrical circuits are best, and are available in various ampere ratings. They can be mounted in fuseholders specifically designed for them and these fuseholders can, in turn, be mounted by means of wood screws to the back of the speaker cabinets.

Table 1 lists fuse sizes to be used to limit the power applied to loudspeakers. Loudspeaker manufacturers generally rate the maximum power handling capacity of their products in their sales and advertising literature, and once this maximum rating is determined, you can select the proper fuse to protect your speaker system permanently.

Occasionally, one element of a speaker may be destroyed while the other drivers remain operative. For ex-

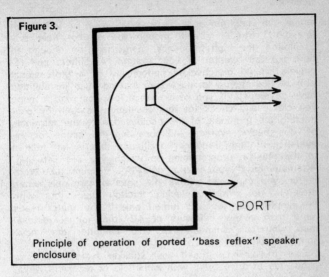

Figure 3.

PORT

Principle of operation of ported "bass reflex" speaker enclosure

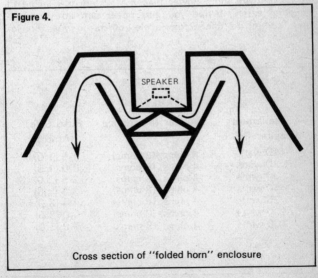

Figure 4.

SPEAKER

Cross section of "folded horn" enclosure

Speakers

ample, an amplifier may be oscillating at a very high (inaudible) frequency and, though you do not hear this oscillation, the high frequency energy may be enough to burn out the tweeter of your system. Amplifiers and receivers should be checked periodically by a professional hi-fi service station to make sure that no such instabilities have developed. If you own even a low cost oscilloscope you can easily check for this oscillation yourself by connecting the terminals of the oscilloscope to the terminals of your speaker systems and observing the 'scope for any evidence of high frequency oscillation that is not related to the musical programming to which you are listening. Alternatively, if you own a good AC vacuum tube voltmeter, you can read across the speaker terminals when there is no program playing through them (but with the amplifier or receiver turned on). If the meter reads more than a few millivolts of AC (the normal residual hum) you can suspect that your amplifier may have some instability.

Even if you have fused your speaker systems, it is a good idea to drive them with amplifiers or receivers which do not put out more power than the system is capable of handling safely. While you may never turn up your volume control to dangerous levels, others in your house-

TABLE 1

Maximum Speaker Power	Speaker Impedance	Fuse Size (Amps)
10 watts	4 ohms, (8 ohms)	1.5 (1.0)
20 watts	4 ohms, (8 ohms)	2.0 (1.5)
30 watts	4 ohms, (8 ohms)	2.5 (2.0)
50 watts	4 ohms, (8 ohms)	3.5 (2.5)
75 watts	4 ohms, (8 ohms)	4.0 (3.0)
100 watts	4 ohms, (8 ohms)	5.0 (3.5)
200 watts	4 ohms, (8 ohms)	7.0 (5.0)

hold may accidentally do so while the receiver or amplifier is off, and then when you go to turn on the system, the initial sharp transient may be enough to destroy one or more drivers in the speaker system.

As a general practice, whenever you go to turn on your hi-fi system, always start with the master volume control all the way counterclockwise. This will prevent popping noises from the speaker on turn-on. While many amplifiers are equipped with protective fuses or even circuit interruption schemes, these devices protect the amplifier from excessive current, but will not protect speakers if their power handling capacity is not equal to that of the electronics driving them.

If your speakers have removable front grills, never operate them with grills removed for long periods of time, as the grills prevent dust accumulation and inadvertent puncturing of woofer cones.

PROBLEMS, CAUSES, REPAIRS

Read speaker warranty carefully. Avoid home repairs if they would void warranties.

Problem: One system of stereo pair produces no sound.

Possible cause	Repair
Open or shorted speaker cables; defect in driving amplifier; defective speaker system itself	Isolate trouble by first interchanging speakers to left and right outputs of amplifier. Make reversal at amplifier end. If same speaker as before is quiet, try new speaker cable. Also check speaker fuse, if supplied. If still dead, trouble is in speaker system. If other speaker dead, trouble is with amplifier and not with speaker.

Speakers

Problem: System produces only low bass sound—no highs.

Possible cause

Tweeter may be defective, or connection to it may have come loose

Repair

If manufacturer permits opening system within terms of warranty, open system and check for continuity of tweeter by using an ohmmeter across its terminals. Reading should be only a few ohms. If "infinite" reading is obtained, tweeter voice coil is open. Replace tweeter with manufacturer's exact duplicate only.

Problem: Raspy, buzzy sound when playing at high volume levels.

Possible cause

Voice coil of woofer or mid-range element may be off-center and rubbing

Repair

With front grill removed, gently depress woofer, applying pressure with all five fingers to center of cone. If rubbing is heard or detected, replace entire woofer with manufacturer's exact duplicate. Follow same procedure with midrange units if found defective. Also check for loose parts (capacitors, coils, screws found loose, etc.) that may be rattling against speaker frame due to sound vibration.

Problem: Reduced sound, intermittently, from one system of stereo pair.

Possible cause	Repair
Defective amplifier or strand of wire shorting across amplifier or speaker terminals	If amplifier is not at fault (check as in "no sound" condition above), check visually for possible single strand of stranded wire cable bridging across speaker terminals or amplifier terminals. Clear "bridging short."

Problem: Mid-range or tweeter system varies in intensity with accompanying static type noise.

Possible cause	Repair
Dirty or defective speaker level controls	Rotate each level control back and forth several times, listening for static type noise with amplifier on, but no music playing. If noisy, spray control element with suitable electronic control cleaning spray. If this does not correct trouble, replace with manufacturer's proper replacement control.

Problem: Bass seems deficient, stereo imaging is vague (after re-connection of systems)

Possible cause	Repair
Speakers may have been reconnected "out-of-phase"	Try reversing connection to *one* speaker only.

Tape Recorders

MAGNETIC RECORDING tape used in tape recorders consists of a thin film of polyester or acetate with a layer of fine iron oxide particles imbedded in a suitable adhesive. These particles can be magnetized in a magnetic field and will retain this magnetization. During the record process on any tape recorder (and this applies to open-reel, cassette or cartridge machines), electronic signals corresponding to the desired sound source are amplified and applied to the coil of a small electro-magnet called the "recording head." This creates a magnetic field which alternates in accordance with the sound's frequency and intensity, in and around a tiny gap between the poles of the magnet. As the tape travels past the recording head, its iron oxide particles are magnetized by the alternating magnetic field. The tape therefore stores the sound information in the form of a magnetic pattern.

In playback, the reverse process occurs. The tape is transported past a playback tape head—another small electro-magnet with essentially the same structure as the record head—and induces a small alternating current in the magnet's coil. This small signal is then amplified and used to drive a loudspeaker.

Track Arrangements

EARLY TAPE recorders used the full width of the tape for a single recorded program. Later, with refinements in tape recorder components, recording tape and techniques, the tape width was divided into two tracks, and then four. In open reel recorders, four-tracks remains the standard today for home equipment; the tracks may be used for recording

TABLE I

TAPE THICKNESS, LENGTHS AND RECORDING TIME
(BASED ON 7½ IPS TAPE SPEED)

TYPE	BASE	THICKNESS (μ)	LENGTH (m)	LENGTH (ft.)	RECORDING TIME (min.) ONE WAY	RECORDING TIME (min.) BOTH WAYS
Standard 100	Acetate	52	370	1200	32	64
Standard 100	Polyester	52	370	1200	32	64
Low Noise high output 100	Acetate	52	370	1200	32	64
output 100	Polyester	52	370	1200	32	64
Long play 150	Acetate	35	550	1800	48	96
Long play 150	Polyester	35	550	1800	48	96
Double play	Polyester	25	740	2400	64	128
Triple play	Polyester	20	1100	3600	96	192

Tape Recorders

two stereophonic programs or a single quadraphonic (four-channel) program, as diagrammed in Figure 1. Of course, if single channel recording is required, four separate programs can be recorded, each using one of the available tracks. Table 1 shows the standard lengths and types of tape available for open reel recorders and indicates recording times available based upon one-direction or two-direction recording.

Tape Speeds

TAPE SPEED is of significant importance in sound quality, especially where high (treble) frequencies are concerned. The higher the tape speed, and the narrower the tape head gap, the better the high frequency response of the resultant recording. Recent advances in recording head technology have made it possible to fabricate ultra-narrow head gaps so that excellent frequency response can now be obtained even at slower tape speeds. Tape speed is, of course, directly related to recording time, and in Table 1, the recording times listed are based upon tape speed of 7½ inches per second, the speed at which all pre-recorded tapes are duplicated. At 2¾ ips, recording time would be double that shown, while at the "professional" tape speed of 15 ips (available on a few home machines) time would be cut in half.

Tape Quality, Bias and Equalization

IN RECENT years, new tape formulations have appeared on the market. These include so-called "low noise" tapes and Chromium Dioxide tapes. In order to utilize these non-standard tape varieties properly, a tape recorder must have switchable bias and equalization. Bias is the name given to a high-frequency signal (usually above 65 kHz) which must be applied to the tape during recording to avoid distortion, while equalization is a deliberate alteration of frequency response during record and playback so as to produce end results which have flat response. The new types of tapes require different bias and equalization from the older standard type, and unless your recorder has specific provisions for making these changes (usually by means of front panel switching), the newer forms of tapes (especially Chromium Dioxide) may end up giving poorer results on your recorder than older, standard tape.

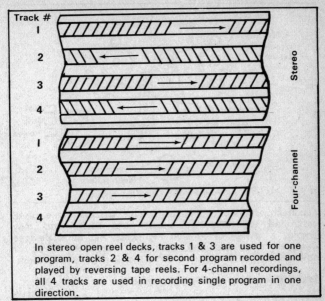

In stereo open reel decks, tracks 1 & 3 are used for one program, tracks 2 & 4 for second program recorded and played by reversing tape reels. For 4-channel recordings, all 4 tracks are used in recording single program in one direction.

Figure I

Tape Drive Mechanism

THE MECHANICAL part of a tape deck (often referred to as the tape transport system) has to move the tape past the recording and playback heads at a constant, specified speed. This is accomplished by a rotating capstan against which the tape is pressed by a pinch roller wheel. The mechanism must also perform two other functions: rapid forward winding and rapid rewinding of the tape reels. All three tasks can be performed by a single motor and a system of belts, pulleys and idler wheels, as shown in Figure 2.

Where greater precision and quality is required, separate motors can be used to drive the capstan and both reels, or three separate motors may be used, one for each reel and one for the capstan drive. In two or three motor deck transports, the capstan and reel motors are of radically different design so that each can perform its task with

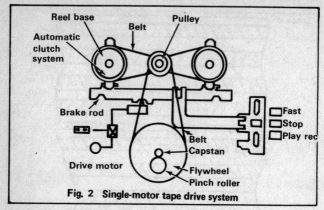

Fig. 2 Single-motor tape drive system

maximum efficiency. Top quality tape transports are often controlled via electronic circuits and relays and may employ a variety of tension regulators and other devices designed to protect the tape from excessive forces or spillage. Figure 3 shows a three motor drive arrangement.

Erase, Recording and Playback Heads

TAPE RECORDERS require at least two heads—an erase head which eliminates the previous magnetization on the

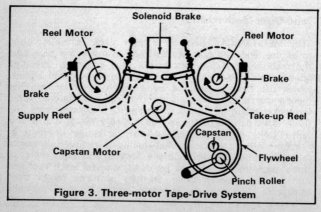

Figure 3. Three-motor Tape-Drive System

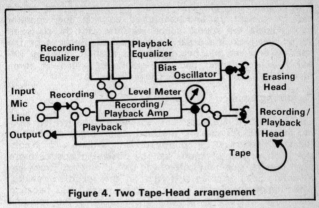

Figure 4. Two Tape-Head arrangement

tape and a combined record/play head. The arrangement for such a two-head system is shown in Figure 4. Better-quality machines will use three heads—an erase head, a record head and a separate playback head. Not only can each head then be designed specifically for its own purpose (and the criteria for a record head differ from those of a playback head), but three heads in a recorder permit "tape monitoring"—a really accurate recording control technique. As the tape travels past the recording head it is magnetized with the program signal. Then, as the tape

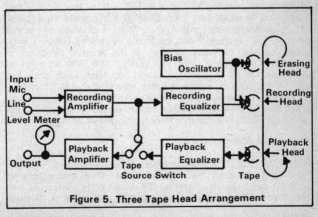

Figure 5. Three Tape Head Arrangement

Tape Recorders

travels past the playback head, the just-recorded sound can be picked up and monitored so that the operator can compare the source sound instantly with the recorded sound and make necessary readjustments. Because of the spacing between the heads there is a short time lag between source sound and tape-monitored sound. A three headed tape record system is shown in Figure 5.

Recording Level

SINCE RECORDING tape has a limited capacity for storing magnetic information, the strength of signal applied to the tape head must be controlled. This is done with a control knob or pair of knobs and by observing one or more level meters, generally referred to as VU meters. Excessive recording level causes distortion in the recorded results, while insufficient level results in noisy, hissy tapes because the program level is not far enough above the residual noise level of the tape particles themselves.

Other Mechanical Features

TO MAKE tape decks even more convenient to use, a number of additional features have been designed and are used in some machines. An automatic stop mechanism is common. It halts the reels when the tape runs out and in some cases even turns off the entire machine. Various automatic reverse arrangements also have been devised, one of which is the sensing foil method. The user applies short pieces of adhesive metallic foil near either end of the tape. Tape guide and tension arm (two parts in the normal tape path) act as switch contact points for a relay and when the metal sensing foil reaches these parts the reversing relay is activated, causing the tape to travel in the reverse direction. If the foil is affixed to each end of the tape, the tape travel will continue to be reversed back and forth each time the end of the tape is sensed by the switch contacts. It should be noted, however, that an auto/reverse deck requires two erase heads and two double-action record/playback heads which generally makes this feature somewhat costly.

Preventive Maintenance

FOR TOP-QUALITY performance, it is imperative that all tape heads be kept clean at all times. Dust and magnetic particles become deposited on the heads after prolonged use and this will rapidly deteriorate sound quality. Heads should be cleaned periodically by rubbing the entire head surface with a cotton swab stick soaked in rubbing alcohol or any of the specific cleaning compounds sold for this purpose.

If magnetic particles from the tape, or other foreign matter, are allowed to accumulate on the pinch wheel and capstan, irregularity in tape transport will occur, detectable as increased "wow" or "flutter." These parts are cleaned in the same manner as the heads. Be sure to avoid the use of chemicals such as chlorothane or other household cleaning fluids, since these may chemically react with the rubber pinch roller, causing it to deteriorate.

Normally, the steel pole pieces which form part of the recording and playback heads become slightly magnetized after extended use. The effect of this magnetization may be the introduction of noise into recordings made on the machine. Head demagnetizing therefore should be performed periodically. This can be done with the aid of a bulk head demagnetizer by bringing it close to the heads and making several circular motions over the entire head surface area as well as around the head housing, if it is constructed of ferrous metal. Always turn off power to the unit prior to demagnetizing of heads and avoid the use of magnetized tools (screwdrivers, etc.) in the immediate vicinity of the heads.

Recorded tapes, when stored for long periods of time, often exhibit an effect called "print through." Because the layers of tape are tightly wound to each other, a minute amount of magnetization from one layer may cause an adjacent layer to become slightly magnetized with its neighboring signal pattern. This can be detected during subsequent plays as a slight echo or pre-echo. Since fast rewind generally winds the layers of tape tighter than would normal-play speed, many professional recordists DO NOT rewind tapes after play, but store them in the so-called "tail out" position, rewinding them only just prior to their subsequent playing. Tapes should be stored at moderate room temperature, if possible, for greatest durability.

Note: Since open-reel tape decks are generally complex electromechanical assemblies, troubles other than those listed below should be referred to qualified service personnel, preferably the service agency specified by the maker of the particular tape deck. Do not substitute parts for those supplied originally, especially parts associated with the transport mechanism, as these are generally custom fabricated for each machine.

Tape Recorders

Problem: Loss of sensitivity and tone quality

Possible cause

Dirty erase head; wrong side of tape facing heads; magnetized head; tape selector switch set incorrectly

Repair

See suggestions under preventive maintenance. Check tape type in use and set machine properly. Check tonal settings on auxiliary amplifier.

Problem: Machine will not record or play. Transport motions are OK.

Possible cause

Pause button may be engaged; tape/source selector incorrectly set; Input and output level controls incorrectly set; Faulty electronics (record or playback preamplifiers)

Repair

Check settings of all controls as noted. Check VU meter readings. If no readings obtained, probably faulty electronics, in which case, refer to qualified service agency.

Problem: Irregularity (wow or extreme flutter) in tape transport.

Possible cause

Dirty capstan or pinch-wheel. Sticky or dirty tape surface. Improperly loaded tape. Slipping belts in one-motor drive system. Incorrect reel tension adjustment

Repair

Check all points referenced for cleaning, per instructions under maintenance. If available, check service manual for adjustment of tension in drive system, etc.

Problem: Tape will not run.

Possible cause

Blown fuse. Power not on because of auto-shut-off feature. Pause button depressed. Twisted or sticky tape. Burned out motor or sticky tape. Burned out motor or transport relays

Repair

Check power cord, fuses, etc. Check power switch. Release pause switch. Check for capstan rotation. Check for defective relays or solenoids; replace if defective.

Problem: Previous recording will not properly erase.

Possible cause	Repair
Dirty erase head. Faulty erase/bias oscillator circuit. Open coil in erase head	If head is cleaned and trouble persists, have bias circuit and erase head continuity checked by qualified service personnel

Problem: Distorted or noisy sound.

Possible cause	Repair
Recording level too high or too low. Input level to auxiliary amplifier too high. Old or defective motor relays	Check all level settings. If OK on recorder, reduce output level on recorder during play, increasing volume setting on associated amplifier. Repeat recording with fresh tape.

Problem: Tape breaks or spills during fast forward or rewind.

Possible cause	Repair
Misadjustment of belt tensions or defective reel motors (on multi-motor machines). Also, defective motor relays	See service manual for proper belt adjustments. Check for proper action of relays and solenoids in multi-motor machines.

Portable Phonographs

PORTABLE PHONOGRAPHS only are the subject of this chapter; stereo components are covered separately. In most of the market, the original portable phonograph has been replaced in recent years by lower-priced hi-fidelity "compacts." CONSUMER GUIDE Magazine endorses the switch to compacts and recommends that you compare quality and pricing of these units from any of the large audio manufacturers before purchasing a portable. Nevertheless, for children, for those concerned with easy mobility, and for those who are looking primarily at the price tag, the portable phonograph still has its place, and probably will for a long time to come.

In essence, the portable phonograph works in the same way as the most complex sound system. Its job is to pick up the variations within the spiraled groove of the record disc and translate it into sound. There are four necessary elements involved: turntable, pickup, amplifier, and loudspeaker.

As a record spins on a turntable at the required speed (45 and 33-1/3 rpm are pretty much standard on discs — even children's records are hard to find at 78 rpm), the stylus or "needle" of the tone arm rests in the groove, moving with the vibrations. The motion of the stylus is used to generate an electric voltage in a cartridge known as a transducer. This voltage is then sent to an amplifier, where another transducer is used to change the electrical impulses into audible sound waves, which are produced through a loudspeaker.

At its lowest common denominator, the entire process is a conversion of energies into different forms: from mechanical to electrical, and ultimately, to sound.

In the portable phonograph, each of these steps (the

essentials of sound reproduction) is accomplished in one assembled unit, although in many higher-priced models, the speakers detach for better stereo separation. Ideally, in the best hi-fidelity sound systems, each of these steps takes place in carefully-designed separate components, but if you are not really an audiophile, a portable can serve your listening needs adequately.

How to Choose a Portable

SOUND REPRODUCTION in a portable phonograph, or any sound system for that matter, fails or succeeds by its freedom from noise generated by the phonograph parts and by the sensitivity of the tone arm and its cartridge which picks up the information coded into the walls of the disc's grooves. Noise-free sound reproduction balance and relative freedom from friction is extremely important. Much of the time, what you think is a defect that requires service is actually a weakness in the system itself. If you buy carefully, you will have fewer causes for complaint.

As with any mechanical device, total elimination of friction is impossible, but it is possible to do away with most of the problem through the use of ball bearings and rubber wheels — even on inexpensive children's phonographs — and a phonograph with low friction will last longer and give better sound from the time you buy it.

The tone arm of a phonograph should have a counterweight to assure that the arm makes a correct arc over the record and to prevent the arm from the vibrations which cause resonance. Almost all higher-priced portable phonographs (those in the $80 to $120 price range) should have decent counterweights, but most of the inexpensive models have extremely flimsy tone arms, one of the primary reasons for their poor sound quality. Before purchasing any model, however, make sure there is some balance. On higher-priced units, there should also be a ball bearing device to reduce friction as the tone arm moves.

Ultimately, however, it is the stylus or "needle" which determines the sensitivity of the phonograph. In most cases today, the needles employed are made of industrial diamonds; however, on the inexpensive portable phonographs, sapphire needles are still widely used. The sapphire needle is inferior to its diamond counterpart, and provides far less listening

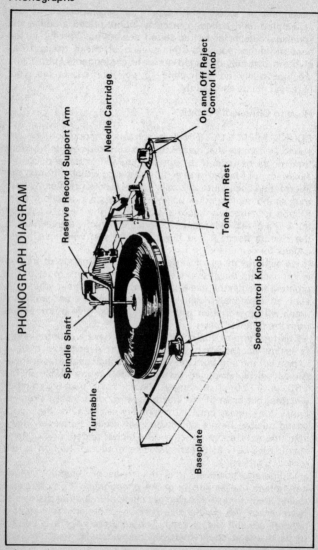

PHONOGRAPH DIAGRAM

Needle Cartridge

Reserve Record Support Arm

On and Off Reject Control Knob

Tone Arm Rest

Spindle Shaft

Speed Control Knob

Turntable

Baseplate

time before requiring replacement. For that reason, unless the unit is going to serve only as a toy, CONSUMER GUIDE Magazine recommends that you consider only units which take a diamond stylus.

As with the tone arm, balance is a key factor in the performance of the turntable. The turntable should have a certain resiliency to allow for variables with the records and with the device which "drives" the turntable or makes it spin. Fluctuations in the speed of the driving mechanism can cause two different kinds of distortions: "flutter," which is a trembling effect caused by erratic speed changes, and "wow," which is a tonal undulation. In the turntable driving device there should be as little friction as possible, and a rubber wheel should be used to assure smooth, noiseless function. Lastly, the turntable should be made of a non-magnetic material, to keep interference with the pick-up of the stylus at a minimum.

These, however, are ideal conditions which are missing on all but the best models in the category. Children's portable phonographs often have turntables made of plastic which appear to be carved out of the base. These turntables, often very poorly designed, are forever getting stuck, as friction wears away the "heavy duty" plastics creating jagged edges and irregular revolutions. Again, only if the phonograph is actually going to be used as a toy should one of these units be purchased.

There is an evident ambivalence in discussing portable phonographs, for we are really talking about two different types of phonographs, one geared for children, the other for inexpensive but serious listening pleasure. The decision on the intent of usage is a prerequisite in choosing any model.

One factor which crosses lines, and is important when picking out a phonograph is portability. There are numerous models on the market which are labeled as "portables" which are actually much too heavy and awkward to be carried from place to place. Be sure to check the size and weight of the unit if mobility is a concern, and the ease with which the model can be carried by its handle. There are also "true" portables available, AC/DC phonographs which can operate on batteries alone, as well as household current, if you want to use the phonograph outdoors.

In picking out a children's record player, you will have to choose every feature. They start with manually operated

Phonographs

monaural units with two speeds and are stepped-up to three and four-speed models with an automatic record changer and separating speakers.

In the high-end of portable phonographs, all of the specifications of more sophisticated stereo equipment should be taken into account, speaker size, EIA power rating, etc. (see section on components) but allowances should be made considering the limitations in this price range. You will rarely find such features as balance control on the inexpensive phonographs (some do not even have any control other than volume) but do not purchase a more expensive portable unless it gives you some amount of stereo balance and bass and treble manipulation.

PROBLEMS, CAUSES, REPAIRS

WITH THE SIMPLE phonographs, it is often very easy to determine what is wrong with the unit and how it should be fixed. The first place to look is at the needle, especially if your phonograph uses an easily damaged sapphire stylus. Because the sensitivity of the stylus is tantamount to the sensitivity of the phonograph, it is critical to keep it free of dust or other foreign matter.

Assuming you want to move your portable around, always make sure the tone arm is firmly locked into place and will not move about when being transported. Not only can this break or scratch the needle, it also can rip the entire tone arm out. Although some of the children's phonos on the market today can take a surprising amount of abuse, the stylus is still a delicate component. In fact, if you have an old model which does not have a good lock, it would be wise to keep a rubber band with the phonograph, and to fasten the tone arm down each time after use.

Tonal undulations, which we called "wow" before, are usually caused either by an unconstant rotation of the turntable, in which case the driving mechanism or the speed changing shaft should be checked, or by the record itself, if the spindle hole is too large. The trembling rapid speed variations of "flutter," on the other hand, are almost always caused by a worn part of the driving mechanism which can be replaced easily.

Vibrations or resonance usually emanate from the tone arm when it fails to make a proper arc across the disc or when it

Phonographs

starts to vibrate with the grooves. For this reason, it is important to have a well-balanced tone arm.

Amplification problems, on the other hand, are much more difficult to deal with. Nine out of ten times the real source of the problem, especially with the one-package portable phonograph, tends to be the loudspeaker rather than the amplifier, which has a much better reliability. The amplification in portable phonographs always has a certain amount of distortion, but it is in the speaker itself that more breakdowns occur. If your speakers separate, always check the connecting wires first, to make sure they are firmly fastened.

There are a number of other small things you can do to maintain your portable phonograph longer. First among these, with automatic record changers, is avoiding the temptation to stack too many records on the spindle. This often throws off the balance of the turntable, and sometimes plays havoc with the tone arm as well. Also, as with most so-called "heavy duty" plastics, keep the unit away from strong sunlight — plastic cracks and melts more easily than you or the manufacturer would like to believe.

Radios

A QUICK LOOK at some of the sophisticated radios on the market today can obscure the fact that the same basic principle of wireless transmission pioneered by Guglielmo Marconi in 1895 is still operating today. While technology has vastly improved since those days, and sophistication is the rule, the essential facts of radio transmission and reception are well within the layman's grasp.

In its simplest form, the radio is comprised of five essential elements: an input circuit to tune the transmitted frequencies, a "demodulation" circuit to separate the audible frequency from the high-frequency carriers, vacuum tubes or transistors to amplify the audible frequencies, and a loudspeaker. Whatever else your radio may do, its primary function is to remove the audio information sent through electromagnetic carrier signals, amplify the "demodulated" signals, and send the information out through a speaker.

Avoiding the highly technical parts of the process, here is how a radio works. A receiving antenna, which today is usually a ferrite rod, picks up the electromagnetic signal transmitted by the broadcasting station, thus beginning the first step of "selectivity" — the radio's ability to screen out signals which are sent at close frequency to one another. The selectivity, however, is minimal and the signal is very weak at this point; so it must be boosted by the "frequency amplifier," which also increases the radio's selectivity.

The incoming signal is then combined or "beat" with unmodulated oscillations generated by a local oscillator to produce a lower radio frequency signal which contains the same audio information as the initial signal. This, in turn, is amplified by an "intermediate-frequency amplifier." In the

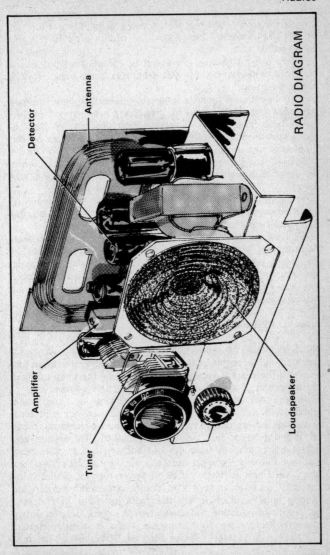

RADIO DIAGRAM

Detector

Antenna

Amplifier

Tuner

Loudspeaker

next stage, a "detector" demodulates the intermediate-frequency signal, and rectifies, filters and amplifies it further. After amplification, the sound is produced through the speaker.

There are, of course, a number of complicated processes involved, and intermediate steps, but this is the basic story in radio reception.

In conventional broadcasting, the electromagnetic signals are sent either through FM (frequency modulation) or AM (amplitude modulation). The reception process for both is fairly similar, although there are important differences on the broadcast end and in the demodulation itself. FM radio signals also are less inclined to distortions by atmospheric conditions or other disturbances which can cause havoc with the AM band.

In addition to AM and FM, there is also the entire realm of short-wave broadcasting, but that is a factor only on the multiband units which are on the market today.

Stereo in radio broadcasting is achieved through FM Stereo Multiplex, a system in which the radio receiver is able to capture two sound channels on one signal. Although there are patents for broadcasting stereo in AM, there has been only minimal experimentation with the systems to date, and their first application probably will be with automobile radios.

How to Choose a Radio

IN SELECTING a radio (we are here confining ourselves exclusively to better-quality AM/FM portable and table-top models) there are a number of considerations to keep in mind to be sure of good performance and fewer service needs.

Preeminent among these considerations is solid state circuitry. In the past, 90 percent of all maintenance problems with radios were due to tubes, so with their elimination most of the big headaches also have vanished. Transistors are much more reliable than the old vacuum tubes; they also subject the other components and circuitry to less heat, so the entire unit is likely to need fewer repairs. Solid state circuitry has been an important feature in the radio industry for a long time — much longer than with its sister TV industry where its introduction and application has come only recently; nevertheless, make sure that your radio is clearly labeled "100% solid state." Those marked 90%, 80% (or any fraction) solid state still contain some tubes, and although the unit is predominantly transistorized, your chances of breakdowns are still higher than with an all-transistor unit.

Another feature which is absolutely essential on FM radios is Automatic Frequency Control (AFC), which automatically locks in the station transmission and prevents drifting to another station. Although radio receivers pick up FM signals with less distortion than AM signals, the feature remains an absolute must, and should not be ignored.

On the other hand, CONSUMER GUIDE Magazine urges you to check the Interference Rejection capability of whatever radio you purchase. Overmodulation, among other factors, can cause serious sound distortions and could send you to a repair shop when in fact there is nothing that can be done. Test every unit before purchasing it.

Similar to AFC is Automatic Volume Control (AVC), a feature which is almost standard on better-quality radios today, attesting to its importance. AVC allows the unit to compensate automatically for volume differences from one station to another.

On multiband radios, CONSUMER GUIDE Magazine is adamant about squelch control, which allows for noise-free reception on the shortwave bands. If you are going to invest heavily in a Public Access or weather-band radio, be sure the unit has a squelch control.

There are many, many other factors to look for when buying a radio. The durability of the plastic on the cabinet and especially on the tuning controls, for instance, is very important. In the near future, if the plastics shortage worsens, and manufacturers are forced to turn to other synthetics, we urge you to take especially careful notice of the strength of the materials employed. As far as tuning controls go, CONSUMER GUIDE Magazine prefers the frontal slide rule controls over the vertical variety, since usually they are easier to manipulate and seem to resist wear longer.

Other considerations to keep in mind for long life are the sturdiness of the antenna, the EIA (Electronic Industries Association) power ratings on larger models, and the inclusion of an indicator light to illuminate the selection controls and jacks to add on accessories. Design and styling are matters of personal taste but make sure the radio sits firmly on a flat surface without rattling about, and that the size and weight of "portables" justify the designation.

Radios

PROBLEMS, CAUSES, REPAIRS

CONSUMER GUIDE Magazine is not going to recommend that you start tinkering with the circuitry of your radio. It is a tricky business and should be left to qualified technicians. For that reason, especially, be sure to read the warranty on whatever unit you purchase. Warranties vary widely from manufacturer to manufacturer, and from model to model, and it pays to do some competitive shopping. Incidentally, some of the largest manufacturers in the United States are not living up to their warranty promises with service technicians at this time, and many servicers are now refusing to service their products. It would be a good idea to check with your local shop before making a big purchase, especially since this is an area where you must depend upon professionals.

There are, however, a number of simple things you can do to extend the lifetime of your radio.

For one, keep the unit free from dust. Minute as they are, dust particles can do more damage than you could imagine when they sift into the inner workings. Similarly, it would be wise to keep your kitchen radio (and studies have found that more and more of every kind of radio find their way into the kitchen) away from the sink — water and electricity obviously make a lethal combination, but, even more, water and the grease from food can corrode the connecting cord and other components of the radio. Also keep the radio away from excessive heat, which can crack and even melt those ''heavy-duty'' plastics.

Lastly, and in all seriousness, be careful of sand. One of the favorite ways to enjoy a portable radio is at the beach — the perfect setting for sand corrosion.

Television

A TV SET — particularly a color TV set — is the most complex consumer product you can buy. It is even more technologically sophisticated than your car. Nevertheless, you can understand how it works, at least in general terms, and you can fix some of the things that may go wrong with it. More important, you can and must learn to operate it correctly for maximum enjoyment and longer life.

To understand how a TV set works, let's start with what you see — the picture tube face — and work backward (first black-and-white; we will add color later). The TV screen on which the picture appears is the closed-off end of a big glass "funnel." On the inside face of the screen there is a coating of phosphorescent material that glows when struck by electrons. A gun which shoots electrons is located at the back of the picture tube, forming the neck of the "funnel." The TV picture is "painted" by this electron gun in a series of thin, tightly spaced, horizontal lines. The beam of electrons shot from the gun sweeps across the screen from one side to the other, starting at the top and working its way down. It moves so fast that your eye cannot follow it and the lines it makes are so close together that they appear to merge, unless you are sitting very close to the set.

As the electron beam sweeps across the screen it is switched on and off at the appropriate instants to create light and dark areas in the appropriate places. The result is a black-and-white picture. Shades of grey are produced by varying the strength of the electron beam when it is on.

Television

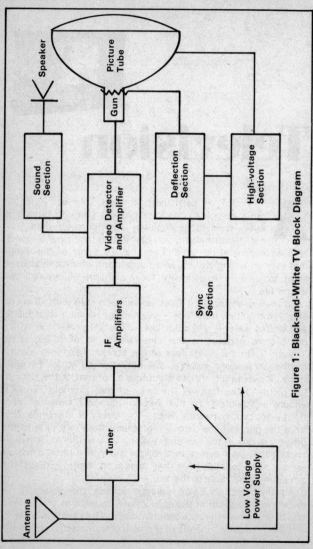

Figure 1: Black-and-White TV Block Diagram

224   CONSUMER GUIDE

TV Information

HOW DOES the TV set "know" when to switch the electron beam on and when to switch it off? To answer that, we must jump all the way back to the beginning of the story, to the TV camera in the studio. Think of the camera as a picture tube in reverse. Light enters the camera from the scene being televised and thousands of photocells sense the amount of light in each tiny area of the scene. The camera scans its photocells in the same sequence and at the same rate as the electron beam in the TV set scans the screen. The camera sends the information from its photocells to the transmitter, which sends it through space to your TV antenna. Electronic circuits in your set process the signal and make the electron beam sweep across the screen, turning on and off in the right places to duplicate the scene in front of the TV camera.

We will take a closer look at the circuits in your TV set that perform these functions later, but first we want to see how a color set differs from black-and-white. On the screen of a color picture tube, tiny red, green and blue dots are arranged in triangular groupings with one dot of each color in each group. There are also three electron guns, one for each color. The beams from the three guns sweep the screen in the same way as does the single gun in a black-and-white set. Red, green and blue are the primary colors, so when all three guns fire at a group of dots with equal intensity, the result is white light. When only one gun is on, you see red only, or green only, or blue only, depending on the gun. When two or more guns are on, firing at different intensities, the result is a blending of the primary colors to produce all the shades of the rainbow.

In the studio or out of doors, the color camera works similarly, with three arrays of photocells, each filtered to pick up one of three primary colors from the scene being televised.

TV Circuitry

THE ELECTRONIC circuits in a black-and-white set are diagrammed in Figure 1. The signal from the antenna travels down the lead-in wire and into your set. Once inside, it goes first to the tuner. The tuner selects out the signal from the station you want to watch; you control the tuner with the channel selector. The signal is then made stronger by the IF

Television

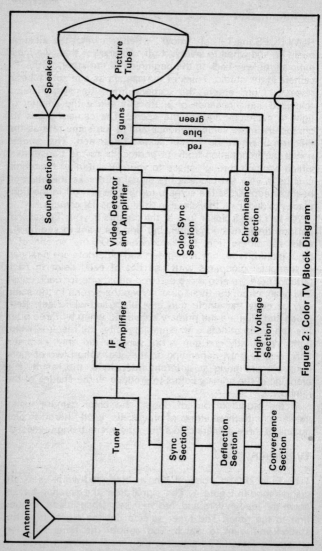

Figure 2: Color TV Block Diagram

amplifier and passed on to the video detector and amplifier, where the video (picture) information is separated from the audio (sound) signal. The sound signal is fed to the sound section where it is further amplified and passed on to the speaker, which converts the electrical signal into sound you can hear.

After being separated from the sound signal, the video signal travels to the sync (short for synchronization) section which separates out part of the signal called sync pulses. These pulses keep the electron beam in your picture tube in step with the camera, so that both the camera and picture tube electron beams start at the top of the picture at the same time, over and over again, many times a second.

The deflection section is next. It actually controls the movement of the electron beam, sweeping it from left to right, returning it to the left in a split second and sweeping it across again. At the same time, it is moving it from top to bottom, so that the horizontal sweeps occur one under the other.

Lastly, the high voltage section controls the intensity of the electron beam. The low voltage section (lower left) merely supplies the energy needed by each section to perform the various functions.

The circuits in a color set are similar to those in black-and-white, with a few additions (shown in Figure 2). At the video detector, color information is separated from the signal and fed to the chrominance and color sync sections. These sections produce three separate signals from the information sent to them, one for each of the primary colors. The signal for each color is applied to the appropriate gun. You will also notice a section marked "convergence." The convergence section makes sure the pictures painted by the red, green and blue electron guns are precisely superimposed on top of each other in the picture you see. When convergence gets out of whack, red, green or blue outlines appear around figures and objects on the screen because one gun is not "aimed" the same way as the others. Repairing this is a job for a professional.

Shopping for a TV Set

IT IS DIFFICULT to judge the quality of a TV set in a store. Salesmen adjust the sets they are most anxious to sell — the slowest sellers or the ones with the best commission or biggest profit margin — to produce the best pictures, and often intentionally misadjust others that actually may be better. The first step, therefore, before you begin to compare any two sets in a store, is to tune the sets YOURSELF. At the same time, you will be discovering how easy or hard each model is to operate. (The section on using and caring for your set will teach how best to tune a set.)

Even with the sets in the store operating at their best, you still may not feel confident in your ability to pick the best unit while standing in the middle of a store with a salesman breathing down your neck. Also, there is no way to judge reliability by simply looking at the picture. So, here are some things to ask for, if you want the very best:

1. Negative guardband black matrix picture tube. Plain matrix is good, negative guardband matrix is better. Non-matrix is acceptable only in very-small-screen sets. Do not take the salesman's word on this — he probably does not even know the terminology. Ask to see a catalog or spec sheet. Black matrix means the color dots are surrounded by black material that enhances contrast and brightness. Negative guardband means the dots are fully illuminated because the electron beam is larger than the dots.

2. Completely solid state chassis. This means there are no tubes in the set except the picture tube. Tubes, like lightbulbs, generate a lot of heat, and they burn out like lightbulbs. Sets which are 100% solid state need fewer repairs, because they have transistors instead of tubes, and require less electricity than sets with tubes.

3. Modular construction. Modular sets have plug-in circuit boards that are easier to fix or replace. Most solid state sets are modular.

4. Automatic frequency control (AFC). This feature makes fine tuning easier. A set with AFC need not be fine-tuned exactly. As long as the set is tuned fairly close to the correct frequency, AFC will pull in the station. AFC affects only fine tuning (the ring around the channel selector on most sets) and not color, tint, contrast or brightness. Many color sets have "magic" pushbuttons for these functions, or claim to be "self-adjusting," but you would be wise to be very skeptical of these claims. The "magic" buttons simply switch control of color, tint, brightness and contrast from the front-of-set knobs to identical knobs on the back, in most cases.

Care, Installation and Use

A TV REQUIRES almost no routine maintenance. There is nothing to oil, no filters to clog, no loose nuts and bolts to tighten. Just clean the screen with window cleaner and avoid these pitfalls:

1. Do not cover air holes in the cabinet that allow air to circulate for cooling.

2. Use a program guide instead of indulging in unnecessary channel changing. Tuners wear out from over-use.

3. Protect portables from falls by using a sturdy table or stand. Any set can be damaged by physical shock.

When your set is installed, pay serious attention to the antenna. A cheap antenna might save you $10, $20 or even $50, but if it is inadequate for your area you will be shortchanging yourself. Learn to tune your set correctly.

If your set is a color set, start by turning the color all the way down. Now tune it just like a black-and-white set. Turn AFC off (if the set has it) and fine-tune the station. When you have the fine tuner at about the right setting, you will notice that turning it one way garbles the sound and picture. Turning it the other way gives clear sound, but as you turn farther, the picture gets "wormy" looking, with lots of wavy lines in it. Adjust for the wormy picture, then turn back the other way just enough to make the worms disappear. Re-activate AFC.

Next, adjust hold controls, if necessary. Vertical hold stops rolling. Horizontal hold straightens up the picture if it is broken into diagonal or slanted bars. If either hold control was severely misadjusted, you may have found it impossible to fine tune accurately. Go back and do it again.

Now you can adjust brightness and contrast to achieve a pleasing, fully-detailed picture. Avoid excess brightness — it makes the picture fuzzy. Contrast controls the blackness of blacks and the whiteness of whites. Start with a very washed-out, gray looking picture and add contrast until details begin to disappear in the shadows.

That is all you do with a black-and-white set. In tuning a color set, your next step is to turn up the color control slowly until you see colors appearing on the screen. Stop and adjust tint for a natural flesh tone. Turning tint one way will add too much green, the other way too much red. Now bring up the

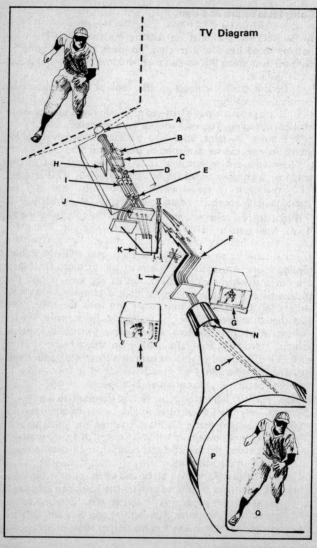

TV Diagram

A. Camera lens collects light rays. B. Reflecting Mirrors C. Separating Mirrors D. Lens System E. Three image orthicon tubes are pocused on the face of each tube and convert the rays into electronic signals for each color. F. Color tubes three electron guns, each shooting a scanning beam, each projecting a color to its corresponding phosphor so picture appears in full color. G. Color Set H. Reflecting Mirror I. Camera Tubes J. The encorder bolsters the color signals and the adder is for forming black and white picture signal to send the broadcast to both types of sets. K. Transmitter relays combined signals. L. Home antenna picks up broadcast and wire connects to the receiving set. M. Black and White Set N. Electron Guns O. Scanning Beams P. Color Picture Tube Q. Screen

color control some more, but without overdoing it. Touch up tint again as needed.

Fixing Your TV Set

AS AN AMATEUR, you would be foolish to work on the innards of a TV set when it is turned on. Voltages in a TV set run as high as 31,000 volts. That could kill you. This puts many repairs out of your reach, but not all.

You can correct some malfunctions without taking the back off your set. Others you can fix by working inside the set, *with it unplugged* — but be careful; some parts of the set store electricity and can shock you even when the set is unplugged. All sets are fitted with safety interlock power cords that automatically disconnect the power when the back is removed because of the hazards of working on a live set. Do not attempt to defeat this protective feature.

How can you minimize the risk of shock from stored electricity when working inside the set? Two parts of the set store electricity — the shell of the picture tube and the filter capacitors. When changing tubes or cleaning the tuner (the only two types of repair you can perform inside the set) you will not have to touch either the shell or the capacitors, but to be on the safe side, you can discharge the electricity from the picture tube shell (the filter capacitors are usually out of harm's way). To discharge the picture tube shell, use a piece of insulated wire with an alligator clip on one end. Attach the alligator clip to any bare metal area of the chassis and touch the other end of the wire to the anode button on the picture tube shell. The anode button is the point where a wire is connected to the outside of the picture tube funnel. Be careful

Television

to hold the wire by the insulation with your right hand. A spark will jump to the wire, indicating the electricity has been bled off.

After making the set safe to work in, you can use the chart at the end of this chapter to attempt a repair. On solid state sets, there is little you can do inside the cabinet because there are no tubes to replace. However, you can still clean the tuner, if that is indicated by the trouble-shooting chart for the symptoms your set is displaying.

In tube-type sets, you will find a tube location guide pasted somewhere on the back or inside the cabinet. This is a map of your set, with tubes labeled by the function they perform. If the trouble-shooting chart indicates you should suspect the horizontal output tube, for example, use the tube location guide to find it. Once you have found it, you can take it to a store with a tube tester (some drugstores and most radio repair shops have one for customers' use) to check it out. If it fails, replace it. If it proves good, and no other tubes are suspected, your problem is more complicated than you thought.

The tube may be bad even if the tester says it is good, because the tester does not measure all of the tube's functions. You could buy a new tube and try it in your set. That might solve the problem and it might not. If it does not, you can console yourself with the knowledge that the old tube probably would have blown eventually, and may well have been weak. If you want to avoid buying a tube that you don't need, and you have tested all the tubes that the chart tells you to suspect and found them all good, then you have no choice but to call a professional. The malfunction may not be caused by a tube at all. Do not adjust any controls that are not accessible from outside the set — it is doubtful that you would improve anything and you could conceivably cause your set to emit harmful x-rays.

The following controls, which are accessible from outside the set (even if they are hidden on the back and are referred to as service controls), can be adjusted by the knowledgeable layman. Your set may not have all of these controls but it probably has some:

●Focus — If the picture is fuzzy, try the focus control. Adjust it so that the horizontal scanning lines that make up the picture (you can see them if you look very closely) are as thin and sharp as possible.

• Vertical Height and Vertical Linearity — Use these two controls if the picture shrinks down from the top and/or up from the bottom. Vertical linearity is probably the culprit if the picture shrinks down from the top only. If it shrinks away from top and bottom, vertical height will have to be adjusted and vertical linearity may be involved also.

• Red, Blue and Green Screens — These three controls balance the three colors that make up a color TV picture. They affect mostly the background, or low brightness, colors in your picture. The drive controls, which we will talk about next, affect the balance of brighter areas. Readjust screen and drive controls when the whole picture develops an off-color cast. The condition will be particularly noticeable between stations or on black-and-white programs. The red, blue or green cast will even be noticeable with the color control turned all the way down, if screens and drives are seriously out of whack. To adjust screen controls, follow this procedure exactly:

1. Turn contrast all the way down and set brightness for a slightly dim picture.
2. Turn color down and tune to an unused channel.
3. Turn all 3 screen controls all the way down.
4. Turn up red screen slowly, stopping as soon as the screen begins to turn slightly reddish.
5. Turn up green screen until the screen turns lemon yellow.
6. Turn up blue screen until the screen looks white or gray. You may have to touch up the other controls to get a perfectly neutral-color screen. Don't get discouraged if you end up starting over a few times. Judging color nuances is tricky.

• Red, Green and Blue Drives — Adjust these after setting up the screens, to balance color in brighter areas. Follow this procedure exactly:

1. Turn contrast and brightness up to normal.
2. Turn color all the way down and tune in a program.
3. Turn all three drive controls down.
4. Slowly turn up red drive, stopping as soon as you notice the slightest pink cast in bright areas of the picture.

5. Turn up the green drive until the bright areas begin to turn orange.
6. Turn up the blue drive until bright areas change to blue-green.
7. Inch up blue and green drives — alternating between them — until highlights turn white. The picture now should be a colorless black-and-white picture. If screens and drives are set correctly, you should see no color tinges in the picture as you rotate the brightness control up and down. When you turn the color control up again, you will have a balanced picture.

PROBLEMS, CAUSES, REPAIRS

THE FOLLOWING table lists only those possible causes for a malfunction that can be dealt with by the non-professional. For any given problem, there also may be other causes than those listed. Many sets will not have some of the tubes which are listed below, because, increasingly, tubes are being replaced in new TV designs by solid state devices. Solid state devices are more reliable than tubes, but they are also difficult for the non-professional to test and replace.

Problems, causes and repairs (or actions to take) apply to both color and black-and-white sets, except, obviously, those sections dealing only with color malfunctions.

Problem: No picture, no sound, no light on screen, tubes not lighted

Possible cause	Repair
1. Wall socket dead	1. Test with lamp.
2. Line cord bad	2. Remove set back and test with test light.
3. Circuit breaker open	3. Press button to reset.

Problem: Screen dark, no sound tubes lighted

Possible cause	Repair
Rectifier tube	Remove & test; replace if bad.

Problem: Screen dark, sound okay

Possible cause	Repair
These tubes: High voltage rectifier; High voltage regulator; Video output; Horizontal output; Damper; Horizontal oscillator	Remove each and test; replace where bad.

Problem: Light on screen, no picture, no sound

Possible cause	Repair
These tubes: Video detector; IF; Mixer-oscillator; RF amplifier; Sound output	Remove each and test; replace where bad.

Problem: Light on screen, no picture, sound okay

Possible cause	Repair
These tubes: Video amplifier; Video detector; Video output	Remove each and test; replace where bad.

Problem: No sound, picture okay, no background noise

Possible cause	Repair
Audio output tube	Remove and test; replace where bad.

Problem: No sound; picture okay; background noise audible; or picture okay, sound poor

Possible cause	Repair
These tubes: Audio output; Audio IF; Audio detector; Audio amplifier	Remove each and test; replace where bad.

Television

Problem: Picture interference that moves with sound

Possible cause	Repair
These tubes: Audio output; Vertical output; Horizontal output; Mixer-oscillator; IFs	Remove each and test; replace where bad.

Problem: Picture shrinks in from sides

Possible cause	Repair
These tubes: Horizontal output; Horizontal oscillator; Damper	Remove each and test; replace where bad.

Problem: Picture shrinks in from sides, top, and bottom

Possible cause	Repair
These tubes: Rectifier; Damper; Horizontal output	Remove each and test; replace where bad.

Problem: Picture shrinks in from top and/or bottom

Possible cause	Repair
Misadjusted vertical height and/or vertical linearity controls	Readjust as explained in section on accessible controls.

Problem: Blooming — picture shrinks and grows as brightness is turned down and up

Possible cause	Repair
In black-and-white sets: High voltage rectifier tube. In color sets, these tubes: High voltage rectifier; Horizontal output; Damper; High voltage regulator; Focus rectifier	Remove each and test; replace where bad.

Problem: Picture bent to side

Possible cause

These tubes:
Horizontal output; Horizontal oscillator; Horizontal phase detector; Sync separator; Noise canceller; any other sync tubes

Repair

Remove each and test; replace where bad.

Problem: Picture out of focus

Possible cause

1. Focus misadjusted
2. These tubes: Focus rectifier; High voltage rectifier; High voltage regulator; Horizontal output

Repair

1. Adjust focus
2. Remove each and test; replace where bad.

Problem: Single white horizontal line on screen (no picture)

Possible cause

Vertical oscillator-output tube

Repair

Remove and test; replace where bad.

Problem: Picture rolls

Possible cause

1. Vertical hold
2. Any sync tube; vertical oscillator-output tube

Repair

1. Adjust control
2. Remove each and test; replace where bad.

Problem: Picture broken into many slanting sections with bars in between

Possible cause

1. Horizontal hold
2. Sync separator; Noise inverter; Vertical oscillator; Horizontal phase detector

Repair

1. Adjust control
2. Remove and test; replace where bad.

Television

Problem: Screen full of horizontal lines

Possible cause
Horizontal oscillator tube;
Horizontal phase detector
tube

Repair
Remove and test; replace
where bad.

Problem: Washed out picture (weak contrast)

Possible cause
1. Contrast control
2. Video output tube;
sound output tube

Repair
1. Adjust
2. Remove and test; re-
place where bad.

Problem: Ghosts that are not dramatically affected by fine tuning

Possible cause
1. Signal reflected by
building or hill

2. Signal being picked up
by lead-in wire

Repair
1. Re-aim antenna, or re-
place antenna with more
directional type.
2. Replace with shielded
(coaxial) lead-in.

Problem: Ghosts that are dramatically affected by fine tuning

Possible cause
These tubes:
Any in tuner; IFs; Video
detector; Video output;
Video amplifier

Repair

Remove each and test; re-
place where necessary.

Problem: Snow

Possible cause
1. Weak signal

2. Dirty tuner

Repair
1. Check antenna and
lead-in wire.
2. Spray contacts with
tuner lubricant and rotate
channel selector.

Television

Problem: Good black-and-white picture with random coloration

Possible cause
These tubes:
Reactance; Burst amplifier; Burst keyer; 3.58 mc oscillator

Repair
Remove each and test; replace where bad.

Problem: Good black-and-white picture but no color

Possible cause
1. Color control
2. These tubes: Bandpass amplifier; 3.58 mc oscillator; Burst amplifier; Burst keyer

Repair
1. Adjust
2. Remove each and test; replace where bad.

Problem: Color cast in black-and-white picture

Possible cause
Color imbalance

Repair
Adjust screens and drives as explained earlier.

Problem: Colors very weak

Possible cause
1. Color control
2. These tubes: Mixer-oscillator; Bandpass amplifier; RF amplifier; Video amplifier

Repair
1. Adjust
2. Remove and test; replace where bad.

Problem: Color snow in black-and-white pictures

Possible cause
Color killer tube; Bandpass amplifier tube

Repair
Remove and test; replace where bad.

Movie Cameras

MOST PEOPLE are more familiar with how still cameras work than they are with how movie cameras work. To understand the movie camera more easily, it might be helpful to take a refresher course in the operation of a still camera and then add to it the distinctions brought into play for motion pictures.

In order to make a still camera function, you need to do two basic things: bring unexposed film into position behind the lens, and expose that film to light. In nearly all cameras, the film is moved by turning a knob or a lever. Then a button is pressed, causing the shutter to open for a fraction of a second, admitting light to the film, and then to close again; the exposure is now complete. For the next picture, you advance the film once more and repeat the process.

These same operations take place in a movie camera, only much more quickly. Movies are actually a succession of still photographs made at the rate of 18 or 24 per second (the number varies according to the purpose of the movie — more about that later).

Film Transport

INSIDE THE MOVIE camera, the film is brought into position by a mechanism called the *film transport.* Once the film is correctly registered behind the lens, it stops moving for a moment while the shutter opens, exposing the film to the light.

Although the shutters of still cameras often are mechanically complex devices, fitted with various kinds of springs,

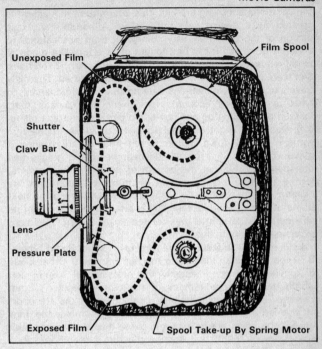

Unexposed Film

Film Spool

Shutter

Claw Bar

Lens

Pressure Plate

Exposed Film

Spool Take-up By Spring Motor

leaves or curtains, the shutters in most movie cameras are much simpler. Of a type known as the *rotary shutter,* they consist of a flat semicircle of some opaque material — usually metal — that spins in front of the film. As it rotates, the metal semicircle moves around in front of the film, blocking it from light; the semicircle continues to rotate until it has turned clear of the film, which is now exposed to light.

The film transport is geared to work in synchronization with the rotary shutter. When the shutter blocks light from the film, the transport moves the film just enough so there will be room for one exposure or "frame" to be made upon it; just before the shutter rotates aside to admit light to the film, the transport stops moving the film; this intermittent movement is created by a device called the *claw*. Although the exact design of the claw may vary somewhat from one camera to another, generally it can be thought of as a fork-like piece of metal whose tines grasp the film by the holes or *perforations* that were punched into it when it was manufactured. The claw travels up-and-down over and over again in a little channel, in what is called an *eccentric movement;* this means that, instead of traveling up-and-down in a perfectly vertical plane, it moves on a slight diagonal so that it is close to the film while it moves down, but retracted from the film when it moves back up. It is on the downstroke that it grasps and transports the film; at the bottom of its channel it retracts, letting the film sit still, while it returns to the top of its channel where it will once again protrude and grasp the next frame of film. It is while the claw is returning to the top of its channel that the shutter has rotated to its "open" position, exposing the film to light.

In all modern amateur movie cameras — super 8 and Single-8 — the claw is all there is to the film transport. Other kinds of movie cameras — notably the professional 16mm and 35mm machines, and many of the older "regular" 8mm cameras — have an additional component in the transport mechanism, the *sprocket wheel,* that helps move the film toward the claw. As its name implies, this is a wheel with sprockets, or teeth, that engage the film perforations; it is present on most movie cameras that use film loaded on reels, but not on cartridge-loading cameras such as super 8 and Single-8.

In cartridge-loading cameras, the film is packaged in a plastic cartridge that can be inserted and removed from the camera instantaneously. In super 8 cameras the film feeds from one side of the cartridge to the other, the side-by-side arrangement being known as a *coaxial* layout; in Single-8 cameras the film runs from a chamber at the top of the cartridge to an identical chamber at the bottom of the cartridge. In both cases, a take-up spindle built into the camera rotates a shaft inside the cartridge that causes the film to wind-up smoothly in the take-up side of the cartridge. However, the actual movement of the film past the lens is caused exclusively by the claw, as described earlier.

TYPES OF MOVIE-CAMERA SHUTTERS

 160° □

Standard Shutter — Opening is 160° for exposure time of 1/40 of a second at 18 F. P. S.

 230° □

XL Shutter—opening is 230°—Larger opening takes 1/28 of a second to move past film.

VARIABLE SHUTTER

Fully open.

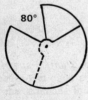 80°

Half closed — Second blade brought partially out, reducing exposure time by 50 percent.

Fully closed — Blades overlap — No light reaches film.

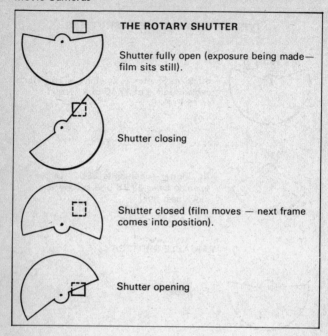

THE ROTARY SHUTTER

Shutter fully open (exposure being made—film sits still).

Shutter closing

Shutter closed (film moves — next frame comes into position).

Shutter opening

Shutter Speed

STILL PHOTOGRAPHERS often refer to *shutter speed,* meaning the length of time the shutter stays open to expose the film to light; it is expressed in fractions of seconds, such as 1/60 sec., 1/125th sec., 1/250th sec., and so on. In the normal course of events, movie cameras do not have variable shutter speeds; where a still photographer selects his shutter speed by setting a dial, most movie makers usually work at the same shutter speed at all times. However, different kinds of movie cameras have shutter speeds of different durations — for example, regular movie cameras have a shutter speed of about 1/40th sec., while the XL or low-light cameras have a shutter speed of 1/28 sec. In a still

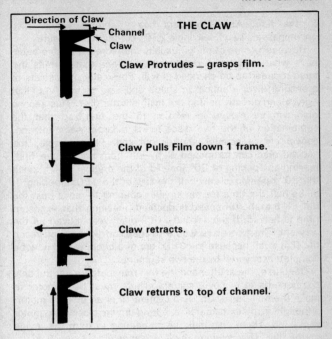

THE CLAW

Direction of Claw

Channel

Claw

Claw Protrudes — grasps film.

Claw Pulls Film down 1 frame.

Claw retracts.

Claw returns to top of channel.

camera, the shutter speed is altered by changing the tension of the springs that drive the shutter; since there are no such springs in movie-camera shutters, how can different shutter speeds be arrived at?

It all has to do with the size of the semicircular disc that forms the movie-camera shutter. If the disc encompasses a large semicircle, it will take a comparatively long time before its rotation in front of the film is completed, meaning that the film will be blocked from light for a longer time and exposed to light for a shorter time. If the disc encompasses a smaller semicircle, the length of time it covers the film will be shorter, and the film will be exposed to light for a longer time. To be more specific, a regular movie camera's disc encompasses a 200° segment, leaving a 160° cut-out to admit light to the film. An XL camera has a shutter whose disc encompasses 130°, leaving a 230° cut-out for exposure.

However, some cameras, usually the more expensive ones, have what is called a *variable shutter,* one that permits the shutter speed to be changed at will. Physically, it consists of a second disc, identical in shape and size to the first, that rides along directly behind the main shutter disc. This second disc can be moved in relation to the first, so that the combination of the two discs forms a larger segment and, conversely, a smaller shutter opening. For example, the second disc can be moved partly out from behind the first, leaving an opening of 80° instead of the original 160°; since the 80° opening is only half the size of the 160° opening, it takes half the time for the smaller opening to move past the film — the shutter speed is doubled, meaning that exposure time is halved. If the second 200° disc were moved all the way out, the two discs would overlap; no light would reach the film at all because the 360° arc of a circle would now be completely covered by the two segments.

Of course, the shutter and the film transport are not the only components in a movie camera. There must be a motor to make them all run. In modern cameras it is an electric motor, although in older cameras a spring-driven clockwork motor was used. There also must be something to form the image on the film. This is where the lens comes in.

The Lens

THE PURPOSE of the lens is to gather the random light waves that reflect from various objects, and to organize them into a coherent image on the film. Lenses come in three basic types: telephoto, normal, and wide-angle. The type is determined by the *focal length,* which is the distance between the film and the *focal point* inside the lens.

In all lenses, the image enters rightside-up, but it goes out the back of the lens (and to the film) upside-down. Obviously, then, there is a place in the lens where the light waves reverse; this is the focal point. If the focal point is a relatively long distance from the film, the lens will be telephoto; if it is closer distance to the film, the lens will be normal; if it is closer still, the lens will be wide-angle. In super 8 and Single-

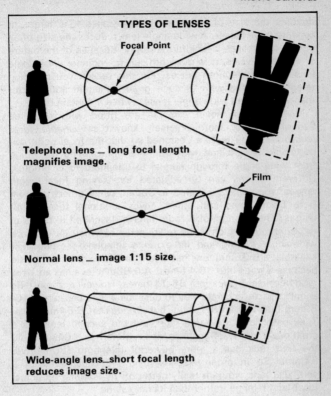

TYPES OF LENSES

Focal Point

Telephoto lens — long focal length magnifies image.

Film

Normal lens — image 1:15 size.

Wide-angle lens—short focal length reduces image size.

8 cameras, a normal lens is one whose focal point is 15mm from the film — it is described as having a 15mm focal length. Any lens whose focal point is further than 15mm will be telephoto, and any lens whose focal point is less than 15mm will be wide-angle. Thus, a 30mm lens has a 2x magnification, a 60mm lens has a 4x magnification, and so on; conversely, a 7mm lens will have half the magnification of a 15mm normal lens. It is the degree of magnification that causes a lens to render an image in a given way; a 30mm lens

doubles the size of an object and, because it is larger, it appears to be closer. A wide-angle lens reduces the size of an object, and makes it look further away. Because of the nature of optical physics, it is more difficult to engineer wide-angle lenses than telephoto lenses. For this reason you can find telephoto lenses with a much greater magnification factor than you can find wide-angle lenses with a reduction factor.

Most modern movie cameras are fitted with so-called "zoom" lenses, more precisely known as *variable focal length lenses*. They are designed so that the focal point can be moved toward and away from the film, running the range from wide-angle through normal to telephoto focal lengths. Different zooms can be adjusted for varying focal-length ranges; some may go from 9 to 36mm, while others go from 6 to 66mm, and still others cover additional focal-length ranges. The strength of a zoom lens is described in terms of its *zoom ratio,* which is the relationship between its extreme wide-angle setting and its extreme telephoto setting. For example, a 9-36mm lens has a four to one (written 4:1) ratio because 9 goes into 36 4 times. A 6-66mm lens has an 11:1 ratio because 6 goes into 66 11 times. However, zoom ratio is only a partly accurate way to describe a lens because a 10-80mm lens has an 8:1 ratio, but so does an 8-64mm lens. They both have the same ratio, but the second lens has a great deal more wide-angle capability (8mm vs. 10mm) while the first lens has a more powerful telephoto (80mm vs. 64mm). So in order to understand the capabilities of a particular lens, you are really better off by learning its actual focal-length range, rather than its ratio alone.

Aperture

ALL FILMS are designed in such a way that a given quantity of light should strike them for correct exposure — neither too much light nor too little. However, the strength of light varies considerably under different conditions when you are making movies — the light on a sunny day is much stronger than the light on a cloudy day. In order to ensure that the proper amount of light reaches the film, all lenses are fitted with a device called the *aperture*. This is an opening whose size is variable; for weak light the opening is large, for strong light the opening is smaller. By being made larger or smaller, the aperture regulates the amount of light reaching the film and, when correctly set, keeps the film constantly exposed to the amount of light that results in correct exposure. If the aperture is incorrectly set to an opening that is too large, the film will be *overexposed* — the image will turn out pale and washed-out on the film; if the aperture is incorrectly set to an opening that is too small, the film will be *underexposed* — the image will turn out dark and murky.

The size of the aperture is described in f/stops, such as f/1.9, f/2.8, f/4, f/5.6, f/11, and so on. The smaller the f number is, the larger the size of the aperture is; for example, f/1.9 is a much larger opening than f/11. Thus, you will use f/1.9 when the light is extremely dim, and f/11 when it is bright. In all but the cheapest movie cameras, the aperture is adjusted automatically by an automatic exposure system, or *electric eye*. This is a device whose light-sensitive sensor "reads" the strength of the light, and causes the size of the aperture to adjust accordingly. In the majority of modern movie cameras, this sensor is located somewhere inside the lens so that it reads the amount of light actually entering the lens; electric eyes of this type are called *reflex, behind-the-lens* (btl), or *through-the-lens* (ttl) electric eyes. A few cameras, particularly the cheaper ones, have electric eyes that make their readings through a separate window. They do a good job, but the reflex electric eye is more accurate under a wider variety of conditions.

Viewfinder

THE FINAL component common to all movie cameras is the *viewfinder* — the eyepiece you look through to aim the camera, and to see what you will get on film. The simplest type of viewfinder is called the *optical* type; it has its own viewing window at the front of the camera, and it is found only on the cheapest movie cameras. The remainder of the cameras have *reflex* viewfinders (also called btl and ttl viewfinders) which do their viewing through the lens of the camera. They are able to see through the lens because the lens contains a small component — sometimes a prism, sometimes a tiny mirror — that reflects a small portion of the

Movie Cameras

light that enters the lens to the viewfinder eyepiece. Reflex viewfinders are more accurate than optical viewfinders because they show exactly the field being "seen" by the lens (optical viewfinders, because they see through separate windows located away from the lens, will take in a slightly different field, especially at close shooting distances). Also, with many reflex viewfinders (but not all) it is possible to see whether the lens is correctly focused for a given subject. Whether or not a particular camera's reflex viewfinder does this depends upon the viewfinder's construction; you can learn this about particular cameras by reading test reports, or by giving them a try in the camera store.

There are many other aspects and features that are popular in modern movie cameras: however, there are so many different kinds on so many different cameras that it would take a complete volume to describe them all. The material here deals with the fundamentals — the features common to all movie cameras. No movie camera could operate without a shutter, a film transport, a motor, a lens, an aperture, and a viewfinder. These are the essentials; additional features may extend the creative and artistic capabilities of a camera, and certainly will widen your enjoyment of movie making. But with the information you have read here, you now should have a basic understanding of how all movie cameras work, and why.

PROBLEMS, CAUSES, REPAIRS

THERE IS one cardinal rule about repairing a movie camera: don't.

Although simple in its basic operations, a movie camera is a complex machine built with a high degree of precision. Modern movie cameras are a jumble of sophisticated electronic, electric, optical, and mechanical devices; all require a great deal of knowledge and skill to repair if something goes wrong. This is no place for an amateur to poke around, for the result will almost inevitably be additional damage. If your camera malfunctions, take it directly to an expert — the professional repairman recommended by your camera's manufacturer or distributor. He has the expertise to do the necessary repair work, and the special tools and instruments to do it accurately.

What you can address yourself to, however, is preventive maintenance; this is something you should do conscientiously, almost religiously, so that you can stack the odds against the likelihood of your camera's ever needing repair.

First and foremost, you should take care to protect your camera from bounces, bumps, and vibrations; this is especially true of the lens, whose alignment is critical within fractions of a millimeter. If you lay the camera down, place it in such a way that its broadest surface is in contact with whatever you place it on; do not put it in a position that will enable it to tip over. If you are traveling in a car or other vehicle, place the camera on the seat — well back, where it can be cradled against the back of the seat. That way, any vibration will be absorbed by the seat's padding — and, if you are forced into a short stop, there is less likelihood that the camera will be hurled to the floor.

When you carry the camera, do not let it merely dangle by its strap. Hold it in your hand, using the strap simply as an additional safeguard. If it dangles freely from your wrist, it can swing about and knock into any number of the malevolent items that were sitting there, just waiting for it to come along.

It is surprising how much damage befalls a camera as the result of pure carelessness and thoughtlessness on the part of the owner. Protecting a camera from the abuses of daily life really is simple and common-sensical. It requires nothing more than an appreciation of the machine's vulnerability to knocks and blows, and the application of logic to protect it against such things. If you pack the camera in a suitcase, surround it with a generous padding of soft material — clothing, for example — to hold it firmly in place; if you store it away for a period, put it in a dust-proof container. Also remember to remove the batteries when you store it; batteries are supposedly leak-proof nowadays, but don't bet on it — protect the camera's battery contacts from corrosion by spending a few moments taking the batteries out.

Aside from run-of-the-mill cautions, however, there are a few other things to keep in mind. For the unfortunate fact is that many of the places you are most likely to want to record on movie film are places that can be lethal to a movie camera. The beach is full of sand that can get into the camera and grind up its moving components; salt air encourages corrosion, and salt water is absolutely deadly. If you ski, or just want to go out and play in the snow, you can quickly find how damaging melted snow can be if it enters the lens or the camera mechanism; if you go boating or canoeing, or if you film family and friends as they swim in a lake or pool, you run the same chance of water damage. Fortunately, you can do a good job of protecting your camera in all these conditions.

The trick is to make a waterproof, sandproof, dust- and dirtproof housing for the camera. What do you make it of? A plastic sandwich bag or freezer bag will do just fine. Put the camera inside it, with the lens facing the bag's opening; then seal the bag around the lens with a rubber band. That's it. The camera is protected from all moisture short of total immersion caused by dropping it into the ocean. The lenses of most cameras are threaded to accept screw-in filters; if you want to do the best job of protecting the camera, buy a Skylight filter and leave it permanently on the lens. This will serve as a barrier against moisture and all the other evils of nature; and in the meantime, it has virtually no effect on lens performance (except that it tends to reduce the excess blueishness that you find on overcast days, or at high altitudes — both desirable attributes of this filter, which is also sometimes called a Haze filter). In combination with the plastic bag, this seals your camera very nicely against the onslaught of hostile elements. The bag should be large enough so that there is plenty of slack all around the camera; this enables you to grasp and operate all the controls.

Of course, it will be necessary for you to remove the bag whenever you want to reload film, and then put the bag back into place again; all this takes a few extra moments. But the time you spend doing this is guaranteed to be shorter than the time it will take to repair the camera.

Incidentally, if you should accidentally drop the camera into salt water, you should wash it out with fresh water immediately. Don't just hold it under a faucet — fill a bucket full of fresh water, and leave the camera in it overnight. Fresh water will do the camera no good, but at least it will not cause the corrosion that salt will. In either case you will have to send the camera in for repair. But the difference between freshwater damage and salt damage is the size of the repair bill.

Movie Projectors

MECHANICALLY, a movie projector is nothing but a movie camera in reverse: using many similar components (shutter, claw with intermittent movement, lens), it transports the film in a replication of the actions performed by the movie camera. The only real difference is that, instead of light entering the front of the lens and going through to strike the film, as in the camera, the projector's light, supplied by a lamp, goes through the film from behind, enters the rear of the lens, comes out the front of the lens, and continues onward to the movie screen.

But how does all this conspire to make pictures that move?

It all depends on the simple fact that many things are quicker than the eye. The eye has a quality, known as *persistence of vision,* which means that everything it sees is retained for an instant; only then does the vision "fade out" from the optic system.

In the section on How the Movie Camera Works, we said that the camera produces 18 or 24 individual pictures, or frames, each second; we also said that the shutter speed of a regular movie camera is about 1/40th second (at 18 frames per second only). Therefore, as the subject that was photographed moved along, its movements were broken down into increments of one one-fortieth of a second, 18 such increments each second.

When the film is run through the projector, the projector flashes each of these frames on the screen for the same length of time, 18 times per second. Individual pictures are coming and going at an extremely speedy rate; a rate so fast that the eye cannot see any particular one of them as a discrete picture. Instead, it sees the increments of motion blended into one another, creating the illusion of continuous movement. Although the projector's shutter closes between frames, blocking all light from the screen (just as the movie camera's does), the eye rarely perceives this because the period of darkness is extremely brief and the eye's persistence of vision retains the sight of the picture even though the screen is momentarily dark.

Frames Per Second

WE HAVE SAID that the movie frames come and go at a rate of 18 or 24 per second. Why this variable? It depends upon the purpose the film is to serve; 18 frames per second (fps) is the traditional rate for silent movies, 24 fps for sound movies. The reason is that most sound movies have the sound track on the film itself. The nature of sound playback is that audio quality is better as the speed of the recording is increased; a given audio signal is stretched out over a longer length of the recording medium (be it a phonograph record, a recording tape, or a movie soundtrack) so that any distortions produced by the medium itself will have a comparatively smaller length of time to affect the sound.

There is another reason for the 24 fps speed. Since the film is moving faster through both the camera and projector, the increments of motion captured by each frame are shorter; a camera that produces a 1/40 second exposure time of 18 fps will produce a 1/54 second exposure time at 24 fps. The image will be sharper because of the higher shutter speed, and the motion of the subject will be reproduced even more smoothly because of the shorter elapsed time between each frame. This is less of a consideration for the amateur, who projects his movies on a relatively small screen. But in movie theaters, where the screen is many feet or even many yards wide, any choppiness in the movement of filmed subjects will become more apparent; so professional films are almost always shot at 24 fps.

Incidentally, although 24 fps has been the traditional speed for sound movies for the reasons mentioned, makers of amateur sound movies will find that they will get excellent audio quality at 18 fps. Sound-recording technology has improved tremendously over the years, letting the running speed of phonograph records drop from 78 revolutions per

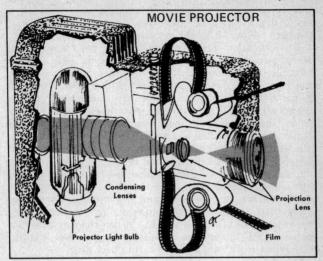

MOVIE PROJECTOR

Condensing Lenses

Projection Lens

Projector Light Bulb

Film

minute (rpm) to 33 1/3 rpm; tape recordings have been even more dramatic in this respect, dropping from an original 15 inches per second (ips) to the 1 7/8 ips of cassette recorders — and yet audio quality is superb, as any stereo buff knows. In view of these tremendous advances, reducing the speed of sound movies from 24 to 18 fps — a reduction of less than 25% — has very little noticeable effect on the quality of an amateur movie's sound track. The fact is that, even at the "slow" 18 fps, the soundtrack is moving along at some 3 inches per second — some 50% faster than the speed of cassette tape recorders. In the meantime, the slower shooting and projection speed saves money, because you use up less film for a given shot.

Sound Separation

IN CONNECTION with sound movies, often you will hear the term "picture-sound separation" or "sound advance". This refers to the fact that, when the soundtrack is on the film, the sound that corresponds to a particular frame of film is not adjacent to that frame; instead, the sound is located ahead of that frame. In super 8, the separation is 18 frames, meaning

Movie Projectors

that if you stretch out a reel of film on a table from left to right, the sound that goes with any particular frame in playback will be 18 frames to the right of that frame.

It might seem more sensible to have the frame and its sound side-by-side (this is called ''dead sync'') but it is not possible in projection. There are two reasons for this. First, the equipment that transmits light through the film takes space in the projector, and so does the equipment that plays the sound; there is not sufficient room for both to be side-by-side. Second, even if there were room, the conflicting requirements of picture and sound playback make dead sync impossible. A sound medium must run smoothly and continuously; for every slight alteration in running speed, you get the audio distortions known as wow and flutter. But a movie film runs intermittently past the lens in a continual stop-and-go. The sound playback equipment must be placed a distance away from the lens in the projector, with enough space between the two so that a loop of film can serve as a cushion between the intermittent movement at the lens and the continuous movement at the sound playback head.

Threading

NEARLY ALL modern super 8 projectors have an automatic threading mechanism in which the projector feeds the film through the film path and on to the take-up reel. This is a great convenience, particularly when you plan to show a large number of short reels, because threading a projector manually can take several moments and is always very tedious. The specific design of the automatic threading mechanism differs from one projector to the next, but all work on the same idea: the film is fed into an entryway, where it is grasped by a sprocket or feed roller and shuttled along through guide channels into the gate (the part of the film path that runs between the projection lamp at the rear, and the lens in front) and from there to additional film channels guiding the film past the sound heads (in a sound projector) and finally, to the take-up reel. Since film is flexible, equally easy to bend in the wrong direction as in the right one, it is essential that the film leader — the first foot or so of film — be in perfect condition. A leader that is bent, torn, too greatly curled, or otherwise damaged or misshapen, stands a good chance of not getting all the way through the automatic threading path. It can jam somewhere inside, while the film behind it continues to come in and pile up behind the jam; the inevitable result is further film damage. For this reason you should be extremely protective of your film leader; you should inspect the first foot regularly and, at the first sign of any kind of damage, splice in a new length of leader film.

PROBLEMS, CAUSES, REPAIRS

AS IS the case with movie cameras, preventive maintenance is the most you really should attempt in the way of projector treatment. Projectors are not nearly as complex as cameras, but they are precise, closely-adjusted machines that require the skill of a trained technician, with the proper tools, to do a really satisfactory job on anything that get out of whack.

Oiling and Cleaning

IF YOUR projector requires oiling, the manufacturer usually notifies you of this in the instruction manual and indicates the oiling points. Never put oil in your projector unless specifically directed by the manufacturer (the one possible exception is in the spindles that hold the feed and take-up reels, which sometimes grow sluggish or develop a squeak as they rotate; more often than not, however, this is the result of dirt rather than lack of lubrication). Under no circumstances should you allow any oil to come in contact with any part of the projector that touches the film; if oil gets on the film, it will spread and degrade the image, and also attract and hold dust and dirt. All oiling (when specified by the manufacturer) should be done with a light machine oil, such as sewing-machine or typewriter oil.

Many household oils have an ingredient that forms a slick that coats the surfaces to which it is applied. This is fine for locks, lawnmowers, and other devices that require both lubrication and protection against rust-producing moisture found in their working environments. But in precision machinery, projectors included, this ingredient will eventually dry out and turn into sludge that will gum up the mechanism; before new lubrication can be applied, the old will have to be removed by solvents. And even before the coating substance

Movie Projectors

dries, its tacky surface will collect and hold dust that otherwise would simply drop off the mechanism's components, compounding the sludge problem. Light machine oils of the type recommended do not have this coating ingredient; they are designed for use on equipment that is not normally exposed to the elements, and their purpose is simply to lubricate.

You should, of course, be especially careful to keep the projector clean; this has less to do with maintaining the projector than it does with maintaining your films, since the smallest speck of dust can permanently scratch your film if it is caught in the projector. You should remove all dust from the projector before each showing, paying special attention to the film gate where the film is held under pressure. A fine camel's-hair brush is a good cleaning tool, although it may spread some of the dust around, transferring it from one point on the projector to another instead of removing it altogether. The best cleaning tool is a lintless cloth dipped in alcohol; this is good for all metallic parts, but to clean the lens you should use a blower, a brush, or one of the special lens-cleaning fluids available at camera dealers.

Belt Repair

OCCASIONALLY the take-up spindle (or the feed spindle, when the projector is being run backwards) fails to turn. Depending upon the specific construction of your projector, and the accessibility of its components, this may be something you can fix yourself. In most designs the spindles are driven by some form of belt that connects with the motor shaft; these belts are usually adjusted so that they have sufficient tension to rotate a large reel loaded with film, but at the same time they have enough slippage so that the film itself will regulate the actual speed of rotation as it feeds onto the reel. Failure of the take-up is most commonly attributed to the belt's stretching out of size, or breaking altogether. Depending on the style of belt used in your projector, you may be able to do repairs, at least on a temporary basis, until you get the chance to turn the projector over to a professional repairman.

The first step is to remove the covers on the backside of the projector, so you can examine the belt, see what style it is, and determine how easily accessible it is. In some projectors, the belt is obscured by other mechanical components, meaning that you would have to dismantle a large portion of the mechanism to get at the source of the problem; better to forget about home-made repairs in this case. In other designs, however, there are no major obstacles between you and the belt. In some cases the belt consists of a tightly coiled spring that can be rejoined by opening up the end coils on both sides of the break, connecting them, and closing the coils again. Other designs have a flat belt made of some kind of fabric — plastic, or nylon. A strong glue, such as contact cement, may prove a successful means for joining a broken belt.

Do your best to join the broken portions in a "butt splice" with the two pieces contacting each other end-to-end, rather than overlapping them; an overlapped splice, because of its extra thickness, may cause the belt to ride high on its drive wheel and slip the track — forcing you to begin the whole process again. Never use staples to join the ends of the belt. Staples are rigid, unable to turn around the circular drive wheel; they will create another situation of the belt riding high, causing it to jump off the wheel. In all cases, the belt should be mended while in its normal running position, connecting the reel spindle with the motor.

Burned-Out Lamp

THE MOST COMMON "repair" you will have to make on your projector is the replacement of a burned-out projection lamp. The instruction book specifies the type of lamp to use, and gives directions on how to install it. The most important thing to remember is *never touch the glass envelope of the lamp with your bare fingers.* In certain kinds of projection lamps, the oil from your fingertips will weaken the glass, causing it literally to melt, bubble and break from its own heat. Many projectors are supplied with a special tool for holding the lamp while you install it. But in all cases, it is best if you perform the replacement while wearing thin gloves such as those used by film editors; the rubber gloves used in household cleaning also can be used.

SLR Cameras

ONLY A VERY few basic components are in a 35mm single lens reflex (slr) camera, but literally thousands of tiny cams, gears, screws, wires, springs, and electronic components are needed to make the basic parts work together as a team.

The most important component of any slr is its lens, which focuses an image of the object you wish to photograph on the film within the camera. Composed of both optical (glass) and mechanical (metal) elements, lenses are interchangeable on virtually all slrs. A lens may be removed from the camera body and replaced with a lens of another focal length (different angle of view and magnifying power) to achieve different effects, or to compensate for different conditions.

Of course, all slrs also have bodies. The body houses most of the camera's mechanisms, keeping the components of the camera system together and aligned to function properly. The body also contains the film in a light-proof environment and provides a path for the film to follow from its cartridge at one end to a take-up spool at the other. Between the cartridge, which is felt-lined to trap light, and the take-up spool, the film passes over a rectangular cut-out, the film plane aperture, located directly behind the lens. In most slrs a device called a focal-plane shutter is located between the lens and the film. This type of shutter is similar in construction to a pair of black window shades, and is positioned behind the lens to prevent light from reaching the film and exposing it before you are ready to make a photograph.

A very few slrs have leaf-type shutters located in their lenses. These serve the same purpose of sealing off light

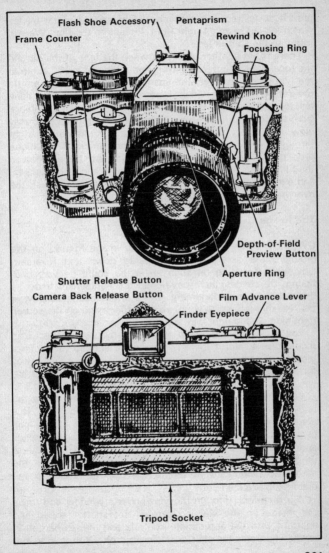

Flash Shoe Accessory
Pentaprism
Frame Counter
Rewind Knob
Focusing Ring
Depth-of-Field Preview Button
Aperture Ring
Shutter Release Button
Camera Back Release Button
Film Advance Lever
Finder Eyepiece
Tripod Socket

until it is desired, but they consist of several metal blades which fan out to admit light from the lens to the film. We will return to the shutter later.

There is yet another object between the lens of the slr and the focal-plane shutter: a mirror. The mirror, at a 45° angle to the film-plane, redirects the image from the lens up to a little ground glass screen which is perpendicular to the film plane and located so that it is optically at exactly the same distance from the lens as is the film. With this construction, you may view and focus the image you wish to photograph right through the taking lens mounted on the camera. This unique property of being able to see exactly what is to be recorded on the film, plus small size, light weight, interchangeable lenses, and overall convenience, combine to make the 35mm slr the overwhelming choice of photographers the world over.

The Image

OWING TO the nature of optics, the image formed on the ground glass screen is both upside down and reversed. Obviously, focusing on such an image could be very confusing. So slr designers developed the pentaprism finder, a five-sided prism arrangement with a little viewing window at the rear through which your eye sees the image on the screen right side up and right-way around.

You have probably begun to wonder by now how you can record on the film if there is not only a shutter but a mirror blocking the image. The answer is, you must move them away for an instant. When you wish to make a photo with an slr, you follow this sequence:

You open the camera body, load the film, and close the body. Then you wind a lever called the rapid-advance. This does several things. It moves a frame of film (1½-inches long by 1-inch wide) behind the filmplane aperture. It cocks (winds spring tension into) the shutter curtains and the mirror mechanisms, and in most modern slrs also cocks the automatic diaphragm mechanism. (We will return to the diaphragm in a moment.)

You then look through the viewfinder's window and focus the image on the viewing screen, set shutter speed and aperture with the appropriate controls and then, when all is ready, you press the shutter release button. With this action, you cause the mirror to pivot upward, out of the way, so that the light being focused by the lens may fall on the film once the shutter curtains open. Next the lens diaphragm automatically closes to the aperture you have selected, the shutter curtains open, the image falls on the film and is recorded, the shutter curtains close, the mirror falls back into place and the diaphragm opens again.

The diaphragm is a device of thin metal blades mounted within the barrel of the lens. It can be opened or closed to regulate the amount of light which passes through the lens. The size of the opening is called the aperture and it is measured in "f-stops." Older or inexpensive slrs have manual diaphragms which must be set by hand before a picture is taken and then reopened, manually, to get enough light for focusing the next shot. Most of the newer, and some of the more expensive old, slrs perform this function automatically.

Shutter speed regulation simply regulates the amount of time the black "window-blind" focal-plane shutter remains open, exposing the film to the light being focused on it by the lens. To determine the settings required by the diaphragm and the shutter, experience teaches you how to estimate them, or the instruction sheet packed with every roll of film lists general rules. For real accuracy, however, you should use an exposure meter.

Many photographers use separate, hand-held meters; modern slrs incorporate built-in meters which actually have their light-sensing elements placed within the pentaprism, or at the rear of the mirror, or sometimes on a tiny plate just forward of the film plane which pivots along with the mirror. These behind-the-lens (btl) meters most often indicate correct aperture and shutter speed as the position of a moving needle. To determine the proper shooting settings the photographer need only set the speed of the film on a little dial, and then manipulate the shutter speed and aperture controls until the needle (visible in the viewfinder) is centered in a notch or is aligned (matched) with another needle. The alignment shows that the controls, which are cross linked to the metering system, are properly set for correct exposure.

Modern slrs perform this metering function at open aperture, so that the image on the viewing screen is bright, and focusing may be carried out at the same time. There is an older, now essentially obsolete system, used with some btl

SLR CAMERA DIAGRAM

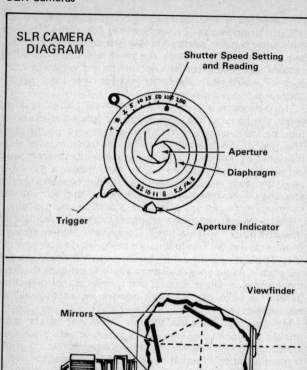

Shutter Speed Setting and Reading

Aperture

Diaphragm

Trigger

Aperture Indicator

Viewfinder

Mirrors

Lens

Film

slrs, called stop-down metering. With stop-down metering the lenses' diaphragm must actually be opened or closed to obtain a meter reading. This is quite inconvenient as it can be slow and clumsy and often darkens the viewing screen.

There are now two kinds of "automatic" 35mm slrs: the aperture priority type which, when "told" the speed of the film and the aperture desired, will automatically pick the right shutter speed; and the shutter priority type which needs to be "told" the film and shutter speeds before it automatically selects the right aperture.

Once all of the film has been used, it is rewound into its light-tight cartridge, by means of a rewind knob, and removed from the slr for processing.

Care and Maintenance

THERE IS virtually no maintenance which the average photographer is able to perform on a modern slr. In this respect, these machines are similar to fine watches and should never be tampered with. In the event of a malfunction, it is always best to return the camera to a shop authorized by its manufacturer or distributor. It usually costs less to do this in the long run because these shops have the specialized tools and knowledge to make repairs in the least amount of time — and time is what you are charged for. However, on occasion you will have to perform routine or emergency tasks. Some of the more common ones are covered in the chart below.

PROBLEMS, CAUSES, REPAIRS

Problem: Unclear Image

Possible cause	Repair
1. Dust on lens, screen or mirror	1. Blow the particles off with a baby's ear syringe. Never use a brush.
2. Finger prints or salt spray on lens, screen or mirror	2. Lightly moisten a padded piece of lens tissue with Kodak lens clean-

ing fluid. GENTLY clean from the center out using a second crumbled piece of lens tissue to move the pad on the lens surface. Never press, and never put your fingers directly on the paper pad or the glass surface.

3. Dust, dirt or salt spray on the body

3. Wipe with a lightly moistened chamois.

Problem: Meter fails to operate

Possible cause

Repair

Battery off or defective

Check to see that the battery is switched on. Clean the battery terminals with a clean dry cloth. Use built-in battery checker or have your dealer check the battery. If the battery is functioning, bring the camera to the repair shop.

Problem: Film cannot be wound with rapid advance

Possible cause

Repair

Film already wound or roll finished

Press the shutter button; the camera may be already wound. Check the frame counter to see if you have come to the end of the roll (20 or 36). If so, push the rewind button and rewind the film into the cartridge.

Problem: Shutter button will not fire shutter

Possible cause   **Repair**

Rapid-advance lever or shutter button not operative

Make sure the rapid-advance lever has been fully wound. Do not force it through! Check to see if you have used all the film. If so, rewind then check the shutter function before reloading. Check to see if the shutter button lock has been released.

If you must store your camera for a long period, remove the batteries and store them separately (or discard them). Place the camera in a plastic bag or container and seal to keep air out.

Bicycles

A BICYCLE at first sight presents no interesting answer to the question, "How does it work?" It seems to suffer by comparison with other more complex and intriguing items in this issue of CONSUMER GUIDE Magazine such as automobiles, stereo systems, and so forth. A bicycle seems simple because it has only mechanical components that require no electricity, chemical reactions or combustion, to do their work.

A bicycle, however, is a well designed piece of machinery with elements of sophistication far beyond its surface appearance. In fact, the bicycle was the progenitor of the motorcycle, the automobile and perhaps even the airplane. The industry spawned by the bicycle was responsible for such developments as the pnuematic tire, the differential, the planetary gear system (which is the heart of most automatic auto transmissions) and modern ball bearings. The bicycle industry was also the first large industrial user of steel tubing. The first automobiles utilized bicycle wheels and chain and sprocket bicycle drive systems and the Wright brothers used bicycle chain to power their first successful airplanes.

A bicycle is an inherently unstable vehicle which works only when controlled and balanced by a rider. Remember your first attempt at learning how to ride? It took a while before you were able to correct quickly and accurately the seeming instability of the bicycle. The role of the rider is a critical one, therefore, in the operation of a bicycle—only he or she keeps it from falling over. The rider continually makes corrections as the bicycle moves forward, instinctively leaning from side to side to keep the mass of rider and bicycle properly balanced. A riderless bicycle with only a power source could not stay upright for long and few devices could provide the necessary corrections on a continuing basis.

When a recording technician was asked what was the most important development in the manufacture of records he replied, "Getting the hole in the middle of the record." As with records, balancing a bicycle is the most important element—all others are basically refinements.

Major Components of a Bicycle

SINCE NO ELEMENT of a bicycle is expendable, it is difficult if not impossible to say which is the most important, but certainly the frame must rank high on the list, since it is vital to a bicycle's basic handling characteristics, overall quality and price tag. Some of the more important aspects of the frame, and their effects on a bicycle's handling, are as follows.

Wheelbase—This is the dimension from the front wheel axle to the rear wheel axle (assuming that both wheels are the same size). If the frame has a short wheelbase (less than 40'') the ride will be very responsive and "quick." If the wheelbase is long (40" or more) then the bicycle will have a softer, less lively feel. On the other hand, the longer frame will absorb a greater proportion of the road shocks encountered by the rider. A bicycle built for racing will have a short wheelbase while the great majority of bicycles built for touring and occasional riding will have a longer wheelbase.

Frame angles—The angle formed by the seat mast and the head with a horizontal line also affects the bicycle's characteristics. The more acute these angles are (the closer to 90°) the livelier and more responsive the ride will be. On the other hand the frame's shock absorbing qualities will be reduced as the angles become more acute. Wider angles contribute to a more comfortable but less lively ride.

Power Transmission

THE POWER required to propel the bicycle is provided by the rider. This power is transmitted from the pedals to the crank, to the front sprocket, then to the chain, the rear sprocket, and the wheel; finally, the force of the tire in contact with the ground pushes the bicycle forward. This power transmission is very effective: power losses due to the transmission account for only about 2 percent of the total power consumed in driving a bicycle forward.

The front sprocket (which is the driving sprocket) is larger than the rear sprocket and a certain mechanical advantage is gained. The larger the front sprocket and the smaller the rear sprocket, the more ground a bicycle will cover with each turn of the pedals.

The gearing on a single-speed bicycle is usually set so that the rear wheel will make approximately 2-1/2 turns for every turn of the front sprocket. Variable gear devices such as the three-speed hub allow the rider to change this basic gearing to accommodate changes in the road. These variable devices make it possible for the rider to "gear down" when encountering head winds or hills or to "gear up" when riding with the wind or when he simply wishes to gain additional speed. The two most popular gearing devices are the three-speed hub, which has a planetary gear system within the rear hubshell, and the derailleur system which derails the chain from one sprocket to a smaller or larger sprocket. Both types are operated by cable-operated shifting levers located on the frame or handlebars.

The Braking System

BRAKING on a bicycle is accomplished either through what is called a coaster brake, that is, a brake built into the rear hub and activated by turning the pedals backwards, or a caliper brake system which operates by closing a pair of brake shoes over both wheel rims. The coaster brake is commonly built in with single-speed hubs and occasionally with three-speed hubs. Caliper brake systems are found on three-speed bicycles and almost always with derailleur-equipped bicycles. Both types of braking systems are positive and very effective. One minor consideration with caliper brakes is that they do not work as well under wet conditions as they do under dry conditions. Hence, extra caution is called for in rainy or wet weather.

Caliper brakes are further divided into two main categories—the sidepull type and the centerpull type. The center-pull type closes more evenly on both sides of the rim and therefore has a slightly better braking action. Center-pull brakes, however, are more expensive, due to having more parts, and they are more prone to adjustment problems.

The Steering System

THE STEERING SYSTEM of the bicycle consists of the fork, handlebars, handlebar stem, front wheel and associated bearings and fittings. The only real difference in any of these components from bicycle to bicycle is the amount of "bend" in the front fork. The amount of bend (or rake as it is called) also plays a role in the handling characteristics of the bicycle. The smaller the rake, the livelier the steering; the longer the rake, the more shock the fork will absorb.

Preventive Maintenance for the Bicycle

SINCE DETAILED repair procedures for all types of bicycles and bicycle components could occupy several volumes, only the most basic items are listed below:

Tires and tubes—It is extremely important to keep tires properly inflated and to treat them as gently as possible. Do not jump curbs; avoid potholes and rough streets; keep oil and grease away from the tires. Bicycle tires lose air gradually and the inflation should be checked regularly with a tire gauge. Inflate tires with a high quality bicycle-tire pump rather than gas station air hoses as these hoses can deliver too much air too quickly, leading to a blowout. When removing and remounting tires and tubes, do not use sharp tools such as screwdrivers, as these will surely cut the tube.

Frame and front fork—Little can go wrong with these items in a strictly "mechanical" sense but check the alignment, especially after a spill or accident. Your best bet is to have the alignment checked by a bike mechanic if you think something is wrong.

Power transmission components—The most vulnerable item in the power transmission system is the chain. It is subject to the most grueling conditions of heavy wear,

Bicycles

dirt, mud and rust. Clean the chain about once a month and lubricate with bicycle oil or one of the specially formulated chain lubricants. Wipe off any of the excess oil to keep it from splattering on the tires. The other components in the transmission system, such as the crank and bearings and the rear coaster brake hub, should give several years of good service without attention. Once every two years, however, it is a good idea to have them overhauled professionally.

Shifting devices—Three-speed hubs need to be fed oil on a monthly basis to keep the many small parts operating properly. The cable also may need occasional tightening as outlined in your owner's manual. Derailleurs should be wiped clean of the inevitable road grit, and moving parts should be lightly lubricated with oil. Cables should be checked for tightness and readjusted if necessary. Most owner's manuals provide information on how this is to be done. On both front and rear derailleurs there are usually two small screws which control the amount of travel of the derailleur. To set these screws, shift the chain to the extreme sprockets (backing off the appropriate screw if required) then turn in the appropriate screw to stop the derailleur from shifting any further.

Cables—Both caliper brakes and derailleurs operate by means of cables which are used to transmit power from the hand lever. If the braking or shifting action seems a little sluggish, remove the cables and lubricate them with bicycle grease. This will make braking and shifting action much easier.

Wheels and spokes—Check the spoke tightness occasionally and keep all spokes uniformly tightened. If you notice the wheels wobbling from side to side this can be corrected by tightening the spokes. Rims should be kept free of dirt and lubricants to allow the brakes to work efficiently.

Caliper Brakes—Lightly oil all moving parts and wipe off excess oil. If the brakes squeal when applied, gently bend in the brake arm so that the front part of the brake block will touch the rim first. Cables should be adjusted with the adjusting barrel so that the brake blocks are no more than 1/8-inch from the rim. If this tolerance cannot be achieved with the adjusting barrel, loosen the cable anchor bolt, pull the cable taut with pliers and retighten the cable anchor bolt.

BICYCLE DIAGRAM

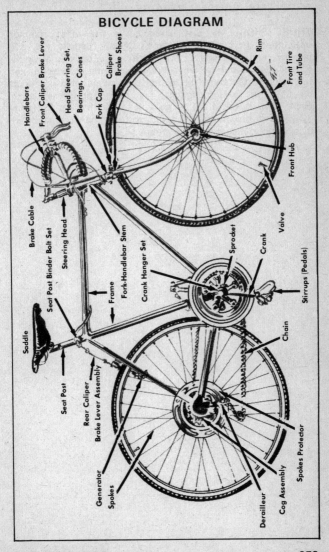

Bicycles

PROBLEMS, CAUSES, REPAIRS

THOSE PROBLEMS just listed cover the most common difficulties bicycle owners face. Causes usually are dirt, neglect, and hard use of the machine, or accidental spills. Since each brand of bicycle will have its own slight differences in features, the owner's manuals always should be used in making repairs. For major problems, a bicycle shop is the place to go unless you have a full complement of bicycle repair tools and extensive practice in disassembly, repair and reassembly.

Bicycle Care

YOUR BICYCLE may require little or no attention at all, beyond keeping the tires filled with air. We know of bicyclists who have done nothing to their bikes for years! But as cycling becomes more popular, and as you spend more time with your bike, you may want to consider keeping your own machine in good repair. You can save money by doing your own repairs, and with a little patience, you can do as good a job on many repairs or maintenance jobs as a professional mechanic.

Tools

THE MOST common tool for bicycle repair is the six-inch adjustable-end wrench, often called a Crescent wrench. Crescent is a manufacturer and not the only one that makes adjustable-end wrenches. Whatever brand or size wrench you purchase, make sure that the movable jaw does not wobble (at least not much), or else the wrench could slip and damage the nut. In addition, the wrench that slips could damage the finish of your bike frame, and most importantly, could injure your hand.

You might find an eight-inch wrench more to your liking than a six. If you plan to do thorough maintenance yourself, then consider owning all of the following adjustable wrench sizes: four-, six-, eight-, and fifteen-inch models. There is a twelve-inch size, but since it does not fit bottom-bracket cups, its use is limited. The fifteen-inch wrench fits bottom brackets, headsets, and freewheel removers, and since it is longer than a twelve-inch, it provides better leverage anyway.

Bicycle Care

Frankly, nonadjustable wrenches — open-end, box, and specially designed bike wrenches — that fit specific nut and bolt-head sizes, are better than any adjustable wrench. Nonadjustable wrenches are less likely to slip, and they wear the nut less. Remember that since most better bicycle equipment employs nuts with metric dimensions, you must use metric wrenches that are properly sized for the nut.

Finally, you can use socket wrenches with a ratchet handle. Fortunately, metric-size sockets are widely available with quarter-inch and three-eighth-inch insert slots. Therefore, if you already have a ratchet handle, you can simply get a few extra sockets for your bicycle needs. Never use a pliers of any kind on bicycle nuts or bolt heads! Smooth-faced pliers cannot grasp a nut at all, and knurled-face pliers invariably chew up a nut and render it ungripable for a proper wrench.

In addition to wrenches, you also need at least one screwdriver. A forged, chrome-vanadium, four-inch blade screwdriver will do for most purposes. You should also have a long-nose pliers with knurled faces and with integral side cutter for pulling cables taut and trimming their ends. Get a set of three tire irons for removing tube-type tires from the rim.

With these four types of tools — an adjustable wrench, a screwdriver, a long-nose pliers, and tire irons — you can do most of the everyday maintenance on your bicycle: tighten and loosen the nuts and bolts; adjust the brakes, gear changers, seat, and handlebar; and change flats or install new tires.

Multiple-gear bikes require that at least the rear wheel, and preferably both wheels, be off the ground for proper adjustment of the gear changers and for checking brake operation. Carbondale makes an inexpensive bike stand for this purpose, but you can simply hang the bike at two points (the seat and the handlebar) from a basement pipe or from ceiling hooks — using ropes, straps, or stretch cords. Or, if you have a convenient empty wall, you can mount two six-inch wall standards with two eight- to twelve-inch shelf brackets, about fifteen inches apart. Pad each bracket (a towel is sufficient), and lay the top tube of the bike over the brackets. For open or ladies' frames, space the brackets to catch the seat and the handlebar stem. If you are on the road or if you cannot hang

Use of Cable Riveting Pliers

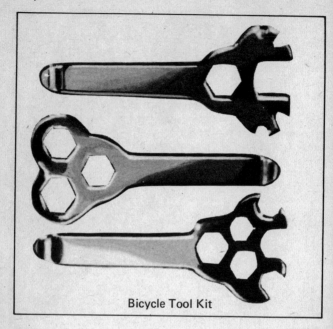

Bicycle Tool Kit

your bike, turn it upside-down and rest it on the seat and handlebar.

For more involved work, you will need a spoke wrench to adjust or replace spokes, cone wrenches to overhaul hubs, and a freewheel remover — absolutely essential to remove a freewheel from the rear hub. If you plan to work on crank arms, chainwheels, and bottom bracket, you need crankset tools and a vise to hold dismounted components as you work on them.

Lubricants, Solvents, and Cleaners

YOUR BICYCLE needs continual lubrication because the moving or bearing parts continuously pick up dirt and grit as you ride. The best lubricants to use are good-quality motor oil

— such as SAE 20 or 30 — or oil made specifically for bikes, such as that by Sturmey-Archer. Use grease for all the ball-bearing parts, for installation of threaded parts, and for installation of tight-fitting parts such as cotterless crank arms on the axle ends. The new spray lubricants such as WD-40 — with the skinny tube attached to the nozzle — are good for pin-point application.

Use oil only for off-bike overhaul of parts. Oil can deteriorate tires and can render brake pads ineffective. In contrast, spray lubricant not only does not do such things, it also — through the force of the spray — helps remove the dirty residue from brake pivots, brake levers, front and rear derailleurs and their levers, and chains.

Grease is primarily used for overhauling components. Use only grease made for bicycles: Lubriplate, Phil Wood, and Campagnolo manufacture the best greases. Remember, oils and greases made for high-speed automotive applications are totally unnecessary for bicycles, since no moving part of a bike runs as fast as that of an automobile. Hence, bike lubricants do not solidify from heat or break down from oxidation at high temperature. Buy grease in squeeze tubes; that way it stays clean and is easier to apply than from a can. If you get grease in cans, use a finger to apply it; no tool works as well. Have a cloth handy before you start to use grease.

For thorough off-bike overhaul or cleaning of components, you will need a good solvent to remove old grease, grime, and grit. Never use kerosene or gasoline! They will explode. The other solvents — lacquer thinner, oleum spirits, turpentine, or turp-based paint-thinner — are flammable, but they are not explosive. Of these, lacquer thinner is the most penetrating, and it evaportates quickly leaving no residue of its own. Nevertheless, be careful when using lacquer thinner around your frame if it is lacquer-finished or epoxy-enamel-finished.

To clean a component, get a metal or glass pie plate and pour solvent into it. Take the component apart and put all the pieces in the dish. Clean each part with your fingers, a toothbrush, and clean cloth. As each piece is cleaned, put it in another clean and empty container or on a clean piece of cloth. Do only one component at a time so as not to mix up pieces, and reassemble each component before starting

Bicycle Care

another.

You should keep your bike clean as well as lubricated. The bike can be washed with liquid detergent and water. If the bicycle is heavily coated with mud, hose it down. This is best done on a warm, sunny day. The waterless spray cleaners — Fantastik, Windex, and Formula 409 — are excellent for cleaning the whole bike at any time of the year. If you live in a northern city and ride in the winter, then these cleaners are especially effective as they help neutralize the salt you pick up. Use these cleaners on the tires as well as on the frame and components; then use a spray lubricant immediately after cleaning.

Bearings

ALL OF THE moving parts of your bicycle run on bearings, usually ball bearings, and these require periodic overhaul. A very small number of components come equipped with needle or roller bearings, and some newer equipment comes with sealed bearings that require no maintenance. Since the needle-bearing type is similar to the ball-bearing type, if you understand one, you will understand the other.

The moving parts all have cup and cone ball-bearing arrangements. This is true of wheel hubs, headset, bottom bracket, and pedals. In each case, a cone holds the balls in a cup, and a locknut holds the entire apparatus in a fixed position. Thus, a rotating axle is entirely supported by the balls. Bicycle grease is used to lubricate this system, as it keeps dirt and grit from interfering with the free running of the balls in the cup and cone. Each bearing assembly may have loose balls or — on some more expensive components — there may be a set of balls held in a cage or clip.

When reinstalling balls, always install as many as the cup will hold. There will always be a little space left over, but this will be less than the diameter of one ball. With caged balls, the cage is always more closed on one side, more open on the other. The open side goes toward the cup, or larger part. To install balls or clips, pack the bearing cup with as much grease as you can, then put the balls in one at a time. The grease will more or less hold the balls in place until the cup or cone is tightened. For hubs and pedals, tighten the cone and

Chain Riveting Tool

lock it; for brackets and headsets, tighten the cup and lock it.

In either case, adjusting these bearings takes a little time. You must tighten the cup or cone involved, adjust it, and lock it. First, tighten the cup or cone a little, say from twelve o'clock to nine o'clock (one-quarter turn). Then, tighten the lock nut. If the component still binds, it is too tight and you must start over. If the axle moves back and forth along its axis, it is too loose. Again, you must start over. Keep adjusting until the axle rotates firmly and smoothly in its bearing without binding and without wobbling. Make sure the lock nut is on tightly, but not so tightly that you are forced to ruin it in order to remove it. Finally, if you want to practice bearing adjustment, get an old adjustable pedal and put it together a few times. The pedal mechanism is roughly the same as all the bearings on the bike.

Finish and Appearance

YOU SHOULD not let the paint and chrome on your bike deteriorate. Paint scratches and chips should be covered with touch-up paint, and the chrome should be polished occasionally with chrome polish, or with toothpaste (yes, toothpaste). Many dealers of well-known bicycles sell factory touch-up paint. If you cannot match colors exactly, it is still better to put on a fair match than to leave the scratches. You can also protect the overall finish with a coat of lacquer or bicycle over-coat.

Since lacquer will lift an epoxy refinishing coat — even if it has dried and set — never use lacquer over epoxy. Actually, you should test any over-coat on the finish of your bike in an obscure place to make sure the finish will not lift. Whether the bike is lacquered or not, give it a wax coating with a clear liquid wax. Do not use the automobile waxes that dry to a cloudy appearance before you wipe them off; they only accumulate in the crevices and catch dirt. If you chip a decal or emblem, it can be touched up with model or touch-up paint.

You might want to refinish the whole frame and fork. Use a good paint stripper and follow directions (be sure to wear rubber gloves). Go down to bare metal; then sand and polish with 120-grit aluminum oxide cloth torn in half-inch strips and used shoe-shine fashion. Give a final wash with alcohol or vinegar; then, roll up newspaper and put a roll through the head tube and one through the bracket. These rolls should fit tightly to keep paint out. At this point you can do one of two things: either prime and paint it yourself, or take it to a car painting place and have them prime and paint it for you. They have a broad selection of colors, and they do an excellent job; you get a finish as good or better than the original, and it should not cost you more than about ten dollars.

To do it yourself, prime the surface with zinc chromate primer, titanium dioxide, or aluminum primer, and let it dry completely. Use spray cans in a well-ventilated, well-lighted area. If your bike has chromed parts, mask them with masking tape and paper. Then use a spray enamel or epoxy enamel, applying two coats and letting the first coat dry overnight. Rub out bumps and runs after the first coat dries with 400 wet-dry sandpaper, and wash the dust away with alcohol before doing the next coat. If you can bear waiting, let it dry a week before you attempt to reassemble the bike.

When you put new decals on the bike it will, hopefully, look as good as new. There is no law that says you must put on the same stickers that came with the bike. For the price of the decal, you can convert your bike from a Peugeot to a Schwinn Paramount. Or get some rub-on transfer letters from an art-supply store. Then you can put your own name on the frame. Whatever you do to your frame, refinishing it is certainly cheaper than buying a new frame or a whole new bike, and the frame's new appearance may give you a whole new outlook toward your bike.

Guns

THE MECHANICAL system that fires a gun has not been changed much in the past 100 years. Some refinements have been made in internal design and storage of cartridges or shells; accuracy as well as smoothness of functioning has been improved to some extent.

How Guns Work

ALL FIREARMS, rimfire as well as centerfire guns, have a hammer to which a firing pin is linked. The hammer is spring-activated, and, when cammed, engages a bar or sear that, at its other end, is hitched to the trigger mechanism. Depress the trigger, and the sear is released, which in turn permits the hammer to move forward or fall. This allows the firing pin to make contact with the primer in the cartridge. In rim-fire guns, the arrangement is similar, except that the firing pin is offset to the side so that the nose of the firing pin makes contact with the rim of the cartridge case, and ignites the priming compound contained in the rim.

In single-shot rifles and shotguns, in side-by-side and over/under shotguns, there is no provision for storing ammunition. The cartridge or shell is inserted directly into the gun's chamber. In all other guns, there is some kind of storage place for ammunition—in semiautomatic pistols there is a magazine and ammunition is fed upward from the magazine into the chamber by the functioning of the gun. A similar system is used in most rifles. The storage of ammunition can be vertical, or in a tubular

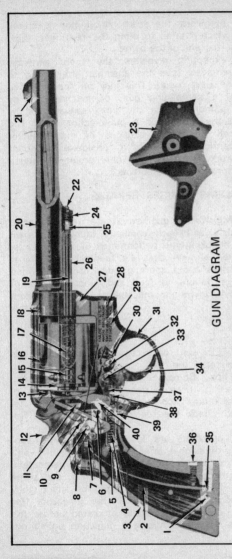

GUN DIAGRAM

1. Stock Pin 2. Stock 3. Frame 4. Trigger Spring 5. Rebound Slide Stud 6. Sear 7. Stirrup 8. Bolt Plunger 9. Hammer Stud 10. Sear Spring 11. Bolt 12. Hammer Nose 13. Hammer Nose 14. Extractor 15. Extractor Spring 16. Cylinder 17. Center Pin Spring 18. Barrel Pin 19. Center Pin 20. Barrel 21. Front Sight 22. Locking Bolt 23. Side Plate 24. Locking Bolt Spring 25. Barrel Lug 26. Extractor Rod 27. Yoke 28. Hammer Block 29. Cylinder Stop Stud 30. Cylinder Stop Spring 31. Trigger Guard 32. Cylinder Stop 33. Trigger Stud 34. Trigger 35. Main Spring 36. Strain Screw 37. Hand Spring 38. Trigger Lever 39. Rebound Slide 40. Hand

Guns

system, as in pump and autoloading shotguns and in lever-action rifles. In revolvers, the spare ammunition is stored in the cylinder which rotates to bring the next live round into line with the rear end of the barrel.

In all guns, excepting revolvers, the spent cartridge case must be removed from the chamber after firing to make way for the next round. This may be accomplished automatically by a selfloading gun, or mechanically by the shooter by either moving the bolt rearward, or by pulling back on the handle of a pump-action gun. The extractor, a small hook that engages in the extractor groove of the cartridge case does a considerable amount of mechanical work and as a rule only prolonged abuse will cause extractor or ejector problems.

PROBLEMS, CAUSES, REPAIRS

ALTHOUGH AMERICAN gunmakers do not operate under a proof law and each company follows its own ground rules in checking the performance of its products, mechanical failures of new guns are relatively rare. Most consumer complaints about sporting guns can be divided into three groups: failure to feed and function; lack of inherent accuracy; downright mechanical failure (seldom encountered).

Failure to Feed

FAILURE TO FEED can have two possible roots—in semiautomatic pistols, the fault is frequently found in bent magazine lips. Borrow a similar and undamaged magazine, and using it as a pattern, bend the lips of your magazine back into their original position with pliers. Work slowly and check the functioning of the gun frequently.

Other feeding problems are found in the feed ramp, which requires professional attention, and in faulty ammunition. Some calibers, such as the 9mm Parabellum or Luger, are notorious for case-size variations, and some pistols are persnickety as to what brand of ammo they will digest without malfunctioning. If the magazine lips are not bent, try changing the brand of ammo before the next step, which would be having a gunsmith polish out the feed ramp.

GUN DIAGRAM

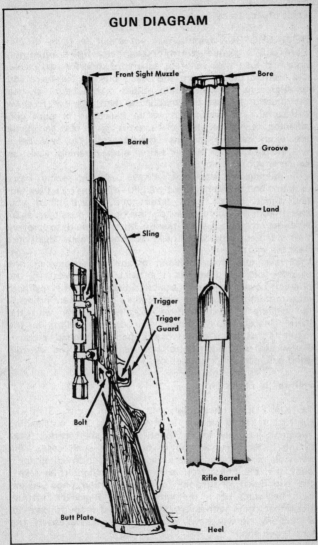

Front Sight Muzzle

Bore

Barrel

Groove

Land

Sling

Trigger

Trigger Guard

Bolt

Rifle Barrel

Butt Plate

Heel

Guns

Lack of Accuracy

BENT SHOTGUN barrels will not shoot to point of aim. Here only a skilled gunsmith can help. Rifles often turn sour and lose their inherent accuracy. Look for two causes —a warped stock where the wood pushes the barrel out of alignment, or worn lands, either in the barrel or near the muzzle. If near the muzzle, a gunsmith can re-crown the barrel. Worn muzzles are an indication of poor gun-cleaning technique. If the barrel is shot out and lands are worn badly near the chamber, only a new barrel will help. Oil left in the barrel after cleaning also can cause erratic accuracy.

In testing for accuracy, always use the same brand of ammo and the same bullet weight—different bullet weights and ammo brands print differently. Always clean your barrel from the breech; when this is not possible, as in lever-action guns, use a plastic Muzzle Guard to prevent the cleaning rod from making contact with the lands near the muzzle.

In revolvers, poor handling of the gun—slamming the cylinder into the frame by the twist of the wrist—is the primary source of gun trouble. Slamming the cylinder into the frame damages the crane, which then prevents the cylinder's chamber from aligning properly with the barrel. Inaccuracy and shaving lead from bullets is the result. Although an expert can sometimes rebend a crane, a new one is a much better bet, especially if you observe good gun manners from then on.

Failures to Function

ACTION RODS, once bent, will lock up a gun. Similarly, the skinny shell carrier in most pump and autoloading shotguns is likely to get bent, or the shell carrier latch spring becomes unhitched or breaks. In such cases, the services of a gunsmith are recommended. In autoloading shotguns, the major trouble is that the shooter, in taking the gun down for cleaning, gets the friction rings assembled backward or in the wrong order. Read the instructions that come with every new gun and learn to care for it properly. It will save you making an unnecessary trip to the gun shop.

Fishing Reels

ESSENTIALLY, a fishing reel is nothing more than a line holder. For most sportfishing a quality reel is absolutely necessary for storing line. In certain types of fishing, a reel is needed that has an excellent "drag" which will help "fight" fish.

Some reels are complicated pieces of machinery, every bit as precision-made as an expensive watch. Other reels are very simply designed. Fishing conditions and the kind of fish to be caught usually determine what sort of reel is needed. For example, a reel used for catching bluegills could never be used in offshore angling for blue marlin.

Basically there are five different types of reels, each fulfilling a specific angling need. There are bait-casting, spinning, spin-cast, fly, and offshore trolling reels. All of these reels work in different ways. And, because of this, each type of reel will be discussed separately.

Bait-Casting Reels

A BAIT-CASTING reel actually is just a tiny winch. The cast lure furnishes propulsive movements to the spool of the reel, pulling line from the reel. The cast is controlled by the angler's thumb. By applying pressure to the reel's spool, a fisherman can slow or stop the line leaving the spool, and thus accurately control his cast.

Most of the newer, more expensive bait-casting reels have anti-backlash devices or "brakes". These mechanisms prevent the reel spool from revolving too fast; they supplement "thumb control". Without a "brake" or proper "thumb control" of the reel's spool, a backlash or line tangle is almost certain to occur.

Many quality bait-casting reels also have lightweight spools that stop quicker than heavy spools; that, too, helps prevent line snarls.

One of the most important parts of a bait-casting reel is its "level-wind" device. This is a metal finger in front of the reel which moves back-and-forth and winds the fishing line evenly onto the reel spool. It makes casting easier because the line is wound and unwound each time a cast is made and then retrieved.

Most bait-casting reels are quadruple multiplying — which means the spool turns four times when the handle is turned once. Thus a lure or bait can be retrieved quickly following the cast.

Quality bait-casting reels also have a button that, when depressed, puts the reel into "free-spool." This is important because then only the spool revolves, not the reel's handle — and that makes for easier casting.

Good bait-casting reels also have a "drag," usually a star-type mechanism attached to the reel handle's spindle. By turning the drag an angler can regulate the pressure necessary to "pull" line from the reel. Drags are helpful in fighting some strong fish.

Spinning Reels

A SPINNING REEL is distinguished from other reels because it has a fixed spool. When a lure is cast, the weight of the lure under forward momentum pulls line from the stationary spool.

A "backlash" or an "over-run" with a spinning reel is impossible because there is no inertia to overcome at the start of a cast. A spinning reel also permits the use of extremely light lures — ones that do not have sufficient weight to start a revolving spool in motion.

To make a cast with a spinning reel, you must open a "bail," secure the line on the tip of your index finger, and flex the rod back, then forward. During the forward movement the line is released from the finger tip and the lure pulls the line off the stationary spool. To slow or halt progress of the lure,

Fishing Reels

you merely drop the tip of your index finger to the edge of the spool, thus contacting the line. With most spinning reels the bail automatically picks up the line to be rewound onto the spool as soon as the reel handle is turned forward.

Virtually all of the better spinning reels have good "drags." Usually the "drag" is located on the front of the reel spool, and works in much the same way as a "star drag" does on bait-casting reels. By adjusting the "drag-knob" on a spinning reel a hooked fish can take line out against the proper pressure, and not break the line.

Quality spinning reels also have an "anti-reverse lock." This is a mechanism that, when put in the "on" position, prevents the reel's handle from turning backwards. Thus line will pay out only against the reel's drag. While the "anti-reverse lock" is "on," fish can be played by tightening or loosening the drag — which leaves one hand free to land the fish. Too, the "lock" is useful in trolling, because when it is engaged the spinning rod can be placed in a rod-holder and the line will not pay out against the reel's tightened drag.

Spin-Cast Reels

A SPIN-CAST reel is just another kind of spinning reel. The difference is that the spin-cast reel has a closed-face spool, rather than an open-faced spool, as do spinning reels. The entire spin-casting reel mechanism is enclosed in a cone shaped hood.

To cast with a spin-cast reel, a thumb push-button (or lever) must be depressed. Then the rod is flexed back, then forward. As the rod is brought forward the push-button is released. The reel's "pick-up pin" then frees the line, and the line is pulled from the stationary spool through a hole in the front of the reel's hood.

Many spin-cast reels have poor drags, if any. Most drags are located on the spindle of the spin-cast reel's handle, and are adjusted by turning forward or back.

Fly Reels

A FLY REEL contributes nothing to a cast. It merely furnishes storage space for the fly line.

For heavy fly fishing, the fly reel must have a good drag. Unless the drag is smooth, a running fish will snap the leader the first time the drag balks. If the reel is not well made, its revolving spool may jam as a fish takes line.

Quality fly reels have a spring drag, operating against a hard-metal ball-bearing washer, and you can alter the tension of the drag with a simple turn. The drag can be adjusted even while a hooked fish is taking line.

Good fly reels are lightweight, single-action types. They have click mechanisms, either silent or audible, to prevent the reel's spool from "overrunning" when line is being "stripped" from the reel.

Offshore Trolling Reels

BASICALLY, an offshore trolling reel is just a larger and more sophisticated model of a quality bait-casting reel.

Most offshore reels have a "free-spool lever," similar to that on a bait-casting reel, which allows the reel's spool to turn without the reel's handle turning. Some of the better offshore reels have two "levers;" one frees the spool completely, the other maintains sufficient pressure to prevent line overrun.

Offshore trolling reels need a free-spool lever because, when a large gamefish strikes a trolled bait, slack line must be given so that the fish takes the bait completely. The reel then is put back "in gear" and the angler sets the hook.

There are two types of drags on most offshore trolling reels. One is the typical "star drag," the other a "lever brake" type. The "lever brake" is preferred because it normally incorporates the "free spool" mechanism and drag into the one lever.

Most trolling reels are geared 3 to 1, which means the spool revolves three times each time the handle is turned.

What to Consider When Purchasing a Reel

GENERALLY, the steps to follow in buying one type of reel also apply when buying any kind of reel.

Once an angler decides on the type of reel he wants (bait-casting, spinning, spin-casting, etc.), he should write to various reel manufacturers for their latest catalogs. The catalogs will enable him to compare the reels of various companies. The important features of reels are detailed in these catalogs, including their line capacities, drag styles, etc.

Usually, you get what you pay for when buying reels. Thus the rule is *purchase the best reel you can afford.*

The best way to be sure you are buying a good reel, is to purchase a name brand reel. Reel manufacturers with good "names" got them by producing dependable reels, pricing them fairly, and maintaining a quality repair service.

Some of the major points to consider when purchasing any reel are smoothness of operation, the availability of parts, special quick take-down features, practical design, a minimum of parts, particularly moving parts, and ease of cleaning and oiling.

Basic Reel Maintenance

TWO OR THREE times a year reels should be taken apart (how to do this is outlined in pamphlets that come with reels when purchased) and the gears cleaned and oiled. The inside of the reel should be rinsed with gasoline, and a toothbrush should be used to scrub all the moving parts. When dry, all moving parts should be lightly oiled, and a small amount of grease applied to the toothed gears. Never apply too much gear grease or oil, and use grease and oil made specifically for use on fishing reels. Such grease and oil can be purchased at sporting goods and tackle stores. In a pinch, any quality light oil can be used, and Vaseline will substitute for reel gear grease.

A reel used in salt water needs special care. Salt water corrodes any reel quickly. It is imperative to thoroughly wash your reel in fresh water following fishing in salt water. Do not wait until the next day; that is too late.

Some experts even take their reels completely apart after salt water fishing. They hold the parts under running water for 10 minutes or more, then dry them carefully. Finally, all moving parts are given a thin coat of reel oil (or grease); then the reel is reassembled.

PROBLEMS, CAUSES, REPAIRS

How to Fix a Broken Reel

MOST BROKEN reels can be repaired by you, at home, at very little cost, provided you can get the needed parts. This is why CONSUMER GUIDE Magazine recommends the purchase of name brand reels. Tackle stores across the nation stock parts for "name" reels.

Bait-Casting Reels

OCCASIONALLY a bait-casting reel is dropped and the handle bent. If this happens, remove the handle, hammer it straight, and replace it on the reel. If the handle is damaged so badly that it cannot be straightened, buy another from a tackle store or the manufacturer.

Occasionally the "level-wind" mechanism on a bait-casting reel will be bent. It may be straightened with pliers.

A common problem with bait-casting reels is that the "level-wind" either doesn't move at the proper speed, skips, or doesn't move at all. If this happens the "level-wind" pawl is worn out. Remove the screw at the end of the "level-wind" bar, withdraw the bar, shake the "level-wind" in your hand, and a small brass gear, called a "pawl," will drop out. Purchase a new pawl, put a drop of oil on it, and reassemble the "level-wind." It will work as new.

Spinning Reels

OCCASIONALLY a spinning reel's bail will not "open" properly for casting. The "bail spring" probably is broken. This spring is located under the large screw that holds the bail to the reel. The screw can be removed easily and a new spring put in place.

When a spinning reel's bail is bent it is almost impossible to straighten it. Buy a new bail and replace the damaged one.

Drags frequently go up on spinning reels. When this occurs, unscrew the drag assembly from the front of the reel-spool, and replace it with a new assembly.

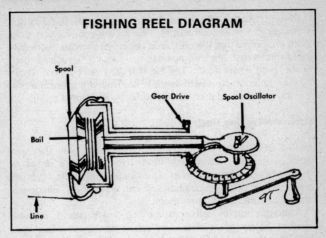

FISHING REEL DIAGRAM

Spool

Gear Drive

Spool Oscillator

Bail

Line

Spin-Cast Reels

MOST SPIN-CAST reels are reasonably trouble-free. However, frequently the fishing line will get jammed behind the reel spool. To fix this, unscrew the reel's hood, remove the line spool, pull the line out, and place the line properly behind the line spool "pick-up pin." Then put the line spool back on, pull the line through the hole in the reel's cone-shaped hood and, finally, screw the hood back onto the reel.

Fly Reels

FLY REELS are very simply constructed. For this reason, compared to other reels, they are considerably more dependable. Not much can go wrong with a quality, well-designed fly reel. Sand and dirt, however, can get into the reel's mechanism. If this occurs the reels should be taken apart and washed thoroughly with water. Then the reel should be dried completely and all the moving parts lightly oiled.

Sometimes a fly reel's click-spring or drag-spring will break. These parts cannot be repaired, so they must be replaced.

One of the world's most famous fly reels, the Fin-Nor, although almost indestructible, has a cork-composition drag. With prolonged use the cork drag becomes smooth, worn by a metal plate that presses against it — much the way a car's brake lining wears down. The Fin-Nor drag can be fixed readily by merely roughing it with sandpaper. This will make the drag ''grab'' and the reel then will be perfectly functional again.

Offshore Trolling Reels

MOST OFFSHORE trolling reels are made so well that very little ever goes wrong with them. However, the drags on these reels occasionally slip. The drags in offshore reels are also made of cork-composition and can wear down. Sandpaper should be used to roughen them.

Although quality offshore trolling reels stand up well against the corrosive effects of salt water, these reels must be washed completely with fresh water after they have been used. Following each salt water fishing trip the line should be run off the trolling reel, the reel should be removed from the rod, and then washed, dried, and oiled meticulously.

Orbital Sanders

THE ORBITAL SANDER is one of the most widely
used tools in the home workshop. Its purpose is to
give wooden surfaces a smooth finish. The orbital
sander gets its name from the fact that sandpaper on
its flat metal plate spins in very small circles (orbits).

Look at the diagrams. Note the motor. Most likely it is the
universal type. Electric current flows through the line cord to
the field coils and armature in the motor frame. The line cord
enters the handle through its very end so that the cord is away
from the work area when the tool is in use. A switch tapped
into the line cord turns electricity on and off.

For a discussion of how the universal motor works, see the
chapter on Types of Motors.

How it Works

IN ORDER to obtain the orbital motion that moves the sanding
plate in small circles, the motor drives the plate by means of a
shaft that is slightly off center relative to the motor armature.
The armature, first of all, rotates a heavy disk. The off-center
shaft extends from the bottom of the disk and, when rotated
by the motor, turns in a bearing centered on the inner side of
sanding plate, causing the plate to oscillate. The part of
the disk opposite the off-center shaft is weighted. This
counterweight tends to balance the load imposed by the off-
center shaft. Thus the motor is not subjected to undue
vibration while the sanding plate is oscillating in its orbiting
motion.

At each of its four corners, the sanding plate is supported

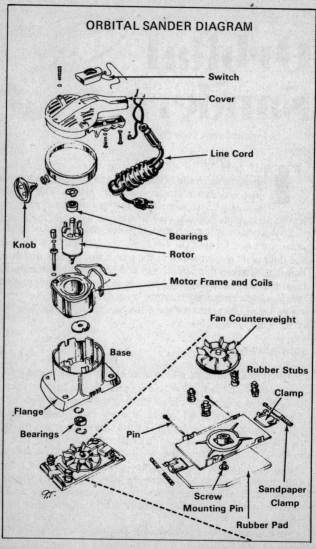

ORBITAL SANDER DIAGRAM

- Switch
- Cover
- Line Cord
- Knob
- Bearings
- Rotor
- Motor Frame and Coils
- Base
- Fan Counterweight
- Rubber Stubs
- Clamp
- Flange
- Bearings
- Pin
- Screw Mounting Pin
- Sandpaper Clamp
- Rubber Pad

by a rubber post. These posts provide the springiness that gives the plate freedom to oscillate while you are pressing down on it.

Located at each end of the sanding plate is a knurled pin that can be rotated by a screwdriver. The ends of a correct-size sheet of sandpaper are inserted under the pins, and the pins turned so that the knurls roll to pull the sandpaper up tight against the sanding plate. A felt pad on the sanding block backs up the sandpaper allowing some flexibility for sanding surfaces not perfectly flat.

PROBLEMS, CAUSES, REPAIR

SOME CARE is needed to preserve the life of your orbital sander. The tool cools itself through ventilating slots in the cover. These slots must be kept clear of sawdust. Carefully scrape the dust from them with a dull-edged tool or wooden scraper, and do it frequently, before the dust builds up.

The air pulled into the sander through the slots in the cover is ejected through holes in the metal base. It is this strong air exhaust which blasts dust away from the work surface as you sand. If the blast seems to be diminishing to a whisper, check these holes for dust build-up.

Be careful how you handle the line cord. Do not pull on it. When home carpenters are enthusiastic and absorbed in their work, they tend to forget the limitations of the cord and stretch it beyond its reach, pulling it out of the wall receptacle, which frays and breaks inner wires. To prevent this, use an extension cord of adequate wire size.

Orbital sanders rarely need lubrication. Bearings are pre-lubricated at the factory for the life of the tool. Never apply oil or anything else through the slots in the cover.

After much, much use, the rubber studs on the flat metal plate may break, causing the plate to loosen. These studs can be replaced. Take off the sponge rubber pad. Pull out the hinge pins and unscrew the stud mounting screws. Replace with new ones made specifically for your drill. A hardware store or home improvement center will have what you need.

Saber Saws

THE SABER SAW is also referred to as the jig saw.
It can be used for a variety of jobs, including intricate cutting of decorative scrollwork and fancy
curved edges; making cut-outs for pipes, electric
cable and wall outlets; and precise notching of studs.

Many home carpenters think the saber saw is designed for
high-speed cutting. It is not. Although it may be used for
relatively heavy work, such as ripping plywood of moderate
thickness and even sawing a 2x4, the blade should never be
forced. Trying to speed action will cause the blade to break.

Generally, the power parts of a saber saw are set up to
provide reciprocating (back-and-forth) motion at the working
end, which is the blade. In this respect, then, the saber saw
works on the same general principle as other reciprocating
appliances and tools, including hedge trimmers.

It all starts with an electric motor, which is positioned
horizontally. As you know, an electric motor functions
because of magnetism. See the chapter on Types of Motors
for an explanation of Universal motors — the kind found in the
best saber saws. Electricity is applied through the line cord to
the so-called field coil in the motor frame. The armature is
enclosed in the frame, but is not attached to it. A variation in
positive and negative poles is established vis-a-vis the frame
and armature. Opposites attract and similarities repel. This is
electro-magnetism, and the attraction and repulsion set up in
the magnetic field cause the armature to spin rapidly.

Getting motor motion to the small, stiff saber-shaped saw
blade extending from the chuck rod is the next task. The blade
must be driven at a speed of 200 to 300 strokes per
minute.

SABER SAW DIAGRAM

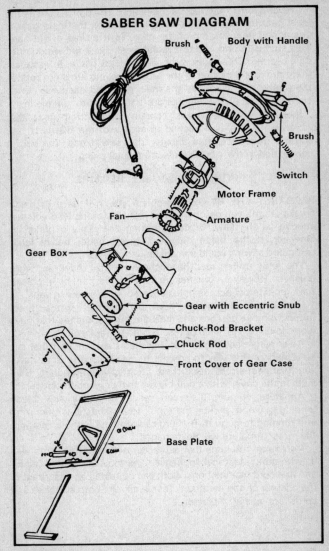

Brush

Body with Handle

Brush

Switch

Motor Frame

Fan

Armature

Gear Box

Gear with Eccentric Snub

Chuck-Rod Bracket

Chuck Rod

Front Cover of Gear Case

Base Plate

The armature shaft moves the pinion. The pinion causes the main gear to revolve. The eccentric stud on the main gear is positioned near the rim of the gear, so it makes a wide arc. This stud is interlocked to a round steel chuck rod which rides on a bearing. This chuck rod bears the saw blade. In essence, then, the rotary motion of the rapidly moving armature rotates the pinion, which rotates the main gear and eccentric. Wide arcing, but rapid movements are transferred to the blade.

Inexpensive saber saws contain an electromagnet that vibrates 120 times a second in step with the 60 hertz line current frequency, and moves the saw blade through a connection to the vibrating electromagnet plunger.

PROBLEMS, CAUSES, REPAIRS

PROBABLY THE BIGGEST problem you will have is blade breakage until you get the feel of just how much load you can impose on the saw. Blades breaking are really a blessing, however. If the blade did not "give" under heavy load, continued sawing could damage an internal part.

The only other real headache you may have is worn brushes. However, brushes in most saws can be replaced through external access holes covered with screw-in caps.

If sawing speed seems less than normal, or the motor falters, remove brushes and measure them. Brushes that have worn down to 1/4-inch or less should be replaced.

An armature could burn out, but that is another part that can be replaced. One way to prevent burned out parts is to make sure that cool air is not blocked. Clear sawdust regularly from slots in the cover with a dull-bladed tool or wooden scraper.

Armature burnout also can result from the saw blade binding in wood, pulling the motor to a standstill with current still running through it. If energized too long without rotating, the motor armature will be damaged.

Two other problems that can occur with saber saws as well as with other electrical appliances and tools are switch failure and line cord malfunctions. Both can be tested as described in the chapter on the continuity test lamp, and both switches and cords are easily replaced.

Circular Saws

THE CIRCULAR SAW, also called the cut-off saw, is surpassed in popularity among home power tools only by the electric drill. The saw is relatively light in weight and can be held in the hand, but it is powerful enough to rip through 2 x 4's and 2 x 6's at a good rate of speed.

A number of models are available. You can buy a circular saw with a blade size as small as four inches in diameter, or you can choose from others in blade size diameters increasing to 12 inches. You can buy a circular saw weighing as little as five pounds or one that weighs as much as 40. Naturally, the heavier saws with larger blades can do heavier work.

Your choices go even further. Special blades that can be attached to most circular saws cut through practically every type of building material from slate to corrugated sheet metal.

Yet, with all these refinements and the wide variety of sizes and designs, there is no great mystery about how circular saws work. In fact, they are similar in operation to an ordinary food mixer, or electric drill.

How It Works

THE OBJECT in designing a circular saw is to attain high speed and considerable power at the blade. The electric motor used by a circular saw, therefore, must be larger and more powerful than the electric motor used by electric drills, food mixers, can openers, and other appliances and tools that employ universal type electric motors.

For example, the electric motor of a 1/4-inch electric drill

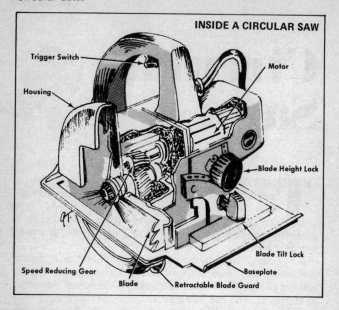

INSIDE A CIRCULAR SAW

Trigger Switch

Motor

Housing

Blade Height Lock

Blade Tilt Lock

Speed Reducing Gear

Baseplate

Blade

Retractable Blade Guard

is rated at approximately 1/2 horsepower. The electric motor in an electric circular saw has a rating of one horsepower to 1-1/2 horsepower.

But whatever the horsepower, the electric motor of the saw and the electric motor of the drill (and of other tools and appliances driven by a universal electric motor) work in exactly the same way.

Still, there is a difference in the gear set-up. In electric drills, the high speed of the electric motor must be reduced substantially to let the drill develop sufficient torque (twisting motion) so the drill bit in the chuck can bite. The overall ratio of the gear train of the average 1/4-inch electric drill is 12:1. This means that the speed of the chuck has been reduced to 12 times less than that of the motor.

For example, suppose the electric motor of a drill has a speed of 3600 revolutions per minute and a gear train having a ratio of 12:1 is used. The working speed of the drill (the

speed at the chuck) would be only 300 revolutions per minute
(RPM) —

$$\frac{3600}{12} = 300.$$

This reduction comes about through the use of successive
gears.

Now, gear trains of electric circular saws have ratios of 2:1
— at most, 3:1. If the motor of the electric saw is rated at a
speed of 3600 rpm, the actual working speed of the blade
would be 1800 rpm. At its lowest (with a ratio of 3:1), it
would be 1200 rpm.

The driven gear of an electric circular saw is driven by a
pinion that is cut into the end of the motor shaft. The saw
blade is attached to the driven gear. The pinion and drive
gears (they are the only gears in a circular saw) are relatively
long, thus giving gear teeth a more substantial contact area so
they are able to bear a heavy load without stripping.

PROBLEMS, CAUSES, REPAIRS

AS ARE OTHER portable electric tools, the circular saw is a
very dependable tool that will last many, many years with
little care. Simple maintenance includes:

• Keep the tool clean of dirt and dust so that the cooling
effect is not impeded.

• Be careful with the line cord, neither stretching nor
yanking it.

• Lubricate the tool when and if called for by the manufacturer (consult service data in the instruction booklet).

• Use the tool for its intended purpose only.

Problems that arise from normal use include: motor brush
wear (brushes can be replaced, usually by unscrewing caps
over access holes in the saw's body, lifting out the old
brushes and inserting new ones); and on-off switch failure
(the switch is replaceable by unscrewing the handle and
removing the switch from its seat by disconnecting wires).

Note: The radial arm (table) saw is a more powerful version
of the hand-held circular saw. It is mounted on a platform and
cuts wood that is placed on a table. Everything that applies to
circular saws as described in this section applies as well to
the radial arm saw.

Fluorescent Lamps

THE COOL, shadow-free glow and even illumination of fluorescent lights have made this kind of lighting popular in both desk lamps and ceiling fixtures. Round and tubular fluorescent bulbs are used. In principle, both are alike; only the shape is different.

It is a recognized fact that, for the same wattage, the fluorescent bulb gives out much more lamp (light) than the incandescent bulb. The reason? In the incandescent bulb, much of the electricity is turned into heat instead of light whereas the fluorescent bulb stays fairly cool. It is a much more efficient way to change electricity into light.

On the other hand, the fluorescent circuit is complete. All the incandescent bulb needs is a socket to feed it current.

Following through the circuit, beginning on the left-hand prong on the plug, current goes through the ballast, through one of the lamp filaments, through the closed switch in the starter, through the other filament in the lamp, and out the right-hand prong on the plug.

Because current is going through them, the filaments in the

lamp glow. There is a gas inside the tube. The glowing filaments electrify the gas in the vicinity of the filament. In the meantime, current is going through the starter, and a small thermostat in it is heating up. Quickly the thermostat trips the starter switch and turns it off.

In turning off, the thermostat switch breaks the entire circuit. But the ballast is of an electrical nature that causes it to generate a momentary surge of high voltage just at the instant its current flow is cut off. This high voltage causes a flash to jump across the tube from one filament to the other through the gas already electrified and ready for the flash to occur.

Once the flash is started it continues. Now, current from the plug goes through the ballast, through the tube, and out the other end. Now the ballast is put to another use. It drops the voltage so that the lamp itself is operating on something like 25 to 50 volts. That is all the fluorescent bulb needs to stay lighted once it is started.

Actually, you do not see the light inside the bulb. It is black light — the discotheque type. What you do see is the glow given off by a chemical powder lining the fluorescent tube. Different powders give different colors: white, green, yellow, blue, and the color called daylight.

The other is the desk lamp with a fluorescent bulb. There is only one difference from the circuit just described — the user is his own "starter."

To turn on the lamp, hold down the start (red) push button just for a moment — then release it. Release opens the switch, cutting off the ballast current flow. When its current gets cut off, the ballast produces its short pulse of high voltage, lighting the tube. For those of you who are technically inquisitive, it is the collapsing magnetic field in the ballast which causes what is called an "inductive kick." Once lighted, the tube stays turned on. To turn off the lamp, push the black button. This is a push-to-disconnect type of switch, and it breaks the entire circuit, causing everything to stop.

Servicing a fluorescent lamp is done by what is called the substitution method. First of all, put in a new bulb and see if

Fluorescent Lamps

that solves the problem. If not, then put in a new starter. If the lamp still does not work, put in a new ballast. Hold off on the ballast replacement until last because you must take the fixture apart to get to it. And, finally, if none of these fix the lamp, then replace the switch.

As the lamp darkens with age, replace it. You will get more light for your money. If the lamp flickers constantly, chances are that the starter is bad and needs replacement. Get the right size starter for the lamp wattage. Ballast faults are rare, but when they occur you can usually tell from the stench of scorched insulation.

A final word. If you need to disconnect the internal wiring — say to replace the ballast — tag the wires to help when you put the appliance back together.

Hedge Trimmers

ELECTRIC HEDGE TRIMMERS work on a principle much the same as electric knives. Two sawtooth blades in contact with each other do the cutting. One blade is fixed in place while the trimmer motor shuttles the other blade. Parts of the hedge caught in the teeth between moving and stationary blades are sheared off by the sharpened edges of the blade teeth. Generally, the fixed blade is at the bottom, with the moving blade located above it. A flat bar on top serves as a guide.

Inside the tool, a reciprocating gear system converts the rotation of the motor into a back and forth motion that drives the movable blade.

The power for an electric hedge trimmer is provided by a universal motor that is exactly the same type used to drive certain other electric appliances and tools. Only size (horsepower) differs. Size depends on the load that the motor is designed to handle. The motor in a hedge trimmer is of moderate size — not as small as the one in an electric knife, but not as large as the one in a table saw.

The chapter on Types of Motors describes the universal motor. In most hedge trimmers, a set of three small gears, called step-down gears, work together to bring motor speed to a level at which trimming action is the most effective.

Keep in mind that the motor is rotating, and that this rotary motion must be transformed into reciprocating (back-and-forth) motion for cutting. This transformation is done by a small pinion gear and a beveled gear. The hedge trimmer diagram illustrates this.

Note that the third gear of the three step-down gears has a shaft. This shaft drives the small pinion gear, which meshes

Hedge Trimmers

with and turns the bevel gear. It is set in such a way that it drives in reciprocating fashion anything that is attached to it.

There is usually a small stud, called an eccentric stud, that is part of the bevel gear. It is the part of the gear that actually drives the moveable blade of the trimmer through a device called the drive block.

PROBLEMS, CAUSES, REPAIRS

ACTUALLY, the bevel gear's eccentric stud could drive the blade directly, but this would cause direct wear on the blade. When the stud wore down the blade sufficiently (the moveable blade would not move), the blade would have to be replaced. This is an expensive matter.

By applying stud movement to the small drive block, only the block must be replaced when it wears out, at a much lower cost than replacing the blade. However, the main reason for using a drive block is to minimize backlash and interference with starting up when on dead center.

Other than this, care of an electric hedge trimmer is not extensive. You must be careful of the way you manipulate the line cord. Make sure the cord is a three-prong type for safety reasons. As with the electric lawn mower and other outdoor tools, you may come into contact with moisture. Unless the tool is properly grounded, you can receive a serious shock. Brush wear can occur, as in other appliances; if you find that the brushes have worn down below 1/2-inch, replace them.

The on-off switch might be a source of trouble in time. Contacts might wear. If they do and the switch does not close, the tool will not start. The switch can be replaced if it fails.

Read the instruction manual that comes with the tool for any directions concerning lubrication of gears. Many manufacturers pre-lubricate parts at the factory, but there may be some that require lubrication.

Also be sure to follow the manufacturer's advice concerning use of the tool. Do not try to use one for sawing down a tree — in fact, do not use one for anything except for what it is intended. You will ruin the trimmer.

IMPORTANT: If cutters jam due to a heavy branch or foreign object, TURN OFF THE MOTOR. Allowing the motor to hum away without turning will do great damage and shorten the life of the armature.

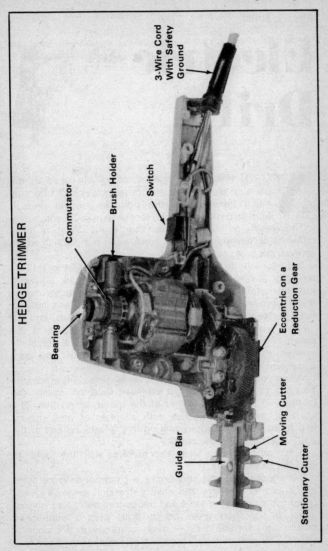

HEDGE TRIMMER

3-Wire Cord With Safety Ground

Commutator

Brush Holder

Switch

Bearing

Eccentric on a Reduction Gear

Guide Bar

Moving Cutter

Stationary Cutter

Electric Drills

NO OTHER power tool is as widely used as the portable electric drill. No other power tool offers as much flexibility as the portable electric drill. It literally puts a motorized tool shop in your hand.

The electric drill is much more than a drill. With its many different accessories, you can sand, saw, buff, polish, drive screws, cut holes, and mix paint.

Yet, for all its versatility, the portable electric drill is basically a very simple tool. It uses an ordinary universal electric motor of the type employed by so many other motor-driven appliances and tools, including blenders and mixers, fans, hedge trimmers, power sanders, routers, saws, and the electric lawn mower. The only difference is the size of the motor. The so-called ¼-inch electric drill has a relatively medium-size motor. The so-called 3/8-inch electric drill has a larger size motor than the ¼-inch.

When you turn on the switch of an electric drill, electricity flows to the motor, creating a magnetic field that causes the motor, and a shaft at the end of the motor, to revolve. The shaft is geared and meshes with a series of other gears, which turn to deliver rotary motion to the working end of the drill, which is called the chuck.

A fan on the motor shaft also revolves with the motor to cool the moving parts.

It is important to note that unlike such motor-driven electric appliances as blenders and mixers, the drill employs gears. Other tools, including saws and hedge trimmers, also employ gears. In operation, gears do for drills what a multi-speed switch does for blenders — they contribute to a change in speed. The gear train reduces the motor speed by a fixed ratio

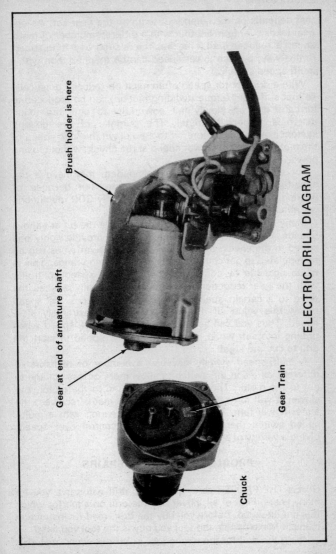

Brush holder is here

Gear at end of armature shaft

ELECTRIC DRILL DIAGRAM

Gear Train

Chuck

that depends on the number of teeth on the gear set. As one gear takes over from another with a different number of teeth, speed is reduced until it reaches the desired operating speed. In this way, a much lower speed can be attained than with a multi-speed switch.

With a drill, motor speed often must be reduced drastically so that sufficient torque (twisting motion) can be produced to turn the drill bit slowly but powerfully to bite into tough materials, especially metal. The purpose of the gearing system in a drill, therefore, is to step down the high speed of the motor to a much slower speed at the chuck, without losing power.

For example, a drill motor, unimpeded, may have a top speed of 3600 revolutions per minute, but because of gearing, the speed at the chuck may be only 300 revolutions per minute.

Many of the newer drills are built to drive the bit at various speeds. Unlike the earlier models, which provided only one speed to the chuck, the trigger on these newer types can be manipulated to get chuck speeds over a varying range. This is made possible by combining a solid state speed controller with the gear reduction system. The gear train reduces the drive to a certain speed; the controller reduces the speed below this value all the way down to an extremely slow speed. Thus you can select a fairly rapid chuck speed when drilling into soft wood, or a suitable slow speed to start the drill to cut into steel.

A multi-speed switch may use a number of resistors of different values in the switch to allow more or less voltage to get to the motor. The less voltage applied to the motor, the slower it will turn; the more voltage the motor receives, the faster it will turn. The combination of gearing with a multi-speed switch therefore means a dual control over speed, giving a variety of choices to the user.

PROBLEMS, CAUSES, REPAIRS

GIVEN THE PROPER care, an electric drill will serve you for many years. First of all, never use the drill on a job for which it is not intended. Before you buy the drill, read its instruction manual. Make certain the tool you buy is the tool you need.

Using the drill for the wrong job, or on the wrong material,

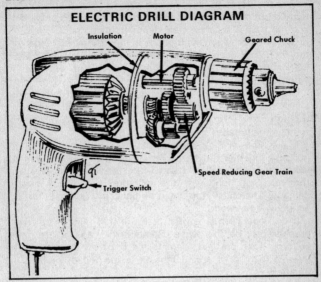

ELECTRIC DRILL DIAGRAM

Insulation   Motor   Geared Chuck

Speed Reducing Gear Train

Trigger Switch

can put an excessive overload on the motor. When the motor is jammed to a standstill repeatedly, and held there for extended periods of time, it becomes overheated. This damages insulation, which affects the armature especially.

Watch out how you handle the line cord. There is no need to belabor this point — it has been mentioned many times throughout this issue of CONSUMER GUIDE Magazine. Do not abuse the cord. More electric drill failures occur because of a damaged line cord than for any other reason, especially since the drill seems to offer extraordinary opportunities for abuse. In particular, pulling the cord at the drill handle, and abrasion resulting from the cord being pulled across the concrete floor, against the edge of the workbench, and so on, cause serious damage.

Make sure the drill is properly grounded before using it. This is vital for your safety. The chapter on "Grounding" explains the best way to do this.

Keep air vents on the sides of the drill clear of foreign matter. The drill "breathes" through these vents. Cooling air enters the vents to help the fan cool off parts, preventing a burned-out motor. Use a dull-edged tool such as a small putty knife or a small brush to clear debris from vents.

Consult lubrication instructions in the manual accompanying the tool. Drill gears can be lubricated either with the kind of lubricant sold at appliance parts stores, or with a #2 automotive grease.

If drill speed seems very sluggish, or the drill fails to run, check the motor brushes to see if they have become worn through use. *Pull the line cord from the wall outlet* and remove the brushes for replacement.

Make sure that all screws that hold the sections of the housing together are tight. They may come loose from the vibration of the drill and should be checked periodically. If they are not tightened, the vibration will cause internal damage. The chuck, too, must be tight; if it is loose, the drill simply will not work.

If drill operation is erratic, or if the drill fails to run, worn brushes may be the cause. Remove the caps on the brush holders. Take out and examine the brushes. If worn shorter than ¾-inch, or if spring tension is too loose, replace the brushes.

Two other power tools — the router and the power screwdriver — are basically the same as an electric drill. The only differences between them are size and the makeup of the working end. A router's working end has cutters that revolve to cut into and shape wood. The working end of a power screwdriver is, of course, a screwdriver tip.

Electric Lawn Mowers

BASICALLY, the electric lawn mower is nothing more than a cutting blade attached to a powerful electric motor. The motor revolves at a high rate of speed; the blade whirls around at a high rate of speed. Refinements make these lawn mowers highly efficient and reliable pieces of equipment.

For example, notice the way in which the wheels are attached to the housing that contains the motor. The back wheels are on-line with each other, but the front wheels are probably staggered. This off-line positioning of the front wheels allows the mower to remain level when it is rolled over uneven ground. Without this feature, the blade would dip too low to the ground (perhaps even strike the ground), cutting grass at or below ground level.

Notice also the strength of the blade. Most are made of 1 / 4-inch-thick steel and are about two inches wide. They are usually one piece, with slightly twisted ends. This slight twist produces a fan effect as the blade revolves, creating an up-draft beneath the mower that lifts the grass blades so they are cut off evenly.

Your blade may be equipped with bolted-on cutting edges near the tips. These cutters are mounted so they will swing back if the blade hits an obstruction. If edges are damaged, they can be unbolted and replaced.

Keep in mind that an electric lawn mower motor is "free-wheeling"; that is, it is not geared, but is permitted to run at a constant, maximum speed. This speed is around 1800 revolutions per minute. The blade, therefore, revolves at this same speed.

PROBLEMS, CAUSES, REPAIRS

ELECTRIC LAWN MOWERS, when they fail, do so usually because of worn brushes or a dirty or damaged commutator. Keep in mind that an electric lawn mower is a powerful, but fairly simple, electric motor similar to the electric motors that drive other tools and appliances found throughout your home and explained in this issue of CONSUMER GUIDE Magazine.

Brushes can be replaced. They are contained in brush holders that in most machines can be unscrewed. A dirty or damaged commutator should be repaired by a professional technician.

The one part of an electric lawn mower that receives the most punishment is the cord. So that you may mow a good distance, the cord is a long one and replacing or repairing it (aside from regular sharpening or replacing of blades) is the most commonly found problem on electric lawn mowers. This is not because of failure (power cords seldom fail), but because of carelessness: users of electric mowers run over the cords, slashing them with the blade.

You should inspect your power cord often. Never take a chance with one that is damaged or showing signs of deterioration (cracked insulation). The danger of receiving serious shock is very real, because cords drag on the grass, which is often damp. This makes you the ground, and electricity can pass from the damaged cord, through the mower housing, to you.

Never, but never, operate an electric lawn mower using anything but a three-wire power cord that is designed for outdoor use. The third wire grounds the machine to the frame. Older mowers do not have grounded cords. Do not use an older mower until you have equipped it with a new cord.

The All-Important Blade

IF YOUR electric lawn mower develops a vibration, which is a fairly common problem, the heavy steel blade has probably been thrown out of balance. Vibration must be corrected as soon as possible to avoid wearing out motor bearings. Once bearings are damaged, your choice is to replace the bearings or replace the machine—both expensive propositions.

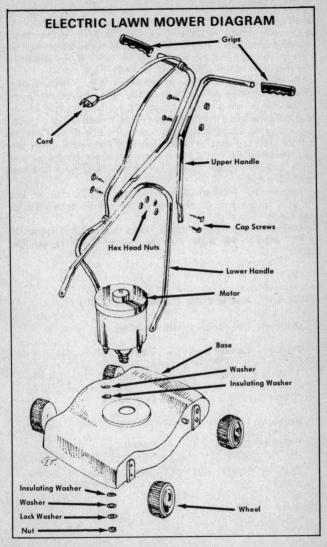

ELECTRIC LAWN MOWER DIAGRAM

Grips

Cord

Upper Handle

Cap Screws

Hex Head Nuts

Lower Handle

Motor

Base

Washer

Insulating Washer

Insulating Washer

Washer

Lock Washer

Nut

Wheel

Electric Lawn Mowers

Check the blade's balance by removing it from the motor shaft (it is usually held by a bolt that can be removed with a properly fitting wrench). Hold the blade in a horizontal position and insert a metal rod (a small screwdriver will do nicely) through the blade's mounting hole. If the blade is not balanced, it will dip toward the heavy side.

Grinding a blade to try to rebalance it is a hit-and-miss process, but less expensive than buying a new blade. Using a fine-cut grinding wheel, grind off a small amount of the cutting edge on the blade's heavy side. Use a light touch. Do not grind excessively, but make only one or two passes before stopping to retest blade balance. Proceed in this manner, grinding a bit at a time, until the blade comes to rest in a straight horizontal position when held by the metal balancing rod.

Incidentally, you can sharpen a blade in this manner, but be sure to grind equal amounts of metal from both sides of the blade.

Caution: In grinding a blade, hold the grinding wheel at a 45° angle to the blade. Do not approach the blade straight on.

PROBLEMS, CAUSES, REPAIRS

Problem: Lawnmower will not start

Possible Cause:	Repair:
1. Worn brushes	1. Replace
2. Dirty or damaged commutator	2. Have repaired by professional

Problem: Lawnmower vibrates excessively

Possible Cause:	Repair:
Cutting blade out of balance.	Grind a little at a time to correct imbalance.

Typewriters

OF ALL THE precision instruments with which people are familiar, the typewriter is probably the most unappreciated for the mechanical wonder that it is. It is a marvelous mechanism, an outstanding feat of engineering that successfully reconciles two opposing mechanical principles: it must be strong so that constant pounding and banging will not knock it out of whack; it must be rapid and light in action so that the dance of fingertips across its keyboard will be all that is required to make the machine go.

From a mechanical standpoint, strength has requirements that conflict with lightness and rapidity; strength means solidarity and mass, but solidarity and mass are the antithesis of lightness and rapidity. Yet typewriters overcome the conflict, as they have for a century (the first typewriter was put on the market in 1874) and uncounted millions of them have been manufactured. Your own typewriter, be it a portable or an office model, manual or electric, represents one of the most brilliantly conceived, carefully crafted, precisely engineered devices that the average citizen can buy.

Manual Typewriters

NOWADAYS, nearly all office typewriters are electrically powered, while most portables are manual. However, used manual office machines are available in abundance; they are not expensive, and more often than not they can be found in excellent operating condition. So although the office manual is a thing of the past as far as manufacturers are concerned, these models remain alive and well in the hands of private

BASIC COMPONENTS

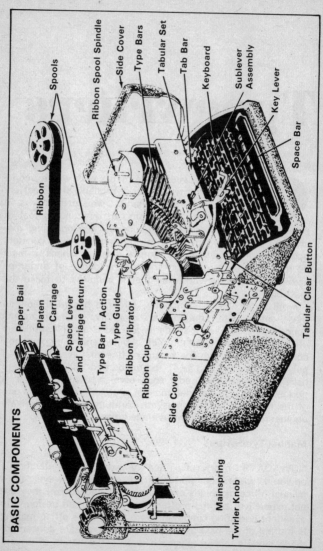

Spools

Ribbon

Ribbon Spool Spindle

Side Cover

Type Bars

Tabular Set

Tab Bar

Keyboard

Sublever Assembly

Key Lever

Space Bar

Tabular Clear Button

Paper Bail

Platen

Carriage

Space Lever and Carriage Return

Type Bar In Action

Type Guide

Ribbon Vibrator

Ribbon Cup

Side Cover

Mainspring

Twirler Knob

users. For this reason, plus the fact that the mechanics of electric typewriters borrow considerably from manual-type-writer technology, we will devote ample space to the principles of the manual typewriter.

To understand how the manual works, it would be helpful first to define the various components essential to its operation. First, of course, are the typewriter *keys;* these are the buttons at the front of the machine with letters printed on them, which, when pressed, activate the machine as a whole. The keys are at the operator's end of slim metal bars called *keylevers;* these lead into the interior of the machine and connect the keys with the other components required to make the typewriter go. The keylevers are connected with the *typebars;* these are the individual metal arms that swing up toward the paper when the keys are pressed. At the tips of the typebars are the *type heads* or slugs; these are the metal components that contain the actual type that strikes the paper and prints the letters.

Inside the machine is a rod that traverses the width of the typewriter and is called the *universal bar;* this is the unit that activates many other parts of the typewriter that do not have to do with actually making the type strike the paper. One of these is the *carriage;* this is the part of the machine that holds the paper and moves back and forth. Mounted in the carriage is the roller, cylinder, or as it's officially called, the *platen;* this is the rubber-covered tube around which the paper is fed line by line while typing. The carriage and its platen are made to move from right to left by the *mainspring;* this is a coiled spring that pulls the carriage to the left, the mainspring and carriage being connected by a belt called the *drawband.* The carriage is prevented from moving to the left, until a key is pressed, by an assembly called the *escapement;* it is attached at the rear of the body, or *frame* of the typewriter. The escapement comes in contact with a bar at the rear or bottom of the carriage (depending upon the particular design) called the *escapement rack;* this is a toothed bar, each tooth representing one space in the travel of the carriage.

The final major assembly in the typewriter is the ribbon mechanism, which consists of two basic groups of components. One is the *ribbon feed;* this is the mechanism that causes the ribbon to move back and forth between its two spools. The other is the *ribbon vibrator;* this is the little holder for the ribbon, directly in front of the point where the

Typewriters

type heads strike the paper, that causes the ribbon to move upward to bring the ribbon into typing position, and downward again so the ribbon will not block your sight of the letters printed.

How it Works

WHEN YOU PRESS a key, many things happen all at once. Most obviously, the keylever goes down and causes the typebar to lift, bringing the type head into contact with the paper wrapped around the platen. But there is more. As the keylever goes down, it comes into contact with the universal bar (in some designs, the typebar itself contacts the universal, or a linkage connecting the keylever with the typebar is what comes into contact with the universal bar) and makes the universal bar move. This movement is transmitted to the escapement by means of another connecting bar or linkage.

When at rest, the escapement prevents the carriage from moving to the left by means of a rigid finger, or *dog,* that holds a spoked wheel called the *starwheel* in place. But when the universal bar is activated, it causes a part of the escapement called the *rocker* to move, bringing the dog out of the way of the starwheel. The starwheel is attached to a pinion, on which the carriage escapement rack rides. The carriage, being pulled to the left by the mainspring, moves, the starwheel turns, and then is stopped by another escapement dog. The rocker returns to neutral position, its dog holding the starwheel, pinion, and carriage in place until the universal bar is activated again.

The escapement acts so quickly, and contains special spring-powered components, that the carriage is allowed to travel only the distance of one tooth each time the escapement rocker moves. That's why the width of the space between letters is always the same — the distance between teeth in the rack is identical to the space required by the type, and the escapement permits the carriage to move only one tooth at a time.

As you can see, there are quite a few things happening inside a typewriter — each time you press a key. Aside from the initial finger tap that activates the keylever, all other energy inside a typewriter comes from nothing but springs. In this sense, the typewriter is mechanically more akin to a fine

THE ESCAPEMENT (Based on Royal)

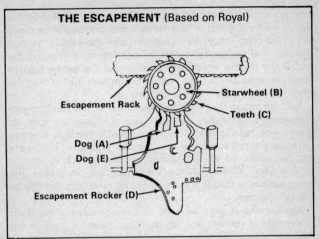

When at rest, Dog (A) blocks motion of Starwheel (B) by contact with Teeth (C). When Universal Bar is activated, Escapement Rocker (D) moves (toward or away from viewer of diagram), moving Dog (A) from Starwheel, which is permitted to turn. Second Dog (E) prevents Starwheel from traveling more than one tooth (or one space in the carriage motion as the Carriage Escapement Rack rides on a pinion connected to the Starwheel).

watch than any other kind of mechanism; yet it is far more complex than the most elaborate watch, containing many times more parts, and undergoing many more different actions.

Moving Parts

BUT THERE ARE still many other things that go on inside a typewriter. In the description of the relationship between the keylever and the typebar, we implied that the two are directly connected together. This is true with many portables; but in most of the office machines, which are larger and whose weight is less of a consideration, there is an intermediate link between keylever and typebar. This is called an *accelerating sublever,* and it is connected relatively loosely between keylever and typebar. When the keylever is depressed, its energy is transmitted to the accelerating sublever, which begins to fly forward — the typebar has not begun to move yet. However, once the sublever has traveled a certain distance and has gained a certain momentum, it engages the end of the typebar inside the machine and makes the typebar move; in other words, it is really the sublever, rather than the keylever, that activates the typebar.

You are acquainted with the space bar at the front of your typewriter's keyboard, and you are well-familiar with its purpose of making spaces between words. The way it works is really a simplification of the keylever principle. The space bar is connected to the universal bar, or directly to the escapement. When you tap the space bar, it moves the universal bar — just as the keylevers do — or acts directly on the escapement.

You are also acquainted with the carriage release, the lever at the side of the carriage which, when pressed, permits the carriage to run freely in either direction. This is a simple mechanism, since the carriage release lever is connected directly to the escapement rack. When you press the carriage release, what you are really doing is lifting the escapement rack away from the escapement, so that the carriage's travel will no longer be inhibited by the escapement — until you let go of the carriage release again, when the escapement rack will engage the escapement pinion once more.

The tabulator works on a similar basis: when you press the tab key, the escapement rack is moved away from the escapement in some designs, or the escapement is held away from the rack in other designs, both approaches enabling the carriage to run freely to the left in compliance with the pull of the mainspring. The only additional component required is something to stop the carriage at the desired point. This is called the *tab stop,* and in nearly all typewriter designs since the 1930's the desired tab stop or stops are set by means of a key on the keyboard labeled "Tab Set." In most designs, the Tab Set key activates a finger or bar at the rear of the carriage. When this key is pressed, the finger pushes against one of a row of detents, or stops, one detent being included for each tooth on the escapement rack; thus you can activate a detent for any particular space in the carriage's travel. When the finger pushes the detent, the detent protrudes through the

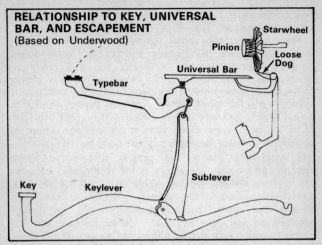

RELATIONSHIP TO KEY, UNIVERSAL BAR, AND ESCAPEMENT
(Based on Underwood)

Starwheel

Pinion

Loose Dog

Universal Bar

Typebar

Sublever

Key

Keylever

When Key is pressed, Universal Bar is moved (in this case by the Typebar) and releases Loose Dog which holds Starwheel in place. Carriage, whose Escapement Rack rides on pinion of Starwheel, is enabled to travel one space before Dog stops Escapement.

other side where it will come into contact with some non-moving part of the typewriter. The outcome of it all is that the tab key releases the carriage for free travel, while the detent stops the carriage at the desired point.

Electric Typewriters

MANY OF THE internal workings of electric typewriters are similar to those of manuals; the real difference is that they are performed by an electric motor instead of by hand. Many people are under the impression that the advantage of an electric is that it works faster than a manual. This is not true. Any modern office manual is capable of operating faster than the fastest typist, and this has been true of almost all standard office machines since just after the turn of the century. The true advantages of the electric include the fact that the motorized mechanism produces a more uniform impression of type on the paper — although a skillful typist can do nearly as well with a manual.

The other advantage is that, during the course of a full day's work, typing can, surprisingly enough, be tremendously fatiguing. Tapping the keys, shifting for capitals, and returning the carriage for the beginning of a new line have been proven to be major consumers of the typist's energy, resulting in tiredness and lack of efficiency. Since the keys of an electric do not have to be tapped quite so hard — they really only have to be touched — and since shifting and carriage return are performed by motor, an electric is less tiring for the operator.

In mechanical terms, the biggest difference between electric and manual typewriters is the relationship between the keylever and the typebar. While a manual's keylever is directly connected to the typebar (or indirectly connected, through the sublever) there is no real positive linkage between an electric's key and typebar. Instead, the key connects with a cam that is placed in line with the typebar. Running across the machine, beneath the row of cams, is the *power roller;* this is a rubber cylinder, not unlike the platen in appearance, that rotates continuously once the electric typewriter is turned on; it is driven by the electric motor. When a key is pressed, it brings the cam into contact with the roller. The rapidly-spinning roller kicks the cam away, hurling it toward the typebar. The cam hits the typebar, and the typebar flies toward the printing point. Since the roller spins at a constant rate, the cam is kicked toward the typebar with the same force no matter how hard the key is pressed, and the typebar strikes the paper with an equally uniform pressure; this is what accounts for the extremely even appearance of an electrically typewritten page.

PROBLEMS, CAUSES, REPAIRS

TYPEWRITERS are extremely complex, but that is not the same thing as complicated. Their mechanics are logical and straightforward: something pushes against something else, which causes something to happen. And although there are thousands of parts put together into dozens of assemblies, there is a considerable amount of repetition in a typewriter's construction. Most typewriters have, for example, about 42

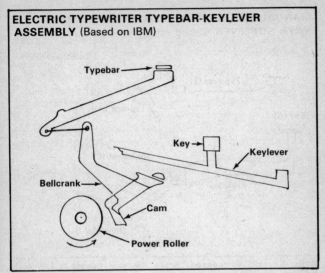

ELECTRIC TYPEWRITER TYPEBAR-KEYLEVER ASSEMBLY (Based on IBM)

Keylever presses down on Cam; Cam contacts Power Roller; Power Roller kicks Cam away, pulling Bellcrank; Bellcrank moves Typebar.

keys; this also means 42 keylevers, 42 typebars, and 42 sublevers when the particular machine is thus equipped. All of these are secured to the frame of the machine, and connected with one another, in a similar fashion. Because of these factors, there are certain kinds of repairs you may be able to make yourself.

In describing these repairs, we will emphasize the manual typewriter rather than the electric. Because electric typewriters are motorized, there is a greater number of areas that require the services of a professional typewriter mechanic.

Maintenance and Preventive Maintenance

BEFORE WE DEAL with the few how-to-fix-its that you can perform on a typewriter yourself, we should consider the measures you can take to prolong the life of your machine and keep servicing to a minimum.

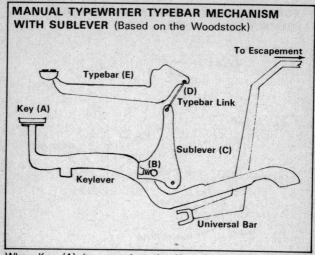

MANUAL TYPEWRITER TYPEBAR MECHANISM WITH SUBLEVER (Based on the Woodstock)

To Escapement

Typebar (E)

(D)
Typebar Link

Key (A)

Sublever (C)

(B)

Keylever

Universal Bar

When Key (A) is pressed, entire Keylever lowers at Key end, thrusting Peg (B) into notch in Sublever (C). Sublever accumulates motion, but does not move Typebar (E) until slack in (D) is eventually taken up. Continued movement of Sublever finally pulls Typebar (E) against platen to print.

First and foremost, keep the typewriter clean. Dust is the enemy of all machinery, but it can be especially vexing in a typewriter. The hundreds of individual joints and linkages in the mechanism are all made to exacting tolerances; an accumulation of dust can cause a sluggish action and displeasing performance — and very often it is harder to get foreign matter out of the typewriter than it is for it to get in. Portable typewriters come with cases; and if your office machine does not have a plastic dust cover, you can and should buy one for a few cents at a stationer's or typewriter dealer's. Cover the machine between uses.

Lubrication

LUBRICATION, of course, is essential to any machine. You should oil your typewriter periodically — at least every six

SPACE BAR THAT ACTIVATES ESCAPEMENT
DIRECTLY (Based on Royal)

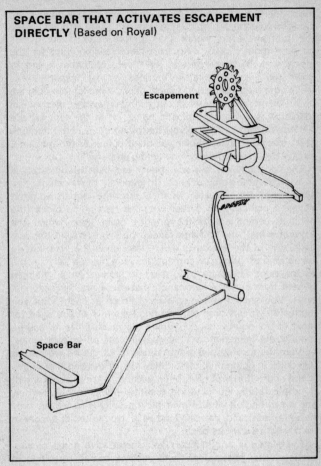

Escapement

Space Bar

months, or sooner if any part of the mechanism squeaks, does not operate smoothly, or grows sluggish — using a non-gumming light machine oil, or the typewriter oil sold by typewriter dealers. Before putting oil into any part of the

Typewriters

mechanism, you should clean that part thoroughly; if oil comes into contact with dust, a gum will likely form and make the problem even worse than before, and cleaning will become more difficult. An excellent cleaning fluid for the mechanism of typewriters is Tri-Chloro Ethylene; it breaks down gum and sludge, evaporates almost instantly, and leaves the metal bone dry. Liberal applications of this fluid are an excellent means to wash out a dirty typewriter mechanism (don't let it get on any plastic parts, or on the typewriter's finish, which it can dissolve!) but oiling is essential immediately afterward at all moving contact points in the machine, because of the fluid's extreme drying properties.

The locations for periodic oiling are usually indicated in your typewriter's instructions. In general, they include: the comb segment in each typebar slot; the ribbon vibrator, where it comes into contact with the type-guide block (the notched component at the printing point upon which the vibrator rides); the carriage races, the keylevers, at the rear underside of the machine, where they enter the typewriter's frame; and all points of contact between moving parts in the escapement. There are other parts of the mechanism that can benefit from periodic lubrication, but these are the essential ones. You should use very, very little oil at each point you lubricate — a tiny drop on the end of a pin is all you need for most of the points listed — since too much oil is as bad as none at all. Immediately after applying the oil to each point, operate the moving part a few times to let the oil work in; if you delay in doing this, the oil may run off the part that needs it and your effort will have been wasted. It takes about a half hour to carefully lubricate the essential points in a typewriter, and it can be dull work. However, it usually is necessary only twice a year, and the dividend is a typewriter that continuously operates at its best.

The platen is another part you should give some consideration. After heavy use it will become scored, resulting in uneven-looking typing. But even if you don't use your typewriter that often, you should expect to have the platen resurfaced with new rubber every few years. In time, the rubber dries and hardens, and this is the source of many troubles. The machine becomes noisier as the typebars slap against the hard surface; ribbons wear out prematurely, and can even be torn by the repeated battering of type on one side and the unyielding surface on the other; a hard platen can cause the type to punch holes through the paper (especially the e, q, o, p, a, c, and period); and, of course, the type itself will wear out more quickly as it pounds against the hard surface. If you do not follow a regular schedule of platen re-covering, the way to tell it is time for one is the appearance of any of these symptoms. If the platen looks shiny (instead of being matte or dull) you can be certain that it needs re-covering.

Some typewriter owners have been known to sandpaper the grooves off a platen that has become scored by heavy use, but this is not a recommended practice at all. First, it will not make a hardened platen soft — and that is the biggest source of platen troubles. Second, the platen should have an exact, pre-specified diameter. The reason for this is that the types cast upon the type heads are slightly concave, so that they will correctly fit the curve of the cylindrical platen; if you change the diameter of the platen by sanding it down, the type will no longer fit properly and you may get letters that are lighter at the tops and bottoms than in the centers.

The cost for resurfacing a platen with new rubber can vary, but usually it is between $5-$10. The least expensive typewriters to re-cover are those that have removable platens — nearly all office machines, and a good number of portables are built so that the platen can be snapped right out — since you can bring the platen alone to the typewriter dealer, and he does not have to charge you for the labor in removing the platen. Typewriters with non-removable platens will cost a bit more, since the dealer has to disassemble some of the carriage components to get the platen out.

Whenever your typewriter is to go unused for a long period of time, it is a good idea to move the paper-release lever into "open" position, moving the feed rollers away from the platen. If the typewriter is allowed to sit for a long time with the feed rollers in contact with the platen under full pressure, it is possible that the sides of the rollers that contact the platen may become flattened. This can result in uneven line-spacing or wrinkling of the paper.

If you observe these points on maintenance and preventive maintenance, your typewriter is bound to give you good service for many years. The proof of this is the number of really old typewriters that are still perfectly capable of a fine job. It is not at all uncommon to find a typewriter 20 or 30 years old that still performs excellently (how many 20 or 30-year-old automobiles, television sets, dishwashers, toasters, or lawnmowers can you find that work so well?). And the fact is that there are typewriters 60 and 70 years old that work nearly as well as new machines, simply because they were kept clean, lubricated regularly, and treated with the respect due any fine instrument.

Operating Problems — Drawband

BUT ANOTHER FACT is that typewriters do get out of order. It is rare for this to happen in the course of a typewriter's normal working life (unless it's a cheap machine whose parts are poorly made from second-rate materials) since the art of typewriter construction was perfected long ago, and the machines are built to last.

The drawband is one of the more likely objects of malfunction. Although made of strong material and well-fastened to both the mainspring and the carriage, it is under constant tension and is obliged to move back and forth in the course of doing its duty. It can work loose from mainspring or carriage, or it can break. If this happens while you are typing, you'll know it because you'll hear the whirr and clatter of the mainspring as it spontaneously uncoils, and then the carriage will fail to respond to the keys or the space bar. If it happens when you're away from the typewriter (a much less likely proposition) you'll simply discover that the carriage does not move when you strike the keys; to confirm that the problem is the drawband, and not some other damage to the carriage itself, depress the carriage release lever and gently try running the carriage back and forth. If the carriage moves freely, the problem is probably the drawband. To make certain, inspect the mainspring — you'll have no difficulty determining if it's disconnected.

If you need a new drawband, write down all the information about your typewriter — brand name, model designation, serial number — and present this to a typewriter dealer; not all dealers stock these parts, nor are all willing to sell them, but you're sure to find one who has what you need or, barring that, you can probably order the drawband from the manufacturer or distributor of your make of typewriter.

Installing a new drawband, or reconnecting an existing one that has slipped out of place, is neither a difficult job nor is it one that should take more than a few minutes. The first step is to locate the part of the carriage to which the drawband connects; this will be somewhere at the bottom of the carriage, at its right end as you face the machine from the keyboard, or the left end of the carriage as you face the machine from the rear (you will probably find it more convenient to work on the drawband from the rear of the machine). On most typewriters the drawband connects with a peg or a hook on the carriage, although some drawbands are screwed to the carriage.

Turn the mainspring until you find the place where the drawband connects; this is often in the form of an oblong hole in the mainspring housing that receives a finger attached to the drawband, although here, too, the drawband sometimes is screwed down. Before attempting to connect the drawband in earnest, practice connecting the drawband to the mainspring so you'll know exactly what to do when the time comes.

Always connect the drawband to the carriage first — if you try connecting it to the mainspring first you won't get anywhere. But before actually affixing it to the carriage, it's a good idea to place the drawband in its working position between carriage and mainspring. In most typewriters it runs beneath the carriage, but you can determine this by standing the typewriter on its side opposite the side to which the drawband connects, aligning your eye directly above the drawband's carriage connection, and looking straight down to the other end of the carriage; the straight line of your sight follows the path of the drawband, since drawbands always go straight from carriage to mainspring. Now dangle the drawband over its path, and carefully lower it down toward the mainspring, taking care not to let it get hung-up on any parts or protrusions on the way. When the drawband emerges from the far side of the carriage, grasp it and either hang on to it or temporarily fasten it to some convenient part of that end of the carriage, so it won't ride up while you are attaching it to the near end of the carriage. Once the drawband is firmly

Typewriters

attached to the carriage, take the typewriter off its side and stand it in normal operating position, with the carriage drawn back far enough to give you clear access to the mainspring.

Before you connect the drawband to the mainspring, you must wind the mainspring up. First thing to do is determine which way you must turn the mainspring to wind it — usually it's counterclockwise as you face the rear of the machine. With your fingertips, you simply start turning the mainspring in the proper direction — but how many times do you turn it? This can vary from one make or style of typewriter to another, but a good starting place is from four to seven complete revolutions of the mainspring drum — the lower number for small machines, the higher number for the big office models. Be mindful that, as you turn the mainspring, it will want to unwind in the opposite direction; you will probably want to wind it with one hand while preventing it from uncoiling with the other. Once you've wound the mainspring as much as you want to, attach the drawband to it; this will take a little care since the mainspring still wants to unwind, which is why we suggested earlier that you practice attaching the band to the spring to learn what to do before you have to fight the spring's tension.

Now do some typing, and see if the mainspring has been wound to the tension that best suits you; the time to be most watchful is when the carriage reaches the end of the line, because it is here that the mainspring has the least tension. If the carriage moves too forcefully, slamming from space to space, you've wound the mainspring too far — you should disconnect the drawband and let the mainspring unwind one or two revolutions. If the carriage seems slow and lazy, particularly at the end of the line, the mainspring should be wound another revolution or two, and, possibly, another one or two revolutions after that if you're still not satisfied. Under no circumstances should the mainspring be wound to its very limit. This will probably damage the mainspring; and it's guaranteed that the carriage will move too fast, possibly even walking the entire typewriter across your desk as you type.

Electric Typewriters

MANY OF THE components of electric typewriters are similar

to those of manuals, but many are also significantly different. The paper feed, the carriage support system, the typebars and comb segment, and several others have remained consistent between electric and manual typewriters; the suggestions presented here on preventive maintenance and minor repairs are as applicable to electric machines as they are to manuals.

However, the motorized components of an electric add new considerations — parts that are less simple to repair unless you have had formal training in electric typewriter mechanics. The majority of electric-typewriter breakdowns come from the power source (the motor) or its allied components — belts, the power roller, etc. It is not such an easy matter to trace the source of a problem in an electric as it is in a manual, where one part so clearly leads to another. A greater amount of disassembly may be required in an electric, and this is work best left to the experts.

Automobiles

WHEN YOU START your car, put the transmission into gear, release the brakes, and begin to move, you are setting into motion the most significant social development of the 20th century. No other invention of this century has had a greater impact on mankind.

Despite this, comparatively few people know how their cars work. Most of us figure that we own an overly complicated machine that only an expert can understand. Nonsense!

There is no great mystery involved. Basically, a car is a simple conveyance made up of a few major components which work together toward one end: to get you where you want to go. These components are: engine, transmission, and differential (or rear end). To begin, we will put things into perspective by explaining what each of these does and how they work together in that common effort.

The Basic Components

ENGINE — The engine produces the power that eventually propels the car. Without the engine, your vehicle would be no more use to you than a wagon without a horse.

The power that an automobile engine puts out is rotating power. The technical term for it is "torque." It is turning effort, and every part of an engine — whether it moves up and down, or around, or in and out — has but one purpose: to produce enough torque to turn a long shaft called a crankshaft which, in turn, allows a large gear called a flywheel to turn. The flywheel is located at the output end of the engine and is connected to the next major component, the transmission.

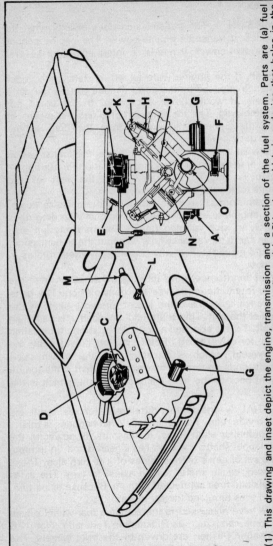

(1) This drawing and inset depict the engine, transmission and a section of the fuel system. Parts are (a) fuel pump, (b) fuel filter, (c) carburetor, (d) carburetor air filter, (e) PCV valve, which is a device that helps in the control of pollution, (f) oil filter, (g) oil pump, (h) valves, (i) rocker arm assembly, (j) hydraulic valve lifter, (k) valve cover gasket, (l) transmission, (m) transmission output shaft, (n) pistons, (o) crankshaft

Automobiles

TRANSMISSION — The transmission does exactly what its name implies: it transmits engine power. The engine cannot transmit its own power. It needs an intermediary for several reasons.

First of all, if the engine were forced to start while under the resistance imposed by the gears needed to turn the car's drive wheels, it would never get going. It just could not overcome the drag. The transmission provides the means of separating (decoupling) the engine from the drag so the engine can get started.

This is what happens when you place the transmission selector level in Neutral (or Park) in preparation for starting — the engine is actually separated from the rest of the components needed to move the car.

The transmission, through a series of different size gears, allows the engine to assume the load gradually so drag does not cause it to stop running (stall). The transmission also permits the car to move backwards. Without the transmission, the car could move forward only since the flywheel rotates in one direction.

Rotary motion (torque) goes into the transmission from the engine and rotary motion leaves the transmission. The parts inside a transmission have the job of turning a shaft at the output end of the unit. This shaft, understandably, is called an output shaft. To it is attached a pretty long, strong tube called a propeller (or drive) shaft. Rotary motion provided by the engine flywheel, which is transferred to the transmission output shaft, ends up turning the propeller shaft. This torque is then sent back to the next major component, which is the differential.

DIFFERENTIAL — Inside the differential (or rear end) are gears that divide rotary motion in two. What happens is this:

As the propeller shaft turns, it transmits its power to the differential input shaft. The shaft has a geared end. In turning, it causes a set of gears on both sides of it to turn also. These gears, in turn, cause shafts (called axles) to turn. The axles have wheels and tires connected to them. Because axles turn, wheels and tires turn, and the car moves.

What we have discussed is the common rear-wheel driven vehicle. Some cars, such as Oldsmobile Toronado, Fiat 128 and Volkswagen Dasher, are driven by the front wheels. The transmission and differential are located in the front of the car, usually right beneath the engine. A few vehicles are even driven by all four wheels for maximum traction. Jeep and Scout are popular four-wheel drive cars.

In simple terms, then, this is the way in which a typical car works. However, in order to appreciate fully this marvel of the 20th century, it is necessary to delve further, especially to get an understanding of what can go wrong, how to help prevent problems, and how to handle a problem when it does arise.

What follows, then, is a discussion of the major systems of the family car.

Engine Operation: Fuel, Spark & Compression

LARGE, multi-faceted automobile engines and small, simple chain saw engines have much in common. To run, both need fuel, spark for igniting the fuel and compression. Two alone won't do. All three must be present.

The difference between auto engines and chain saw engines is the way in which the three operations are accomplished. A chain saw is a two-stroke engine. An automobile engine is a four-stroke engine.

This means that the four processes involved in internal combustion in each cylinder of the engine take place over a series of four up-and-down strokes of the piston in that cylinder. These four processes are intake of fuel, compression of fuel, ignition of fuel (the power stroke) and exhaustion of waste gases.

The power stroke of a four-stroke internal combustion gasoline engine, then, occurs every other revolution of the crankshaft.

The crankshaft? That is what the operation is all about. All the pistons of an automobile engine (depending on the engine, it could be four, six or eight pistons) are attached by so-called connecting rods to a shaft that extends the length of the engine. This shaft is the crankshaft.

Each piston moves up and down in synchronization with other pistons to provide connecting rods with reciprocating motion, which turns the crankshaft. The rotary motion provided by the crankshaft is transferred to the flywheel, to the transmission, to the propeller shaft and on to the wheels and tires.

Automobiles

Only one of the four strokes occurring inside a cylinder during a complete cycle is a power stroke. The other three strokes result from the tremendous surge of power produced during this power (ignition) stroke.

All told, each piston in a typical engine goes through twenty complete cycles of four strokes each in one second if you are driving the car at sixty miles an hour. This allows the crankshaft to revolve approximately 2500 times per minute.

Now, before explaining exactly what happens in a cylinder during each phase of the four-stroke operation, we must go into the workings of the valve assembly. The assembly for each cylinder consists of one intake valve and one exhaust valve, and rods and parts needed to make them move.

The actual moving force is a long shaft, which, like the crankshaft, extends the length of the engine. However, it is smaller in diameter than the crankshaft and is interrupted over its length by devices that have peaked (high) spots. These devices are called cams, and, not too surprisingly, the shaft is called a camshaft.

The camshaft rotates, because the crankshaft rotates. What we mean is this: both the front of the crankshaft and camshaft have gears. These gears are connected together by a thick link-type chain called a timing chain. As the crankshaft is turned by the pistons, it turns the camshaft via this timing chain.

Each valve has its own individual cam. Thus, in an eight-cylinder engine you will find at least 16 cams on the camshaft to operate the 16 valves. In a six-cylinder engine, there would be at least 12 cams for the 12 valves. And in a four-cylinder engine, you would have at least eight cams for the eight valves.

As a cam rotates to bring its high spot up under another surface, it raises that surface.

In the case of a typical valve, the valve is opened and closed by its cam through an ''extension'' rod assembly. As the high spot of the cam comes beneath the far end of this rod assembly — the ''end'' is called a valve lifter — it pushes up. A long rod (called a push rod) extends from the valve lifter to move a connecting device called a rocker arm. The valve stem is connected to the other end of the rocker arm, and obviously the valve stem is attached to the valve face.

The rocker arm "rocks" back and forth, lifting the valve off the port of the cylinder and allowing it to settle back down over the port in relation to cam position.

Now, here is what happens during the four strokes of a complete cycle inside each cylinder of a four-stroke internal combustion engine:

1. Intake stroke. The piston starts down from the very top of the cylinder. The exhaust valve's rod assembly is on the "flat" of its cam; hence, the exhaust valve is closed. The intake valve's rod assembly is on the "high" point of its cam; hence, the intake valve is open. As the piston starts downward, a vacuum (sucking-in action) is created in the cylinder through the port left open by the intake valve.

2. Compression stroke. The piston has reached the bottom of the cylinder and is on its upward stroke, pushing hard against the fuel mixture that has been taken into the cylinder. Both valve rod assemblies are on the "flats" of their respective cams; hence, both valves are closed. As the piston pushes higher and higher, it compresses the fuel mixture to an eighth of its original volume.

3. Ignition stroke. When the piston is at or nearly at (or, in some engines, just past) the top of the cylinder, a spark is emitted from the tip of a spark plug. The tip of the spark plug extends right inside the cylinder. This spark ignites the compressed fuel mixture, which expands rapidly to exert a tremendous amount of pressure over the entire head of the piston. Note that the fuel mixture does not explode — it burns smoothly, spreading its force outward like ripples over water. The valve rod assemblies are still on the flats of their cams, so both valves are still closed.

The tremendous amount of force resulting from ignition causes the piston to be pushed down rapidly and with overwhelming force to turn the crankshaft. Notice that the ignition stroke is the only power-producing stroke of the four-stroke cycle. Piston movement occurring during the other three strokes results because of the crankshaft rotation that happens during the power stroke.

4. Exhaust stroke. The piston has been shoved to the bottom of the cylinder by expanding gases and is moving up again. The exhaust valve's rod assembly is on the "high" point of its cam; hence, the exhaust valve is open. The intake

Automobiles

valve remains closed. As the piston moves up, it forces waste gases resulting from combustion of fuel out through the uncovered exhaust port. When the piston reaches the top of the cylinder, the exhaust valve has again closed and the intake valve has opened. The intake stroke is about to start once more.

The Care and Feeding of Engines

ONE ABSOLUTE requirement of an engine is proper lubrication. Lubrication is provided by motor oil, pumped through the engine to lubricate moving parts. This reduces friction that would cause rapid wear and overheating of parts. If parts get too hot, they would literally weld themselves together, seizing the engine. Keep in mind that combustion temperatures exceed 4000° F.

Oil is pumped from a reservoir called an oil pan (or sump) by an oil pump. It passes through a filter, which prevents dirt and contaminants from being transferred to the interior of the engine where they could abrade parts. After lubricating critical parts, oil drips back into the oil pan.

One demand an engine makes on you as the car owner is that you keep it filled with an adequate amount of *clean* oil of the proper type for the engine (oils differ as engines differ). It is also very important to replace the oil filter periodically.

Instructions on frequency of changing oil and oil filter, and what type of oil to use in your engine, are provided in the owner's manual that comes with your automobile.

Important: If you are going to give an engine the care it needs, you should have this owner's manual. If you have lost it, secure another by writing the Technical Publications Department of the manufacturer of the vehicle; be sure to include the model and year of the vehicle.

ENGINE: PROBLEMS, CAUSES, REPAIRS

NOTE: In these troubleshooting charts, the "Repairs" are followed by a number. If the number is **1**, it means that the repair can be handled by a completely inexperienced person. If the number is **2**, it means that a moderately experienced owner can handle it with ordinary tools. A number **3** means that only an experienced mechanic with specialized tools should make the repair.

Problem: Valve leakage; discovered by compression test (a test done with a gauge to determine if compression meets engine needs)

Possible Cause
Leaky valve seals; carbon on valves; valve part wear

Repair 3
Grind valves and valve seats, replace springs, seals and parts as needed.

Problem: Noisy valve lifters; discovered by clicking noise coming from engine and engine "miss"

Possible Cause
Loss of oil (most valve lifters are hydraulic); dirt causes sticking

Repair 3
Replace.

Problem: Loose or leaking valve cover gasket; discovered by loss of oil (oil spreads over outside of engine)

Possible Cause
Loose cover or damaged valve cover gasket

Repair 3
Tighten cover; replace gasket if leak prevails.

Problem: Worn piston rings and/or engine bearings; discovered by loss of compression; noise

Possible Cause
Oil pump failure; overloading engine (driver fault); normal wear after many, many thousands of miles

Repair 3
Replace parts. Problem can be put off with proper changes of motor oil, oil filter and air cleaner (filter).

Where Does the Fuel Come From?

FUEL COMES, of course, from the fuel tank, but also from the

Automobiles

air. The fuel mixture burned in the cylinders is composed of approximately 15 parts of air to one part of gasoline. If fuel contained too much gas and not enough air, it would not burn. Similarly, if it contained too much air and not enough gas, it would not burn.

The typical route that gasoline follows is from the fuel tank to the fuel pump to the carburetor to the intake manifold to the cylinders. The typical route that air travels is from the outside through the radiator to beneath the hood, into the carburetor through the air cleaner where it mixes with gas, and on to the cylinders. Both gasoline and air are cleaned by filters before reaching the carburetor.

The heart of the fuel system is the fuel pump. Most pumps are mechanically driven by the camshaft. An arm on the pump rides on a cam. As the camshaft rotates, the arm is activated, causing a diaphragm inside the pump to pulsate.

As the diaphragm rises, it creates a partial vacuum that pulls gasoline from the fuel tank through a fuel line into the fuel pump. As the diaphragm falls, gasoline is pushed through a small one-way valve through the fuel pump and into another fuel line that goes to the carburetor.

Fuel enters the carburetor fuel bowl. The bowl is a holding tank where gas is kept until it is needed by the engine. Gas gets from the carburetor to the engine because of the vacuum created by the up-and-down strokes of pistons. It literally pulls the gas.

The amount of gas allowed to enter the bowl is dictated by the float assembly, which is similar to the plumbing in your home's toilet bowl. As more gas is needed, the level falls and the float drops, pulling a valve (called a needle valve) off an inlet seat and allowing gasoline to flow. As the need for gas declines, as it would, comparatively speaking, when the engine idles or is running at a slower speed, gas that fills the bowl causes the float to rise, which pushes the needle valve on the inlet seat and shuts off gasoline flow.

Gasoline is pulled into the body of the carburetor at a narrow point, called the venturi, where it mixes with air that is coming down from above it. Air, too, is taken in because of the pull of engine vacuum. Gasoline and air mix together.

The air has been filtered through a filter element in the carburetor air cleaner, which is the large usually-black-painted container that sits in the middle of the engine. Air must be filtered to prevent airborn dust from entering the engine where it would damage engine parts.

Gasoline, too, is filtered before it enters the carburetor, to keep impurities from lodging and blocking the flow of gasoline and also from entering the engine. Gasoline that comes from the pump at your local gasoline station is not always pure.

The gas-air mixture is pulled from the carburetor into the intake manifold. The intake manifold is nothing more than a distribution device through which the fuel mixture is parceled to each cylinder.

How to Care for a Fuel System

FUEL SYSTEM maintenance involves the following (identified by numbers: **1** for an inexperienced owner; **2** for a moderately experienced do-it-yourselfer; **3** for an experienced technician with special tools):

1. Replacing (or cleaning) the carburetor air cleaner filter as often as the manufacturer suggests (consult your owner's manual). **1**

2. Replacing (or cleaning) the gasoline filter as often as the manufacturer suggests. **1**

3. Cleaning dirt off carburetor linkages and external pivoting points. Linkages are rods that control certain carburetor actions, such as choking action needed to start a cold engine. When an engine is cold, it needs a greater concentration of gasoline (less air) to start than it needs when warm. To provide this, in most cars a plate automatically closes over the top part of the carburetor to block off air flow. As the engine warms up, a thermostatic spring releases tension on the plate and allows the plate to open. Dirt on the linkage that controls choke action and/or dirt on choke plate pivot points may cause faulty choking, which would lead to hard starting, and stalling, in cold weather. **1**

4. Having the carburetor adjusted periodically to compensate for wear and loss of adjustments that affect the flow of fuel mixture under various engine speed conditions. For example, the engine is designed to idle most efficiently at a certain speed — say, 600 revolutions per minute, but this varies from engine to engine (*your* engine's actual idling speed usually can be ascertained by consulting the owner's

manual). Engine idling speed is controlled by the amount of gasoline which is allowed to enter the carburetor idling circuit that feeds gas to the engine. If the idling circuit's adjustment screw has worn or has lost calibration, idle speed would be thrown out of synchronization. This can cause a speed-up in engine speed at idle and a waste of gasoline. **2, 3**

FUEL SYSTEM: PROBLEMS, CAUSES, REPAIRS

NOTE: Rated for difficulty by number, **1** being the simplest; **3** being the most complex.

Problem: Engine will not start

Possible Cause
Fuel pump failure

Repair 2
Test; replace if faulty.

Problem: Engine hard to start; stalls

Possible Cause
Clogged fuel filter

Repair 1
Replace filter.

Problem: Engine stalling, missing, rough idling, flooding, hard to start; excessive gas consumption

Possible Cause
Carburetor dirty and/or parts worn

Repair 3
Disassemble, clean and overhaul; or replace.

Problem: Engine hard to start, stalling; consuming excessive gas

Possible Cause
Clogged carburetor air filter

Repair 1
Replace filter.

Problem: Engine misses

Possible Cause
Defective cables

Repair 2
Test — replace if faulty.

Where Does the Spark Come From?

THE SPARK that ignites the fuel mixture in the cylinders comes from the car's ignition system, which consists primarily of a coil, distributor, spark plugs, and interconnecting wire and cables. Technically, the ignition circuit is broken into two circuits: primary and secondary.

The purpose of the primary circuit is to carry a charge of comparatively low voltage (12 volts) provided by the battery or alternator through the coil and to the distributor when a set of contact points inside the distributor is closed.

When points are closed, the current is permitted to flow by way of the distributor to ground on the vehicle frame (usually) and then back to the battery. This completes the primary circuit.

But when the points open, current does not flow to the distributor points. Instead, it is amplified in the coil about 2000 times, which transforms the original 12 volts into more than 25,000 volts. This voltage is sent from the coil to a part called the rotor, which sits on the distributor shaft beneath the distributor cap.

The rotor turns 360°, providing the current to each spark plug through contact points in the distributor cap. In other words, the metal contact of the rotor touches each metal contact in the cap to transfer current from the rotor to the cap. The distributor cap contacts and spark plugs are connected to each other by means of high tension cables.

The most important function of the ignition system, other than actually producing the high voltage required to ignite the fuel mixture, is to deliver that voltage to each spark plug, and thus to each cylinder, at the right time. If this timing is off, such problems as missing and excessive fuel consumption can result. The actual timing is controlled by rotor rotation, of the distributor shaft.

The rotor, as we said, sits on the top of the shaft. The shaft is turned by the engine camshaft. If timing is not properly adjusted, a readjustment can be made by turning the distributor so the shaft is brought back into proper relationship with the rotor, and the rotor is brought back into proper relationship with distributor cap contacts, and hence with spark plugs.

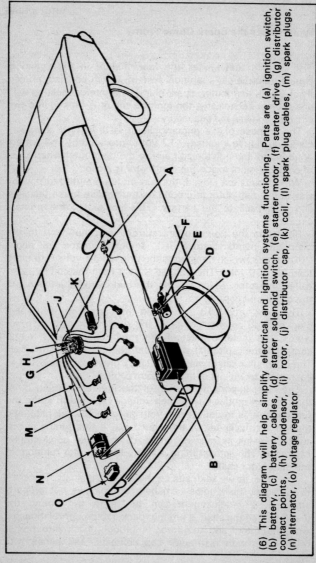

(6) This diagram will help simplify electrical and ignition systems functioning. Parts are (a) ignition switch, (b) battery, (c) battery cables, (d) starter solenoid switch, (e) starter motor, (f) starter drive, (g) distributor contact points, (h) condensor, (i) distributor cap, (j) rotor, (k) coil, (l) spark plug cables, (m) spark plugs, (n) alternator, (o) voltage regulator

How to Care for an Ignition System

IGNITION SYSTEM maintenance involves the following (rated for difficulty by numbers ranging from **1** for easiest, to **3** for maintenance requiring specialized training or tools):

1. Replace spark plugs periodically (the average life of plugs is considered to be about 12,000 miles). Plugs wear out, causing an interruption in the flow of current to the fuel mixture in the cylinder. When electrodes at the tip of spark plugs are worn, the voltage needed to fire the fuel mixture cannot jump the space (gap) between electrodes. Misfire results, and fuel that otherwise would have been burned is expelled through the exhaust cycle and wasted. **1**

2. Clean and gap (or replace) distributor contact points when they become worn. The contact points are a switch. Inadequate contact point performance means that switch failure has resulted. If a switch in a room of your home fails, the lights cannot be turned on and off. If distributor contacts wear out and the space (gap) between them becomes too large, current cannot be delivered. The engine will not run. **2**

3. Time the delivery of the spark. If timing goes out of adjustment, as it generally does within 12,000 miles or so, the problems mentioned above would occur. One indication of the need for timing adjustment is a "pinging" sound from the engine, especially on a pull, such as driving up a hill. **2, 3**

4. Replace high tension (spark plug) cables periodically. If cables become brittle and crack, loss of current would result which would cause the engine to malfunction and fuel to be wasted. **2, 3**

What Can Go Wrong with the Ignition System

THE FOLLOWING are some of the more common problems that can affect your car's ignition system and what you must do to overcome them:

IGNITION SYSTEM: PROBLEMS, CAUSES, REPAIRS

NOTE: Rated from easy to repair **1** to complex and requiring a specialist **3**.

Automobiles

Problem: Loss of engine power; loss of gas mileage

Possible Cause
Worn distributor contact points

Repair 2
Replace (useful life is about 12,000 miles). Also replace point condenser, which absorbs surges of electricity from point operation. It is likely to be near the end of its useful life.

Problem: Engine will not start

Possible Cause
Damaged distributor cap

Repair 2
Clean off contacts and clean out terminals. If contacts are badly burned or cap is cracked, replace.

Problem: Engine will not start

Possible Cause
Burned out coil

Repair 2
Test — replace if faulty.

The Electrical Units

A CAR'S ignition system will not work without electricity. Neither will a car's lights, horn, radio, gauges, etc.

Units that provide electricity are the battery and alternator. The starter motor also will be considered here as part of the electrical system, because it does create electricity and works hand-in-hand with the battery to start the engine.

The battery — more aptly, the storage battery — is a component that stores chemical energy and converts it to electrical energy when electricity is needed. It has one primary purpose: to provide the electricity needed to activate the starter motor and thus to start the engine.

Once the engine starts, the production of electricity is assumed by the alternator. In other words, once the engine is running, the battery is no longer needed.

The battery consists of layers of negative and positive lead plates. The catalyst that permits interaction between negative and positive plates is electrolyte, which is an electricity-conducting fluid composed of water and sulphuric acid. The battery is kept in a charged condition by the alternator.

Follow the progression: electricity fed to it by the alternator is stored by the battery through the medium of electrolyte. This is chemical energy. Electrolyte acting on a series of negative and positive charged lead plates results in the conversion of chemical energy to electrical energy, which is sent on to the starter motor (and which, incidentally, is also used to operate electrical components — lights, radio, heater, etc. — when the alternator is not in operation).

As a battery remains in use, lead sulphate particles from the plates flake off and start building up in the battery case. When these particles reach a plate and touch it, a short circuit results. This is what happens when a cell shorts out. The battery at this point is on its last legs.

There is no way to prevent shorts, but there is a way of delaying them. There is also a way of preventing the battery from self-discharging.

Self-discharging is what the name implies — the battery creates a substance (electrolyte salts, which result from vapors given off by the electrolyte) that combines with dirt on the battery case. This provides a conductive path which saps energy from the battery. It can discharge itself.

Ways of preventing self-discharging and of delaying short circuits are discussed in the section on maintenance.

Alternator

THE ALTERNATOR is a generator of electricity — more technically, its name is alternating-current (AC) generator. After the engine is started by the battery and starter motor, the alternator is driven by the car's drive belt. The alternator rotor, which is similar to an armature in other types of electric motors, interacts with a stator, which does the work that the field coils do in other types of electric motors, to produce alternating current.

This alternating current — alternating current is current that changes direction — must now be channeled to the components that need it. This is the task of the diodes in the alternator. These are pick-up devices that act like valves. They accept the alternating current and direct it to the car's electrical components. They are, in essence, devices that convert alternating current to direct current.

An alternator running at high speed can produce too much electricity. Excess current will cause electrical components to burn out, and will cause the battery to overcharge. An overcharged battery will short out rapidly.

To keep this from happening, some sort of device is needed to act as a traffic cop on the alternator. This device, not surprisingly, is called a regulator.

Regulator

WHEN MORE electricity is called for by the car's electrical units, the regulator, through a set of contact points, allows it to pass. When electricity is not needed, the regulator holds the alternator back.

As we said, the alternator converts mechanical energy (remember: it works only when its shaft is turning — this is mechanical energy) to electrical energy. Conversely, the starter motor converts electrical energy to mechanical energy. This is how it works:

When you turn on the ignition key, you send a small charge of electricity from the battery to a device on top of the starter called a solenoid. A solenoid is a "plunger" type affair. A magnetic field is established that jerks the starter drive, on the end of the starter motor, into mesh with the engine's flywheel.

You may remember that at the beginning of this chapter we mentioned that the flywheel is a large geared wheel on the output end of the crankshaft.

The starter drive has a gear called a pinion gear that meshes with the geared flywheel when the solenoid is activated.

At the same time as the gears mesh, electricity from the battery flows to the starter motor. The starter motor is a direct current electric motor that is like the motor used in such appliances and power tools as food mixers, drills, and circular saws. It has an armature and field circuit, and when electricity is introduced a magnetic field is established that allows the armature to revolve inside the field at tremendous speed and with great force.

You can see what happens. The armature turns the starter

drive pinion. The pinion turns the flywheel, which turns the crankshaft. This permits piston rotation, which starts the four strokes of the combustion cycle. Fuel flows and spark is provided by the ignition system, which is simultaneously being fed electricity from the battery through the ignition circuit.

The engine starts and you release pressure on the ignition key. When you do, you break the circuit between the battery and starter. The solenoid retracts the starter drive pinion from the flywheel. If it did not do this, either or both of the two gears would be damaged.

How to Maintain Electrical Components

UNLESS YOUR car is pretty old, the only electrical component that requires maintenance is the battery. In older cars, the generating motor (in the past, a direct current generator was used) and the starter motor had lubrication points. That is no longer true.

Battery maintenance involves the following:

1. Check battery water once a week and keep water to the level marks. Lack of water hastens sulphation, which leads to premature short circuiting.

2. Once every six months, remove the battery from the car and wash it thoroughly on all sides with a mixture of baking soda and water. Then, hose it down with fresh water until the baking soda solution is removed.

Be careful not to let the baking soda solution inside the battery where it will neutralize electrolyte. Cover the battery caps with small strips of masking tape. Caps have tiny vent holes in them that allow electrolyte vapors to escape, thus preventing a buildup of pressure inside the battery. Washing a battery removes these salts and prevents self-discharge.

What Can Go Wrong

THE FOLLOWING are some of the more common problems that can strike a car's charging and starting systems and what to do to overcome them:

ELECTRICAL UNITS: PROBLEMS, CAUSES, REPAIRS

NOTE: Rated for difficulty from **1** — a problem that

can be handled by an inexperienced owner, to **3** — a problem for an expert mechanic with special tools.

Problem: Engine will not start

Possible Cause
Dead battery

Repair 1
Test. If no short, recharge. If shorted, or charge does not hold, replace.

Problem: Hard starting; engine will not start

Possible Cause
Loose or bad battery cables

Repair 1
Tighten cables and clean off electrolyte salts to assure good contact. If cables are frayed, replace.

Problem: Lifeless growls from engine (hard starting)

Possible Cause
Bad starter solenoid

Bad starter motor

Repair 2 , 3
Test. Replace solenoid if faulty.
Test. Replace or rebuild starter motor if faulty.

Problem: Whine emitted when starting is attempted, but engine will not start

Possible Cause
Bad starter drive

Repair 3
Replace starter drive.

Problem: Hard starting; ammeter needle on dashboard shows discharge

Possible Cause
Damaged alternator and/ or regulator

Repair 3
Test both units. Rebuild or replace a faulty alternator; replace a bad regulator.

How Components Are Kept Cool

YOU MAY BE wondering why the tremendous heat (as much as 4000° F.) resulting from the combustion process does not burn up the engine components. The reason is simple: a most efficient cooling system dissipates heat rapidly.

Most cars use a liquid medium to cool the engine: a few use only air. We will concentrate on the so-called water-cooled cooling system, because it predominates. However, the term "water-cooled" is a misnomer in today's cars. A coolant mixture consisting of ethylene glycol (an anti-freeze) and water is usually used.

Ethylene glycol possesses chemicals that inhibit the formation of sludge and rust. Water does not. Ethylene glycol protects the engine from freezing in cold weather. Water does not. Ethylene glycol allows you to use your air conditioner without having your engine overheat with the added load of air conditioning. Water does not.

Water freezes at 32° F. and boils at 212° F. An ethylene glycol solution can be composed that will not freeze until -60° F. is reached and will not boil until 270° F. is reached. You should use nothing except ethylene glycol solution as the medium for cooling your car.

The job of the cooling system is to allow an engine to operate at its most efficient temperature, which is about 200° F. Notice the spread — 4000° F. to 200° F. You can appreciate the enormity of the task that the cooling system must accomplish.

The cooling system consists of a radiator, water pump, hoses, thermostat, fan, and jackets inside the engine. Here is the sequence that allows your engine to shed heat:

The radiator is the reservoir for coolant and consists of two tanks — one on top and one on the bottom (or one on one side and one on the other side). The top tank (or one side tank) is the inlet side. Coolant coming from the engine enters this tank. The bottom tank (or the one on the other side) is the outlet tank. Coolant leaving the radiator to the engine departs from this tank.

The two tanks are connected to each other by tubes that allow coolant to flow from the top tank to the bottom (or from one side to the other). These tubes are surrounded by fin-shaped metal objects which, as a conglomerate, are called the radiator core. As hot coolant coming from the top (or side)

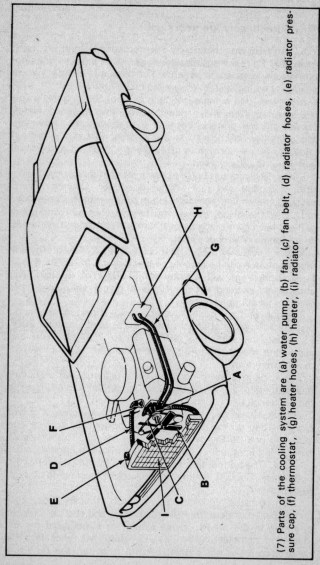

(7) Parts of the cooling system are (a) water pump, (b) fan, (c) fan belt, (d) radiator hoses, (e) radiator pressure cap, (f) thermostat, (g) heater hoses, (h) heater, (i) radiator

tank flows to the bottom (or the other side) tank, it is cooled by air that flows through the radiator core.

Assisting in this cooling process is the fan. As it revolves, it permits the coolant to dissipate heat. Coolant keeps flowing in a complete circuit. It is drawn by the water pump from the radiator's bottom tank through a hose into passages (jackets) surrounding hot engine parts. In making its route, the coolant absorbs heat from these parts. It makes a complete circuit around the engine and re-enters the top tank of the radiator through another hose. Then the whole route starts all over again.

The thermostat is a critical component. When the engine is cold, some means of heating it as quickly as possible must be used. An engine operates most efficiently at a particular temperature range — generally around 180° to 200° F. If an engine remained cool all the time, condensation would result and mix with oil to form sludge that would coat moving parts. Furthermore, a cold car is an uncomfortable car in winter. The heater will not put out heat unless the engine is warm.

The task of getting the engine warm as fast as possible is given to the thermostat. When the engine is cold, the thermostat is closed. This blocks coolant from entering the top tank of the radiator. Instead, when the engine is started, coolant circulates continually through the engine, getting hot quickly as it absorbs engine heat (again, remember, combustion can raise the temperature to almost 4000° F.).

As the engine warms up, the warm coolant acts on the thermostat to relieve spring tension on its valve. This causes the thermostat to open and permits coolant to flow into the top tank of the radiator. If the thermostat did not open, the coolant would get hotter and hotter, and would reach its boiling point. Then, the engine would overheat.

The car's heater is integrated into the cooling system. It is simply a miniature radiator like the one up front. Hot coolant is diverted to it. Heat is drawn from the hot coolant by the heater motor (blower) for circulation inside the car. The coolant is then reintroduced into the main stream.

Maintaining the Cooling System

TO PREVENT the disaster of overheating, abide by the following maintenance schedule:

Automobiles

1. Once a month, remove the radiator cap when the engine is cold and check coolant level. There is a level mark on most radiators. Add coolant if necessary, but be aware of the fact that if much coolant is needed, or the loss of coolant from month-to-month seems appreciable, a leak may exist that should be found and fixed before it gets worse and real trouble ensues.

2. Drain and flush the cooling system every year or every two years (as recommended by the manufacturer; see your owner's manual). Use chemical cleaners and flush with fresh water to clean out sludge and rust. Add fresh ethylene glycol in the proportion recommended on the container for the coldest anticipated temperature in your area.

3. Check radiator hoses every year by squeezing them. Replace a hose that shows cracks or feels mushy.

4. Clean debris and dead bugs from the radiator core periodically.

5. Check the water pump drive belt (fan belt) every six months. If it is cracked or frayed, replace it.

COOLING SYSTEM: PROBLEMS, CAUSES, REPAIRS

NOTE: Rated for difficulty from easy (for a novice) — **1**, to difficult but manageable — **2**, to only for an experienced technician — **3**.

Problem: Coolant leaks from pump; when appreciable amount is lost, overheating occurs

Possible Cause	Repair 3
Water pump failure	Replace.

Problem: Engine overheats and alternator stops working (same belt generally drives both)

Possible Cause	Repair 2
Fan belt snapped	Replace.

Problem: Coolant is lost and overheating occurs

Possible Cause	Repair 2
Radiator hose leaks	Replace.

Problem: Overheating

Possible Cause	**Repair 1**
Radiator pressure cap fails (cap seals and maintains working pressure of cooling system)	Test cap. Replace if faulty.

Problem: Engine is slow to heat up, or overheats (depends on whether thermostat fails in closed position or in open position)

Possible Cause	**Repair 3**
Thermostat failure	Test. Replace if faulty.

Problem: Engine overheats and/or radiator leaks coolant

Possible Cause	**Repair 3**
Radiator clogs or springs leak	Clean out radiator or replace. Some leaks can be repaired.

Problem: Cold air blows from heater into car with engine warm

Possible Cause	**Repair 3**
Dirt in heater; hoses leaking or clogged	Clean or replace heater core; replace hoses.

How You Stop Your Car

YOUR LIFE depends on your car's braking system. Two types of brakes prevail: drum brakes, an older design; and disc brakes. Your car has one of three different set-ups —
- Drum brakes on all four wheels
- Disc brakes on all four wheels
- Disc brakes on the front wheels and drum brakes on the rear wheels.

Furthermore, your car may be equipped with a device that makes braking effortless. Simply resting your foot on the

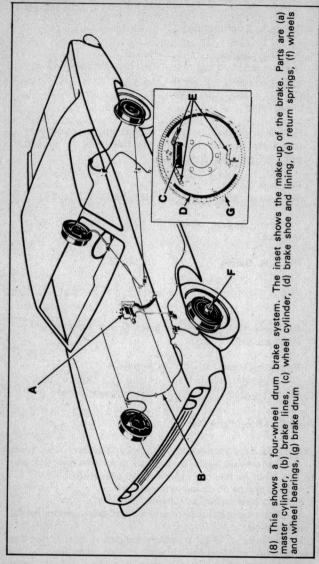

(8) This shows a four-wheel drum brake system. The inset shows the make-up of the brake. Parts are (a) master cylinder, (b) brake lines, (c) wheel cylinder, (d) brake shoe and lining, (e) return springs, (f) wheels and wheel bearings, (g) brake drum

brake pedal activates brakes; in other systems, the driver must press down hard on the brake pedal. This device is the brake power assist unit, or, as it is more commonly called, the power brake.

No matter what set-up you have in your car, the process starts at the brake pedal. When you step on that pedal, what you really are doing is sending hydraulic (fluid) pressure to the braking mechanisms at each wheel. This hydraulic pressure that you exert has a force of up to 1000 pounds at each wheel.

When you step down on the brake pedal, you send a piston forward in a component called the master cylinder. The master cylinder is the brake fluid reservoir. It is located on the firewall of the car — that is, in the engine compartment just in front of you. The brake pedal and master cylinder piston rod are connected by means of a brake pedal linkage.

The master cylinder piston pushing against fluid causes hydraulic pressure to be exerted on the mechanical parts of the brake at each wheel. Before discussing what happens there, let's consider for a second the role of the power brake.

If you lift the hood of your car, you can see the power brake — a large cylinder attached to the firewall on the left side of the vehicle (the left side of a car is always considered to be the driver's side). A large diaphragm — almost the same diameter as the cylinder itself — is the chief power component.

Notice that the power brake unit is attached to the firewall — not the master cylinder. In cars without a power brake, the master cylinder is attached to the firewall. In cars with power brake, the power brake unit is attached to the firewall and the master cylinder is attached to the front (output) end of the power brake unit. Both sides of the power brake diaphragm are in equilibrium, kept stable by the maintenance of equal pressure on both sides of the diaphragm. When you step down on the brake pedal, you disrupt this equilibrium by opening a port to the atmosphere, allowing air pressure to enter the power brake unit at the rear of the diaphragm.

At the front of the diaphragm, a vacuum is maintained. This is made possible by, of all things, the engine pistons performing their four-stroke combustion cycle. A hose extends from the power brake unit to a port on the engine. This

Automobiles

hose makes it possible for the engine to "pull" air from the front of the diaphragm, which creates a partial vacuum.

What exists then, when you press down on the brake pedal, is vacuum (low pressure) on the front side (master cylinder side) of the power brake diaphragm and atmospheric pressure (high pressure) on the brake pedal side of the power brake diaphragm. You can see what happens — the diaphragm "collapses" with great force toward the master cylinder.

Attached to the diaphragm is a pushrod that, in turn, is attached to the master cylinder piston. The powerful force you put into action by applying the brake pedal is ample to send the pushrod and piston forward with the diaphragm to apply hydraulic pressure to braking components at the wheels.

When you release foot pressure on the brake pedal, the atmospheric port is closed and spring pressure returns the power brake diaphragm to its "equal" standing.

Now, at the wheels — if braking components comprise a drum brake set-up, here is what happens when hydraulic pressure puts them into action:

1. Fluid pressure is exerted on two pistons inside a component called a wheel cylinder. A wheel cylinder is a small metal component that has symmetry — two of everything in equal balance. At the ends of the wheel cylinder are pushrods. The two wheel cylinder pistons exert outward force on the two wheel cylinder pushrods, causing them to push out against the brake shoes.

2. Brake shoes provide the stopping force. A brake shoe is attached to each side of the brake backing plate (the brake backing plate holds all stationary brake components). Brake shoes have bonded or riveted to them an asbestos friction material referred to as a lining. When the wheel cylinder pushrods apply equal outward pressure to both brake shoes, the shoes expand with equal force pressing linings against the revolving brake drum.

3. The brake drum is a separate braking component. It is a large hardened metal cylinder to which the wheel and tire are attached. The drum, wheel and tire revolve together when the car is in motion. But when intense frictional pressure is placed on the brake drum by the brake linings, the drum, and hence the wheel and tire, are brought to a halt.

4. When you take your foot off the brake pedal, you relieve

364

CONSUMER GUIDE

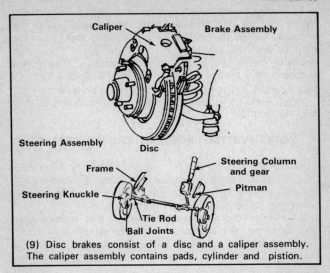

Caliper · Brake Assembly

Steering Assembly · Disc

Frame · Steering Column and gear

Steering Knuckle · Pitman

Tie Rod · Ball Joints

(9) Disc brakes consist of a disc and a caliper assembly. The caliper assembly contains pads, cylinder and pistion.

the hydraulic pressure on wheel cylinder pistons and, therefore, on wheel cylinder pushrods. Heavy springs attached to the brake shoes, called return springs, pull shoes away from the brake drum.

Disc brake components work in quite a different fashion. There is no brake drum encasing stationary components. Quite the contrary — the stationary braking components encase the revolving braking unit.

The revolving braking unit in a disc brake set-up is called the disc or rotor. The disc, wheel and tire are all connected so they revolve in tandem when the car is driven.

Now, positioned over the disc is a fairly large assembly called a caliper. The caliper contains two shoes — an outboard brake shoe and an inboard brake shoe. As their names suggest, the outboard shoe is positioned on the outside of the disc; the inboard shoe is positioned on the inside of the disc. The shoes literally have the disc in a "squeeze."

Each shoe has asbestos brake linings bonded or riveted to it but, with a disc brake setup, the linings are often referred to as pads.

Now, step on the brake pedal and exert hydraulic pressure. When you do, the pressure activates a large piston that presses against the inboard shoe, sending that shoe into contact with the revolving disc. At the same time, fluid pressure forces the caliper to move laterally, forcing the outboard shoe against the disc. The disc is sandwiched in a vice-type grip between the two shoes and is brought to a halt.

When hydraulic pressure is released, parts return to their original position.

BRAKE SYSTEM: PROBLEMS, CAUSES, REPAIRS

YOUR CAR'S braking system requires practically no maintenance. The only thing you should do is check the fluid level in the master cylinder every so often. The fluid should be no lower than ½ inch from the top of the cylinder.

If fluid is needed, add no other type than that recommended for your car by the manufacturer (see your owner's manual).

Important: If a fluid refill is needed often, it is possible that fluid is leaking. Examine each fluid-carrying component for leaks.

To be 100 percent brake-safe, it is wise to remove wheels from the car every 12,000 miles and make a visual examination of brake assemblies for wear and damage. Replace parts that are worn or damaged.

The following chart will allow you to make a diagnosis of a brake problem should it occur (repairs are rated for difficulty from **1** for the easiest to **3** for the most technical).

BRAKE SYSTEM: PROBLEMS, CAUSES, REPAIRS

Problem: Excessive pedal pressure needed to stop (hard pedal); low pedal; spongy pedal; pedal falls away under foot pressure (fading pedal)

Possible Cause	**Repair 3**
Master cylinder leaking	Overhaul master cylinder if possible; replace if not.

Problem: Spongy pedal; hard pedal; fading pedal; grabbing or pulling when brakes are applied

Possible Cause	**Repair 3**
Damaged brake line	Replace damaged brake line.

Problem: Hard pedal; fading pedal; grabbing or pulling

Possible Cause	**Repair 2**
Faulty wheel cylinder or disc brake cylinder	Repair cylinder if possible; replace if not.

Problem: Low pedal; hard pedal; grabbing or pulling; noise on brake pedal application (squeak, click, scrape); brakes chatter or shutter on application

Possible Cause	**Repair 3**
Worn or contaminated brake linings or pads	Replace bad linings or pads.

Problem: Low pedal; spongy pedal; fading pedal; grabbing or pulling; noise; chatter or shudder

Possible Cause	**Repair 3**
Worn or damaged brake drum or disc	Repair if possible, replace if not.

Problem: Extremely hard brake pedal

Possible Cause	**Repair 3**
Power brake failure	Check for damaged parts (vacuum line and check valve); overhaul or replace unit.

The Steering and Suspension Systems

THE STEERING SYSTEM consists of the steering wheel, steering column, steering gear, steering linkage and steering knuckle assembly. A power unit that makes steering easy to perform also may be included. The job of the steering system is to transfer your directional orders to the car's wheels.

Automobiles

The job of the suspension system is to support the weight of the car and provide comfort to its passengers. The suspension, front and rear, consists of shock absorbers, springs and control arms. Wheels and tires also may be considered part of the suspension.

When you turn the steering wheel, movement is transferred through the steering column to the steering gear. The steering gear is a complex arrangement of gears or ball bearings that transfer motion to one side or the other, depending on where you want to go.

Motion is transferred to steering linkage parts on that side. The purpose of steering linkage parts is merely to continue the transfer of motion. They pass it to the steering knuckle assembly. One part of this assembly is the wheel spindle to which the wheel and tire assembly is bolted. Thus, motion is transferred to the wheel, and the car moves.

If the car includes power steering, hydraulic force is used to help parts of the steering gear transfer motion. This takes that part of the job off your shoulders.

There is nothing particularly complex about the workings of the suspension system. Shock absorbers are cylinders that are filled with hydraulic fluid, or air, that absorbs road shocks. Springs are also provided to help ease the bumps and stabilize the vehicle. Two control arms — upper and lower — support shock absorbers and springs. Wheels contain bearings on which they (and tires) revolve.

STEERING SYSTEM: PROBLEMS, CAUSES, REPAIR

THE MOST IMPORTANT maintenance function to perform for both the steering and suspension systems is lubrication of key parts as often as the car manufacturer recommends. Lubrication keeps parts in good working order and prevents them from wearing out prematurely. These parts include steering linkage pivot points, ball joints (part of the steering knuckle assembly which pass steering motion to the steering knuckle and to the wheel spindle) and wheel bearings.

Other maintenance procedures involve checking and filling the steering gear with fluid, if necessary, and doing the same thing for a power steering unit. A key maintenance function is to keep tires properly inflated. Tire pressure should be checked weekly, and air added or reduced to bring pressure into line with car manufacturer recommendations. Incorrect air pressure causes rapid tire wear.

Problems and repairs follow, rated for difficulty from **1** for the easiest to **3** for the most complex.

STEERING SYSTEM: PROBLEMS, CAUSES, REPAIRS

Problem: Vibration in steering wheel

Possible Cause
Worn or damaged steering linkage part

Repair 3
Replace bad part.

Problem: Vibration in steering wheel; steering not stable; car weaves over road

Possible Cause
Damaged or worn ball joint

Repair 3
Replace bad ball joint.

Problem: Bumpy ride; body sways on turns; front end dips when braking; clunking noise when hitting bump

Possible Cause
Worn or damaged shock absorber

Repair 2
Replace bad shocks.

Problem: Noise (usually clicking) as wheels revolve; hubs hot to touch after drive

Possible Cause
Wheel bearings damaged or not adjusted properly

Repair 3
Disassemble, lubricate and adjust to specification if not damaged; replace if damaged.

Problem: Tire thump on drive; vibration

Possible Cause
Wheel balance faulty (wheels, tires and brakes have to be balanced with each other so no "heavy" spot exists to throw assembly out of balance)

Repair 3
Have wheel assemblies balanced whenever tires are put back on wheels or if wheels are switched around.

Problem: Vibration; car pulls to one side on level road when you take your hands off steering wheel; car weaves; premature tire wear

Possible Cause
Wheel alignment out of whack

Repair 3
Have wheels aligned (once every 15,000 miles is considered necessary).

Plumbing

FOR SOMETHING that is such an important part of our everyday lives, it is surprising how little-understood the plumbing system is. Perhaps this is because much of it simply can't be seen; like veins and arteries in the body, the pipes hide in the house structure. Or, perhaps it is because, in many peoples' minds, it falls under the forbidding category of "mechanical things" — something not unlike brain surgery in complexity. Whatever the reason, you could retire — handsomely — just collecting a penny from everyone in America who doesn't know what happens when he or she turns a faucet on.

Actually, house plumbing is simple. It consists, basically, of two systems. One supplies fresh water, hot and cold, where needed; the other drains waste and used water away.

Fresh Water System

ALL WATER enters the house through a main pipe at the water meter, where it is duly recorded. From there a network of thin pipes, like branches of a tree, carries the cold water to various fixtures — tubs, sinks, toilets, and showers. Appliances — dishwasher, washing machine, garbage disposer — are also tied into the network. This water is always under pressure.

Another network of thin pipes carries hot water from the meter to the fixtures that use it. This water is hot because it is fed first, by a pipe, through the hot water heater. Usually, both networks of pipes — cold and hot — travel parallel to each other through the house.

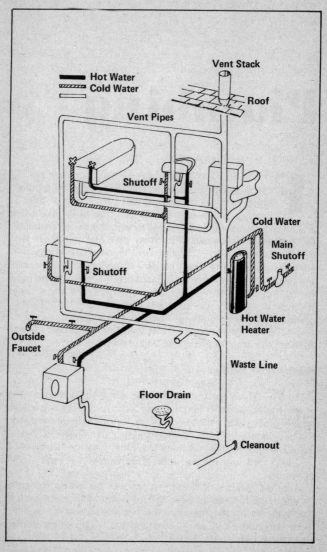

Hot Water
Cold Water

Vent Stack

Roof

Vent Pipes

Shutoff

Cold Water

Main
Shutoff

Shutoff

Hot Water
Heater

Outside
Faucet

Waste Line

Floor Drain

Cleanout

At certain points in the system there are little wheels called shutoff valves. These work like faucets — they let you turn the water on and off in a particular section of pipe and/or fixtures. These valves are handy for repairs. Turn off a valve and you can repair a pipe section or a fixture, without the water shooting out like Old Faithful Geyser. If you wish, you can shut down all the water in the house — hot and cold — by turning off either of the two valves at the water meter.

Drainage System

THE OTHER SYSTEM, the drainage one, is technically known as the Drain-Waste-Vent system, also known as the DWV system. As you might expect, its job is to drain off used water and waste and to get rid of gases that would otherwise accumulate in drain pipes.

The drainage system is like the fresh water system in the sense that it is composed of a network of pipes. Unlike the fresh water one, however, those pipes are large (from 1-inch to 4-inches as opposed to 3/8 inch to 1-inch) in inside diameter. And the system operates by gravity, rather than pressure: all the pipes are slightly pitched so the waste runs out under its own power.

There is a drain or waste pipe for every fixture in the house. These pipes lead to other pipes, and all ultimately lead to the main house sewer line, which in turn leads to the septic system, cesspool or city sewer line (pipes by the way, get larger as they near the sewer line). All the drain pipes in the house also are connected to vent pipes, which usually lead to one or two vent stacks; gases travel through the various pipes and up and out the stacks, which protrude through the roof.

Also, to prevent these gases from backing up and out of the fixtures into the rooms of the house, each drain pipe has a bent section, either S or U shaped, which is kept filled with water. These water-filled bends seal off the pipes, thus keeping the gases out. Not surprisingly, these bent sections are called traps.

Every DWV system also has cleanout plugs located at various points. These can be opened by a plumber for clearing a blockage, no matter where it may be.

That, basically, is the plumbing system: one system to get

Plumbing

the water distributed throughout the house, one system to carry waste away. Some rainy afternoon, try to trace it. Start at your water meter and work your way through your house. (Tip: Hot water pipes will feel warm). You'll find it fun, and the next time something goes wrong you won't feel so helpless.

Simple Repairs

THE TWO parts of a plumbing system that give the most trouble are the sink and toilet. Pipes, to a lesser degree, can also develop maladies that need correcting. But most of the things that go wrong can be simply corrected. Let's take a look.

Leaking Faucet

THERE ARE various types of faucets, and they look different, but all work basically the same way.

On each there is a handle, attached to a shaft, or spindle, which is inside the faucet body — the visible part on the sink. This shaft, threaded at its very end, sits in a hole, or seat, in the body. It is from this hole that the water (remember, it's under pressure) is constantly trying to get out. The shaft end holds the water back; however, when you turn the faucet on, the shaft screws up and out of the hole, and the water rushes up, then out the faucet spout.

Now if the shaft were just plain metal, it could not seal off that hole very well. But on the end there is a washer — a fiber or rubber device shaped like a small black donut — held on by a small screw. This washer presses against the edges of the hole like a cork. It prevents that constantly-pushing water from sneaking out past the edges of the shaft — in other words, it prevents a drip.

With time, though, washers wear out, or get chewed up from repeated contact with the seat, and they no longer seal the hole wall. A little water gets by — and then you do have an annoying drip.

When this happens, the impulse is to turn the faucet handle tighter in its "off" direction. And this will likely stop the problem because the washer will be forced tighter against the hole. But, inevitably, a few days or weeks later the washer will be so damaged that it simply will not be able to seal the hole properly anymore.

The answer, of course, is to install a new washer.

To do this, first turn off the water. Remember the valve we mentioned? All you have to do is find the one controlling the flow to the dripping faucet.

Usually, this valve — and another for the other faucet — will be right below the sink. If there are a number of valves there, and you are not sure which to turn off — turn them all off. No harm done.

If the valve is not below the sink, check the wall nearby. None there? Check the basement. See if you can locate the pipes leading up to the sink, then simply turn off the appropriate valve. If all else fails, turn off either main valve at the water meter. Of course this will shut down the hot and cold water supply to the entire house, but the repair does not take long, so there will be no great inconvenience.

Next, take apart the faucet. How you do this depends somewhat on the type you have, but all are basically the same. Unscrew or turn those parts that look like they can be unscrewed or turned and the faucet comes apart. It really isn't complicated at all.

One common type of faucet has the shaft, or spindle, held to the body by a large, shiny nut (called the bonnet or cap nut) on the outside. To disassemble this type, first wrap the nut with tape or bandaids to protect its finish, then loosen it with a wrench whose jaws open at least one inch. Then, turn the handle as if you were turning it on and the shaft unscrews up and out. There, on the end of it, you will see the washer held on by a tiny screw.

Unscrew the screw and replace the washer with one the same size. (You can buy a single washer, but most people buy a packaged assortment of washers in various sizes.) While you're at it, replace the little screw; make sure it is brass (other metals don't stand up well to water).

In another type of faucet, the big nut is not visible. The handle covers the shaft. To disassemble this, first use a Phillips screwdriver (made to fit into screws with crisscross slots rather than one straight slot) to take out the screw holding the handle on. Lift the handle off. If it balks, just tap

Plumbing

upward on the bottom with a screwdriver handle, then lift off.

With the handle off, you will see the big nut. Using a wrench (or pliers, in a pinch) loosen this nut. Then replace the handle on the shaft and turn as if you were turning the faucet ON. The shaft will come up and out; on the end, of course, will be the washer. Replace with one of the same size.

Some faucets look like they can't be taken apart: there doesn't seem to be anything to turn. But there is. With a screwdriver, or a fingernail, whichever works, pry up the little disc on the top of the handle. When you do you'll see a screw. Just take this out, pry off the handle — and there will be the big nut, ready for turning.

Sometimes, things don't go smoothly when you work on a faucet. For example, the screw holding the washer on, or the big nut holding the shaft, may not yield to the urgings of your screwdriver or wrench. The answer in both cases is penetrating oil. This is available in small cans at hardware stores. Just squirt a little of the oil near the threads of the stubborn part, and give it five minutes to seep down around the threads and break up the rust and corrosion causing the obstruction. Then turn. If this doesn't work, try a little more oil.

Another problem: In trying to remove a stubborn washer screw you may break off the head. If this happens, use a nail file or screwdriver and pry out the washer. Apply penetrating oil to the screw, wait five minutes, then get a grip on the screw shank with a pair of pliers and turn it out.

One other problem: When reassembling the faucet, the big nut occasionally will not seem to go on straight. The answer here is to work slowly and carefully. Don't force. Just place the nut in position and fiddle with it until it turns easily.

If a new washer does not stop the leak, the problem is likely with the faucet seat — the hole through which the water flows. It is probably worn or chewed up; the effect is that the washer cannot make a tight seal against it. You can buy a faucet-seat reaming kit for about one dollar at hardware stores. Instructions are on the package. Inside you will find a small toothed tool that lets you grind the seat smooth again.

If even this does not help, the seat is probably damaged beyond repair. Depending on the faucet type you have, sometimes you can unscrew the seat itself (all it takes is an inexpensive little Allen wrench) and replace it. Ask your hardware store dealer about it.

Dribbling Faucet

THIS IS nowhere as common as a leaking faucet, but it sometimes occurs when the faucet has the large nut on the outside. Water dribbles out around the top of the nut.

First, try tightening the nut (don't forget to wrap tape around it first). If this does not work, the problem is the packing: the graphite-impregnated string under the nut that prevents water from escaping is worn out.

Turn off the water valve and disassemble the faucet. You'll spot the packing immediately. Discard it, and replace with fresh packing. Just wrap it around the shaft three or four times, snip off the excess, and push the packing up under the nut. Then reassemble. (You can use regular packing — string — for this, but a better choice is soft black plastic that looks like string but can be molded easily with the fingers and is easier to manage. Packing costs less than twenty-five cents at hardware stores.) Turn on the water; if the faucet still leaks, take it apart again and add some more packing.

Some faucets do not have packing, but use a big rubber washer called an O ring. If you find one of these, take it to your hardware dealer and get one just like it.

Stopped-up Sink

KITCHEN, bathroom and other sinks in the home are basically the same. Unfortunately, they all are subject to the same problem: getting stopped up. To clear a sink, you try a number of things. One method or another should get the water flowing again.

First, feel around the drain strainer (take care if it is a kitchen sink; sharp utensils may be in it) to see if anything is blocking the drain. Soap, lint, hair, food particles or the like can quickly accumulate. Pick out the obstruction with your fingers. If the water goes down, pick out anything else you can see; a pair of tweezers is sometimes helpful.

If the problem is not caused by a clogged drain, go to the next thing, the plunger. A plunger, also known as a ''plumber's friend'' and technically known as a force cup, consists of

Plumbing

a bell-shaped rubber cup with a handle that looks like a sawed-down broomstick. In use, it gets the water in the drain pipe to rock back and forth, which may push the blockage out; it also creates suction that may pull it free.

Get a good plunger, 6-inches in diameter (the cost is about $3 — it does not pay to buy a low-quality tool) with a bulb on the end. (It also can be used on a toilet, when necessary.) The bulb can be snapped inside the cup, out of use, when using the plunger on the sink; when snapped out for use, the bulb fits snugly in the hole in the bottom of the toilet bowl.

Before using the plunger, make sure the sink has at least six inches of water in it. Place the cup squarely over the drain and press down, compressing it. Lift up about half an inch, then press down again. Continue in this way, up and down, in a steady rhythm. Every thirty seconds or so, jerk up extra hard and check to see if the water is draining. If it is, continue plunging until all the water is gone. As a test to see if the pipe is clear, run the water full blast. It should go down the drain quickly.

By the way, if you are plunging a sink with an overflow drain, or one that has a companion sink, the overflow or other sink drain must be stoppered with a soaking wet rag (you'll need a helper). Otherwise the pressure and suction the plunging creates will be somewhat dissipated.

If five minutes of plunging does not clear the sink, stop. No amount of plunging is going to clear it, so you try the next thing, which is clearing the trap.

You'll remember that a trap is a bent section in the pipe that traps water and serves as a seal against waste pipe gases backing up into the house. A sink trap also, unfortunately, is a perfect place for forks, knives, bottlecaps and a variety of other items to get trapped when they fall down the drain; they eventually can block water flow.

There are two common types of traps. One has a plug on the very bottom. Place a large pail under the trap and loosen this plug with a wrench; then unscrew with your fingers. The water in the trap and sink — plus the blockage — will run into the pail. If just a trickle of water comes out it means the pipe — the trap — must come off. To do this, after placing your pail beneath the trap, loosen the nuts at the top of each leg of the U, then lift them upwards. Gently rock the trap back and

378   CONSUMER GUIDE

forth until it comes off. Some nuts, by the way, are friction fit; just sliding them upwards with your fingers frees them — no wrench is necessary. Probe inside the trap with a piece of hanger wire.

When the trap is clear, resecure it. Make sure you get the pipe section, and the nuts that hold it on, straight. Take your time, and take care. If the nuts or trap do not go on straight, the trap can leak.

Finally, run the hot water for five minutes or so. This will help clear out any grease collected at the point in the trap where the blockage was.

If you find no blockage in the trap, then the obstruction is beyond the trap — somewhere in a drain pipe (which, you may remember, will ultimately connect to the main line that goes to the sewer or septic system).

Hopefully, the blockage is close enough to the sink so you can reach it with a "snake." This is a flexible wire cable with a point on one end and a crank handle on the other. Such a tool commonly is available at hardware stores. Get one that is eight or ten feet long and is of good quality (it will cost about $2, but, again, poor-quality tools will cause more problems than they will solve).

Take the trap plug off, or the trap itself, and feed the end of the snake into the pipe that disappears into the wall. When it is firmly in place, slide the crank handle within a couple of feet of the opening, and lock it in place by turning the little setscrew on it. Then, while pushing the snake into the pipe, turn the crank handle.

If the snake becomes jammed, it could mean that you've located the blockage; it could also mean that the snake is ensnarled in the pipe. Push and turn until it goes through. Or, if it feels like you've hooked onto something, pull it out.

Repeat the procedure until the entire length of the snake is in the pipe. If you have not located the blockage by then, it means that either the blockage is located too far down the pipe for the snake to reach it; or, if you could only get part of the snake in, it means that the blockage is wedged in too tightly. In either case, it also means that it is a job for a plumber who will come in with his electric, 25-foot long snake to clear it. If he can't do it through the pipe under the sink, he may open one of those cleanout plugs mentioned

Plumbing

earlier and attack it with his snake from there.

Toilet Problems

THIS FIXTURE is by far the least understood one in the house. Like the plumbing system itself, though, it is not really complicated.

Most of the troubles with a toilet come about because something malfunctions in the water closet, the squarish

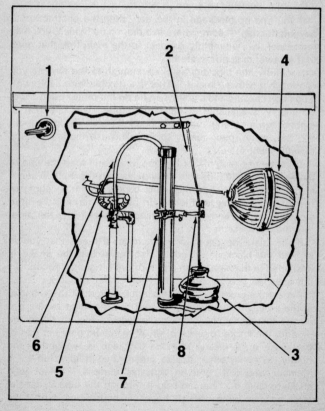

porcelain box that holds water and the toilet works. Before going into the repair of some common ills, it is necessary to describe how the closet — the toilet — works. Let's take a look.

Referring to the sketch, here's what happens when you flush the toilet.

You press on the handle (1), which is connected by a metal bar to a rod (2) or two wires (or chain) which in turn are connected to the flush ball (3). The ball sits in a hole in the bottom of the tank. The rod (or chain or wires) lifts the ball out of the hole, and the water in the tank rushes out into the bowl flushing the waste away.

The tank fills up again automatically because as the water goes down the float (4) also does down. The rod on the float is connected to the water inlet valve (5) and, moving down, opens the valve, letting new water rush into the tank. At the same time the flush ball, which has been held out of the hole by the water rushing out the hole beneath it, plops back into the hole as soon as there is no more water to hold it out. This seals the hole, of course, so the new water gradually fills up the tank.

As this happens, the float — and the rod it is on — rises until the rod end gradually closes off the water inlet valve, stopping water flow. Also, as the tank is filling, a little tube, called refill tube (6) shoots a small jet of water into the overflow tube (7) which leads to the bowl and fills it.

On paper the procedure sounds more complicated than it is. Just flush the tank a few times, observing what goes on, and you'll understand it with no trouble at all.

Now let's take a look at the problems that commonly occur and how to solve them.

Water Keeps Running Into Bowl

IF THIS occurs, take off the tank lid (be careful, by the way; it chips — and breaks — easily) and look into the tank. You will see that the tank is not filling up all the way.

The problem here is with the flush ball. For some reason or other, it is not doing its job of sealing the hole, so the water just keeps running out.

It may be that the chain, or lift wires, or rod that the ball is attached to are entangled in some way, so the ball can't reach the hole. If so, you'll see this. Just disentangle the parts so the ball can reach the hole.

It may be that the hole in which the ball sits is clogged with dirt or scale. Even though the ball looks like it's sitting in it watertight, it isn't. The answer here is to rub the hole edge clean with fine-grade steel wool. To do this, you have to drain the tank and turn off the water. So, just flush the tank and turn off the tank shut off valve — this is usually under the tank on the toilet side. Another way: Lift up the float rod and tie it to something above it, such as a medicine chest doorknob. This shuts off the water inlet valve.

Another reason the flush ball may not be sealing is that it is slightly misaligned with the hole. On many toilets there is a guide arm (8) that is supposed to keep the rod or lift wires properly aligned. But the guide itself may be misaligned. To correct, loosen the guide by loosening the little screw holding it to the overflow tube, and fiddle with the guide until the ball drops squarely into the hole.

One other cause of a leaking tank may be that the flush ball itself is bad — misshapen or damaged in some way. If all else fails, replace it. Just unscrew it from the rod or wire it's on, or unhook it from the chain, and get a new one like it at a hardware or plumbing supply store. If, by the way, the rod or wire holding it was bent, get a new one of these, also.

Another toilet tank problem is that the tank fills up, but the water continues to run until it flows out the overflow tube. When this occurs you'll not only be able to see it, but you'll hear it — it makes a hissing noise. The culprit is either the water inlet valve, the float, or the rod it is on.

First, lift up the rod. If the water flow stops, it means that the water inlet valve is not defective, leaving the rod or float as the problem.

As before, flush the tank and turn off the water. With your hand, unscrew the float. Shake it next to your ear: is there water in it? If so, get a new one at your hardware store and simply screw it in place.

If the float is okay, the rod is the problem. Turn the water on and flush the tank, filling it. Then, grasp the rod with both hands at the middle and bend so the float is lowered. Flush the toilet again and observe where the water stops; ideally, it should stop about an inch from the top of the overflow tube. If not, bend the rod down some more. The idea is to get it riding lower, so the rising water will press up against it sooner — and turn off the water.

If you found that the water inlet was at fault, it is probably just a washer in the valve that is worn. An examination of the valve will show you how to disassemble it to get at the washer. Or, you can replace the entire assembly, called a ballcock. Hardware stores sell kits containing all the parts you need, complete with instructions on how to do the job. Cost is about $6, a lot easier on the budget than a plumber.

Stopped-up Toilet

WHEN THIS OCCURS, the inclination of many people is to run for some towels. The necessity of mopping up a floor covered with water, however, can be avoided simply by turning off the water. As previously mentioned, just turn off the valve under the toilet tank, or lift up the float rod and tie it in that position. This done, you can work on the toilet in peace.

Toilet bowls have built-in traps, and this is where the blockages — anything from a diaper to a child's toy — usually occur.

The first thing is to clear the bowl with the plunger. If you have the kind with the rubber bulb part that snaps out, so much the better.

Before plunging, ladle some water out of the bowl. You don't want it spilling all over the place as you start to plunge. But leave enough water in the bowl so the plunger is covered at all times while plunging.

Fit the bulb part of the plunger into the bowl hole. Press down, compressing the rubber, then lift up a half inch or so. Press down again, lift up, and so on, every now and then jerking up hard. Check to see if the water is going down.

If the water level does seem to be lower, flush the toilet and watch the water. Does it appear normal? It does? Then give it the acid test: Wad up a fairly large ball of toilet paper and try to flush this down. If you can, the problem is solved.

If plunging does not solve the problem, the last try to clear the toilet is with a closet (after "water closet") auger. This

Plumbing

functions like a sink "snake," but is specially designed to clear a toilet. It consists of a flexible cable with a pointed end and a crank handle. There is also a slightly bent bar that rides along the cable. As with a snake, get a good auger. One that costs $3 to $4 and is six feet long should work fine.

To use the auger, pull the cable all the way back until the pointed end is at the end of the tube. Stick the pointed end into the bowl hole as far as you can. It's then you'll see the purpose of the bar: it aims the pointed end upwards, and holds the cable in position so that, once you start pushing the cable in, it will clear a hump inside the bowl and reach the trap.

Start pushing the cable in. If it feels like you've contacted the blockage, turn the crank handle. This will turn the pointed end, which will, hopefully, hook onto the item so you can pull it out.

Keep pushing the cable in, occasionally turning. Sometimes, when the blockage is a bar of soap, for example, you may drive right through it and break it up.

If you get the cable all the way in, and the blockage is still not removed or broken up, there is one other do-it-yourself solution available. It may be that a fork or toothbrush or other such item is causing the blockage and the auger cable is not able to hook onto it, missing it when it pushes through the trap. Stick your arm in a large plastic bag (such as a leaf bag) and reach down into the toilet, then upwards into the hole; you may be able to grab the item and pull it out.

If these techniques don't work, you could try to get the blockage out by taking off the toilet bowl and turning it upside down and then knocking the blockage out. While this is not as difficult as it may sound (you just unscrew the bolts that hold the toilet to the floor and then detach it from the tank), it may turn out that the blockage is deeper in the drain line and you will have removed the bowl for nothing. Call an expert.

Leaky Pipes

IT IS understandable that water pipes occasionally spring a leak. For years, they conduct water under pressure, and are subject to attack by various chemicals in the water. If they are especially old they are especially susceptible.

A large leak — a burst pipe — is a job for a plumber. This involves taking out the bad pipe and replacing it with a new one. Your involvement should be only to turn off the valve that controls the water supply to that particular pipe; or, if you don't know which one that is, turn off the main valve. (In your leisure, and perhaps with the help of someone who is familiar with plumbing, label all the pipe valves as to the pipes, fixtures and appliances they control.)

Leaks of the pinhole variety — far more common than big ones — are well within the skill of the novice handyman or woman.

There are two ways to make the repair. The first is with a pipe repair clamp. These are available at hardware stores and plumbing supply houses in various sizes from 1/2 to 2 inches. To get the size needed for the pipe, wrap a piece of cellophane tape around the pipe to get its circumference. Bring the tape down to the dealer and let him figure out the diameter clamp you need.

The clamp is simple to use. It comes with a rubber, bicycle-type patch. After turning off the water, place the patch over the hole, then slip the two halves of the clamp on the pipe and tighten the halves together with the bolts provided. This squeezes the rubber tightly against the leak and stops it. While some people regard this as temporary — and technically it is — it will plug the pipe for a long, long time.

The pipe clamp is a good tool when, for some reason (probably because you can't find it), you are not able to turn off the valve controlling water flow to the leaking pipe and must turn off the main valve, shutting down the entire house. When that happens, you want a quick, easy repair so that you can get your water turned on again as soon as possible, and tightening a pipe clamp takes only about five minutes.

When you do locate the individual valve to turn it off, or when the leak is around a pipe joint where the clamp will not fit, make the repair with epoxy compound. Many different brands are available at hardware stores.

First (after turning off the water) clean the hole area with steel wool. Then, plug the hole with wax or a small piece of cellophane tape — use as little material as possible. Finally, following label directions, smear on the epoxy. That's it, except that epoxy takes hours to dry — the main reason it is

Plumbing

not good when you have to shut down all the water in the house.

Epoxy, by the way, can be used to repair leaks in drain pipes.

Noisy Plumbing

IN OPERATION, a plumbing system should be quiet. When it makes noise, it means that something is wrong. It's a good idea to get it taken care of right away. Noise means vibration, and vibration is the worst enemy of things mechanical.

If you turn on the hot water and the pipes hammer or shudder, it means there is steam in them — the hot water is simply too hot. Turn down the thermostat on your water heater to about 140° and the hammering should stop.

If you turn off a faucet — either cold or hot — and the pipes hammer, this is a symptom of a malady called "water hammer." This is caused by the water (which moves at a high rate of speed) coming to a sudden stop. In modern plumbing systems there are usually two- or three-foot pipe extensions, or spurs, called air chambers, which act as cushions to absorb the water's momentum. A plumber can install them fairly easily; or, he may use special shock-absorbing fittings. If you have air chambers and the water still hammers, it's likely that the chambers are filled and need to be drained. A temporary solution to water hammer is to close the faucets more slowly.

Another brand of pipe noise, also normally heard when the faucets are turned on, is the pipes themselves banging. This happens when pipes are not securely held in place at some point in the system. Pipes need to be solidly anchored, at frequent intervals, with hangers or wood blocks, especially wherever they change direction. If pipes sag, water running through them will make them vibrate. A plumber will have to solve this problem if you cannot locate the exact spot where the sagging occurs.

If the pipes make a whistling or humming sound, they may be too small or clogged with scale. The cure here is replacement, but you can reduce the sound by installing pipe insulation, available at plumbing supply stores. All you need do with this material is wrap it around the pipes.

You'll also get a chattering noise if a washer on a faucet is loose. The cure is to replace or tighten the washer.

CONSUMER GUIDE